THE CHRISTMAS CONFERENCE

for the Foundation of the General Anthropoposophical Society

1923/1924

Rudolf Steiner

•

THE CHRISTMAS CONFERENCE for the Foundation of the General Anthroposophical Society 1923/1924

•

The Laying of
the Foundation Stone
Lectures and Addresses
Discussion of the Statutes
Dornach, 24 December 1923 to 1 January 1924

•

Foreword and Conclusion by Marie Steiner
Introduction by Virginia Sease
Translated by Johanna Collis
Verses within the text
translated by
Michael Wilson

TRANSLATED FROM THE ORIGINAL GERMAN
DIE WEIHNACHTSTAGUNG ZUR BEGRÜNDUNG DER ALLGEMEINEN ANTHROPOSOPHISCHEN GESELLSCHAFT 1923/1924, GA 260.
THIS TRANSLATION IS MADE FROM THE 4TH EDITION IN GERMAN DATED 1985 WHICH WAS PUBLISHED BY THE RUDOLF STEINER NACHLASSVERWALTUNG ON THE BASIS OF THE ORIGINAL EDITION PUBLISHED BY MARIE STEINER IN 1944.

ISBN 978-1-62148-251-2

DESIGN BY JUDITH LERNER
TYPESET BY: STUDIO 31/ROYAL TYPE

PRINTED IN THE UNITED STATES OF AMERICA

Contents

The Programme of the Christmas Foundation Conference 14

Introduction by Virginia Sease 19

Preface to the 1985 German Edition 21

PART ONE
INTRODUCTORY

The Close of the Year and the Turn of the Year 1923/24
Foreword by Marie Steiner to the first German edition in 1944 25

The year 1922: The culmination of Rudolf Steiner's work in public and the commencement of acts of sabotage. The burning of the Goetheanum. Dr Steiner forcefully stresses the tasks of the Anthroposophical Society. The establishment of the General Anthroposophical Society. The Christmas Foundation Conference bound up with infinite tragedy. What it meant for Rudolf Steiner to take karma upon himself. The grave illness of Rudolf Steiner at the beginning of 1924 and his lectures until 28 September 1924.

Introduction to the Eurythmy Performance by Rudolf Steiner
23 DECEMBER 1923 33

Eurythmy as an original art stemming from Anthroposophy. Art only flows into human evolution when it can make use of supersensible forces; it cannot flourish on a basis of materialistic thinking. The relationship of Imagination, Inspiration and Intuition to eurythmy and to recitation and declamation.

PART TWO
THE PROCEEDINGS OF THE CONFERENCE

The Opening of the Christmas Foundation Conference *by Rudolf Steiner*
24 DECEMBER, 10 O'CLOCK IN THE MORNING 41
The significance of the fact that the Goetheanum and the Anthroposophical Society have their centre on Swiss soil. Thanks to Albert Steffen for his lecture.

Rudolf Steiner's Opening Lecture and Reading of the Statutes
24 DECEMBER, 11.15 IN THE MORNING 43
The ruins of the Goetheanum are a symptom of conditions in the world. The Anthroposophical Movement as a link with the primeval sources of human evolution in the spiritual world, and the Anthroposophical Society as a dwelling for the Anthroposophical Movement. Lessons learnt from experience over ten years. Reasons for the decision to take on the Presidency. The General Anthroposophical Society; its Statutes; complete openness to the public; release of the manuscripts for publication and their protection by moral means. Undisguised public work on behalf of the Anthroposophical Movement using the examples of eurythmy, recitation and declamation, and medical therapy. Reading of the Statutes with explanations. Rudolf Steiner suggests the members of the Vorstand.

The Laying of the Foundation Stone of the General Anthroposophical Society through Rudolf Steiner
25 DECEMBER, 10 O'CLOCK IN THE MORNING 68
The spiritual laying of the Foundation Stone with verses that sum up the essence of the most important spiritual findings of recent years and renew the ancient word of the Mysteries: 'Know thyself'. The Christmas Verse and its harmonizing knowledge of man. Call to found a true community of human beings for Anthroposophia for the progress of the world.

The Foundation Meeting of the General Anthroposophical Society
25 DECEMBER, 11.15 IN THE MORNING 78
Reports from representatives of the national Societies.

Meeting of the Vorstand and the General Secretaries of the National Societies and their Secretaries
25 DECEMBER, 2.30 IN THE AFTERNOON IN THE GLASS HOUSE 84
Answers to questions concerning the admission of members, the Classes, election of General Secretaries, dissemination of anthroposophical knowledge amongst the general public.

Continuation of the Foundation Meeting
26 DECEMBER, 10 O'CLOCK IN THE MORNING 98
The Anthroposophical Society, fully open and yet deeply esoteric. The Foundation Stone Verses with explanations by Rudolf Steiner. Reports of the General Secretaries. Reading of the Statutes. Practical arrangements.

Continuation of the Foundation Meeting
27 DECEMBER, 10 O'CLOCK IN THE MORNING 110
The Foundation Stone Verses with explanations by Rudolf Steiner. General debate: Contributions on the journal *Das*

Goetheanum. Tasks of the central Vorstand. The relationship of the Anthroposophical Society in Switzerland to the branch at the Goetheanum. The Classes and the Sections. Detailed debate on Paragraphs 1 to 3.

Continuation of the Foundation Meeting
28 DECEMBER, 10 O'CLOCK IN THE MORNING 138
The Foundation Stone Verses with explanations by Rudolf Steiner. Detailed debate on Paragraphs 4 and 5 (Rudolf Steiner's suggestions as to the leaders of the Sections), and Paragraphs 6 to 14. Addition of Paragraph 15 naming the founding Vorstand. Answers to questions. Note to Paragraph 2. Adoption of the Statutes at the third reading.

Rudolf Steiner's Contribution during the Meeting of the Swiss School Association
28 DECEMBER, IN THE AFTERNOON IN THE GLASS HOUSE 166
Present social circumstances make it impossible to finance a large number of Waldorf Schools. The importance, particularly in Switzerland, of founding a truly independent school as a model. The financial basis for an independent school in Switzerland.

Meeting of the Vorstand of the General Anthroposophical Society and of the General Secretaries of the National Societies together with their Secretaries and the Swiss Branches
29 DECEMBER, 8.30 IN THE MORNING IN THE GLASS HOUSE 170
The Swiss Anthroposophical Society and its relationship to the branch at the Goetheanum and to the General Anthroposophical Society. The standard amount per member to be paid to the General Anthroposophical Society. Contributions by General Secretaries regarding the membership fee. Rudolf Steiner and Marie Steiner reflect on their work in Berlin.

Continuation of the Foundation Meeting
29 DECEMBER, 10 O'CLOCK IN THE MORNING 183
Foundation Stone Verses with explanations by Rudolf Steiner. Contributions from delegates on the subjects of the opposition to Anthroposophy and of the Free Anthroposophical Society.

Continuation of the Foundation Meeting
30 DECEMBER, 10 O'CLOCK IN THE MORNING 192
Foundation Stone Verses and Christmas Verse. Contributions of delegates on the subjects of the youth movement, the work in England, the independent school in The Hague. Problems of the Society as regards continuity and work in public. On the content of the reports for the supplement to *Das Goetheanum*. The opposition in Holland. The financial situation of the Waldorf schools. Eurythmy in North America.

Continuation of the Foundation Meeting
31 DECEMBER, 10 O'CLOCK IN THE MORNING 204
Foundation Stone Verses and Christmas Verse. The resistance of some sciences to the views of spiritual science. The need to unite all the sciences in an overall view of the world. The Anthroposophical Society must give the impulse for bridging the abyss between art and science. The successes of anthroposophical research. It is urgent for anthroposophical research to link up with present-day civilization.

The Idea of the Future Building in Dornach
Lecture by Rudolf Steiner
31 DECEMBER, IN THE MORNING 210
The rebuilding of the Goetheanum: financial considerations; the form it will take. Concrete as a new building material. The difficulty of achieving an artistic style in concrete. The ground plan to combine round and rectangular shapes. Arrangement of rooms and halls in the new building. Roof

constructed of flat surfaces. Changes in the Anthroposophical Movement since the building of the first Goetheanum mean new demands will be made on the new Goetheanum. On Paragraphs 5 and 7 of the Statutes.

Open Discussion of Swiss Delegates under the Chairmanship of Rudolf Steiner

31 DECEMBER, 2.30 IN THE AFTERNOON 218

Presidency and administration of the Swiss national Society. The representatives of its branches at delegates meetings. Explanations of the Christmas Foundation Conference in public and within the Society. Courtesy as an unwritten paragraph of the Statutes.

The Envy of the Gods — the Envy of Human Beings
Looking back to the burning of the Goetheanum on New Year's Eve 1922/23
Lecture by Rudolf Steiner

31 DECEMBER, 8.30 IN THE EVENING 231

The burning of the temple at Ephesus and the saying from Antiquity about the envy of the gods. The Mysteries as places where human beings and the 'good gods' encounter and understand one another. The envy of luciferic and ahrimanic gods. The deed of Golgotha by the God capable of supreme love. What was once the affair of gods and human beings becomes in the age of freedom the affair of human beings in physical life. The modesty with which divine wisdom presents itself on the earthly plane in the Middle Ages. Instruction of a Rosicrucian master to his pupil: the relationship of physical, etheric and astral bodies to the earth; their membership of the hierarchies; the special relationship of the human being to warmth. The 'language' of new spiritual revelation in the forms and picture content of the Goetheanum. The statue of the goddess at Ephesus — the statue of the representative of mankind in the

Goetheanum. The burning of the Goetheanum and the envy of human beings. The transformation of pain into faithfulness and activity with regard to the spiritual impulse of the Goetheanum.

Continuation of the Foundation Meeting
1 JANUARY 1924, 10 O'CLOCK IN THE MORNING 244
Foundation Stone Verses. Contributions of delegates on the subjects of the opposition and of books.

The Rebuilding of the Goetheanum
Lecture by Rudolf Steiner
1 JANUARY, IN THE MORNING 249
On the shaping of the doorways, windows, pillars, columns and the roof in the new Goetheanum. Internal and external forms making up an organic building. Contributions of delegates on the financing of the new building. Answers to questions on the membership contribution.

On the Right Entry into the Spiritual World. The Responsibility Incumbent on Us
Lecture and words of farewell by Rudolf Steiner
1 JANUARY, IN THE EVENING 260
The future goal of anthroposophical endeavour: to prevent mankind from failing to make the historically imposed step over the threshold through misuse of the capacity to form ideas by applying this capacity exclusively to the material world. The task of Dornach as the place where spiritual realities must be openly spoken about. The need to be uncompromising and truthful with regard to the impulse of Anthroposophy in the various branches of practical life. The hope which is united with the Christmas Foundation Conference. The Foundation Stone Verses.

On Behalf of the Members 274

PART THREE

CONCLUSION & APPENDICES

Conclusion
by Marie Steiner to the first German edition of 1944 279

Rudolf Steiner's work following the Conference. His lectures, books and essays in continuation of what had been inaugurated by the Christmas Foundation Conference.

Rudolf Steiner's Words of Welcome at the Social Gathering 1 January, 4.30 in the afternoon 282

Notes on the Verses 283

NOTE ON THE VERSES IN THE 1985 GERMAN EDITION 283

NOTE ON ELEMENTAL AND ELEMENTARY BEINGS 284

The Printed Version of the Verses in German 286

Three English Versions of the Verses 289

Notes 298

List of Names with Biographical Notes 308

Manuscripts and Blackboard Sketches

(following page 288)

Facsimile 1 II

Handwritten copy of the 'Statutes of the Anthroposophical Society' ready for printing.

Facsimile 2 VI

The printed Statutes, with handwritten alterations and additions arising during the debate on the Statutes.

Facsimile 3 X

The version of the meditation for the laying of the Foundation Stone used during the Christmas Conference.

Facsimile 4 XV

The 'Rhythms' as Rudolf Steiner wrote them on the blackboard.

Facsimile 5 XVIII

Sketches referring to the constitution of the School of Spiritual Science and to the rebuilding of the Goetheanum.

Facsimile 6 XXI

The version of the meditation for the laying of the Foundation Stone prepared for the Supplement to *Das Goetheanum*, Vol. 1, No. 1, 13 January 1924.

Notes on the Facsimiles 307

CONFERENCE PROGRAMME

FOUNDATION MEETING OF THE INTERNATIONAL

	Monday 24 Dec 1923	Tuesday 25 Dec 1923	Wednesday 26 Dec 1923	Thursday 27 Dec 1923
Morning 10:00	Lecture by Albert Steffen: 'On the Historical Destiny of the Goetheanum'	Laying of the Foundation Stone of the International Anthroposophical Society through Dr Rudolf Steiner	Meeting of Members. Theme: The future work of the International Anthroposophical Society and of the national Societies	Anthroposophy and Natural Science Dr Guenther Waschsmuth: 'The Face of the Earth and the Destiny of Mankind'
11:15	Opening Lecture by Dr Rudolf Steiner	Foundation Meeting of the International Anthroposophical Society		
Afternoon 4:30	Paradise Play	Nativity Play	Eurythmy	Three King' Play
6:00	Paradise Play (repeat)			
Evening 8:00	1st Lecture Dr Rudolf Steiner	2nd Lecture Dr Rudolf Steiner	3rd Lecture Dr Rudolf Steiner	4th Lecture Dr Rudolf Steiner

Lecture Cycle: 'World History in the Light of Anthrosophy

We wish to point out that the *first two days* in particular are the most important of the whole Conference. In his opening lecture on Monday, 24 December, Dr Steiner will give guidelines for the Christmas Conference and for the future work. On Tuesday, 25 December, the International Anthroposophical Society is to be consecrated in the laying of the Foundation Stone through Dr Rudolf Steiner. In the subsequent Foundation Meeting on Tuesday, 25 December, the General Secretaries or the Chairmen of the various national Societies will report on the development and the foundation of the Society accomplished in their own countries, after which the foundation of the International Anthroposophical Society is to take place.

Those friends who wish to take an active part in the shaping of the Conference are therefore requested to arrive in Dornach not later than Sunday, 23, December. We would ask the General Secretaries or Chairmen to give sufficient emphasis in their countries to this request.

CONFERENCE PROGRAMME

ANTHROPOSOPHICAL SOCIETY DORNACH CHRISTMAS 1923

Friday 28 Dec 1923	Saturday 29 Dec 1923	Sunday 30 Dec 1923	Monday 31 Dec 1923	Tuesday 1 Jan 1924
Anthroposophy and Art Jan Stuten: 'Music and the Spiritual World'	Meeting of the Anthroposophical Society. Introductory talk: Louis Werbeck: On the Opposition to Anthroposophy. Reports and Discussion on problems of the Society, Education etc.	Anthroposophy and Religion Dr Karl Schubert: 'Anthroposophy, a Leader towards Christ'	Meeting of the Anthroposophical Society: Reports and Discussion, Medicine, Research, etc.	Meeting of the Anthroposophical Society: Reports and Discussion, Anthroposophical Literature, Journals, etc.
Eurythmy	Nativity Play	Eurythmy	Three Kings' Play	Social Gathering
5th Lecture Dr Rudolf Steiner	6th Lecture Dr Rudolf Steiner	7th Lecture Dr Rudolf Steiner	8th Lecture Dr Rudolf Steiner	9th Lecture Dr Rudolf Steiner

and as a Foundation for Knowledge of the Human Spirit'

Those who have not yet made arrangements for accommodation should contact Fräulein Dr Vreede, Dornach bei Basel (Switzerland), Haus Friedwart, 1st Floor. Please direct all correspondence regarding the Christmas Conference to: The Secretariat of the Anthroposophical Society, Dornach bei (Switzerland), Haus Friedwart, 1st Floor.

The price of a ticket for all the lectures is 15.00 F. Separate tickets will be available for the eurythmy performances and the Christmas Plays.

Since the Christmas Conference is exclusively for members of the Anthroposophical Society, friends are requested to bring their membership cards.

FOR THE ANTHROPOSOPHICAL SOCIETY IN SWITZERLAND:

Albert Steffen   Dr Guenther Wachsmuth

Gründungs-Versammlung der Internationalen Anthro-

	Montag 24. Dez. 1923	Dienstag 25. Dez. 1923	Mittwoch 26 Dez. 1923	Donnerstag 27. Dez. 1923
Vormittags 1000	Vortrag von Albert Steffen: **„Aus der Schicksalsgeschichte des Goetheanums"**	**Grundsteinlegung** der internationalen Anthroposophischen Gesellschaft durch **Dr. Rudolf Steiner**	Mitglieder-Versammlung. Thema: Die zukünftige Arbeit der Internationalen Anthroposophischen Gesellschaft und der Ländergesellschaften	Anthroposophie und **Natur-Erkenntnis** Dr. Guenther Wachsmuth: **„Erdenantlitz und Menschheitsschicksal"**
1115	Eröffnungsvortrag von **Dr. Rudolf Steiner**	Gründungs-Versammlung der Internationalen Anthroposophischen Gesellschaft		
Nachmittags 430	Paradeis-Spiel	Christ-Geburt-Spiel	Eurythmie	Drei Königs-Spiel
600	Paradeis-Spiel (Wiederholt)			
Abends 800	1. Vortrag: Dr. Rudolf Steiner	2. Vortrag: Dr. Rudolf Steiner	3. Vortrag: Dr. Rudolf Steiner	4. Vortrag: Dr. Rudolf Steiner

Vortragscyclus: **„Die Weltgeschichte in anthroposophischer Beleuchtung**

Wir weisen darauf hin, dass gerade die beiden ersten Tage der Veranstaltung die allerwichtigsten sind. In seinem Eröffnungsvortrag am Montag, 24. Dez., wird Herr Dr. Steiner die Richtlinien für die Weihnachts-Tagung und für die zukünftige Arbeit geben. Am Dienstag, 25. Dez., soll in der Grundsteinlegung durch Dr. Rudolf Steiner die Internationale Anthroposophische Gesellschaft ihre Weihe erhalten. In der anschliessenden Gründungsversammlung am Dienstag, 25. Dez. werden die Generalsekretäre bzw. Vorstände der verschiedenen Ländergesellschaften über den Werdegang und die vollzogene Gründung in ihrem eigenen Lande berichten, woraufhin die Begründung der Internationalen Anthroposophischen Gesellschaft erfolgen soll.

Diejenigen Freunde, die an der Gestaltung der Tagung aktiv teilnehmen wollen, werden also gebeten, schon spätestens Sonntag, 23. Dez. in Dornach einzutreffen. Wir bitten die Generalsekretäre, bzw. Vorstände, dies in ihren Ländern genügend bekanntzugeben.

[This Programme[1] was printed in *Das Goetheanum*, Vol 3, No. 19, 16 December 1923]

posophischen Gesellschaft, Dornach, Weihnachten 1923

Freitag 28. Dez. 1923	Samstag 29. Dez. 1923	Sonntag 30. Dez. 1923	Montag 31. Dez. 1923	Dienstag 1. Januar 1924
Anthroposophie und **Kunst** Jan Stuten: **„Die Musik und die geistige Welt"**	Versammlung der Anthroposophischen Gesellschaft. Einleitendes Referat: Louis Werbeck: Zur Gegnerschaft der Anthroposophie. Referate und Diskussion über Probleme der Gesellschaft, Pädagogik etc.	Anthroposophie und **Religion** Dr. Karl Schubert: **„Anthroposophie, ein Führer zu Christus"**	Versammlung der Anthroposophischen Gesellschaft: Referate und Diskussion, Medizin, Forschung etc.	Versammlung der Anthroposophischen Gesellschaft: Referate und Diskussion, Anthroposophische Literatur, Zeitschriften etc.
Eurythmie	Christ-Geburt-Spiel	Eurythmie	Drei Königs-Spiel	Rout
5. Vortrag: Dr. Rudolf Steiner	6. Vortrag: Dr. Rudolf Steiner	7. Vortrag: Dr. Rudolf Steiner	8. Vortrag: Dr. Rudolf Steiner	9. Vortrag: Dr. Rudolf Steiner

und als Grundlage der Erkenntnis des Menschengeistes"

Wegen Unterbringungsfragen, soweit dies nicht schon geregelt ist, wende man sich an Frl. Dr. Vreede, Dornach bei Basel (Schweiz), Haus Friedwart, 1. Stock. Alle Korrespondenz, welche die Weihnachtstagung betrifft, bitten wir zu richten an: Das Sekretariat der Anthroposophischen Gesellschaft, Dornach bei Basel (Schweiz), Haus Friedwart, 1. Stock.

Für sämtliche Vorträge wird ein Beitrag von Fr. 15.– erhoben werden. Für Eurhythmie und Weihnachtsspiele sind Einzelkarten zu lösen.

Da die Weihnachtstagung ausschliesslich für Mitglieder der Anthroposophischen Gesellschaft ist, werden die Freunde gebeten, ihre Mitgliedskarten mitzubringen.

FÜR DIE ANTHROPOSOPHISCHE GESELLSCHAFT IN DER SCHWEIZ:

Albert Steffen. Dr. Guenther Wachsmuth.

Introduction

Events which occur in human history are always marked by their own peculiar destiny. Some acquire instantaneous recognition, others remain unnoticed for decades, for centuries and sometimes forever. They are all inscribed, however, in the supersensible sphere in a form often designated as the Akasha Chronicle.

The record of the event of the Christmas Conference for the Foundation of the General Anthroposophical Society which is contained in this publication became accessible in printed form in the original German version prepared by Marie Steiner in 1944, some twenty years after Christmas 1923. The Foundation Stone verse, however, which resounded each day during this Christmas Conference was printed by Rudolf Steiner almost immediately. In the many lectures, letters to the members, and articles which occupied Rudolf Steiner in the months after January 1, 1924 until his death on March 30, 1925, he also made frequent and penetrating reference to the event of the Christmas Conference and the Laying of the Foundation Stone.

The effect of this twenty year span of time between the Christmas Conference itself and the printed proceedings was that those eight-hundred people from many different countries who attended the Conference shared their impressions, memories, inspirations and resolutions with the members at home. Thus an oral tradition arose around the event itself, whereas the Foundation Stone verse, which was immediately accessible, became an inner meditative reality for countless people and was soon translated into various languages, including English. Over the decades which followed, numerous translations of this verse arose out of the anthroposophical work in various English-speaking countries. Besides the translation used in the following text, three other translations have been included at the end.

During the more than forty years between the original publication in German and this first publication in English two basic translations in typescript form served as a working basis for the people to whom they were accessible. Frances Dawson of California made a translation which served some members' groups of the Anthroposophical Society. John Jeffree of England translated the German version soon after it appeared for the English Section meetings led by Harry Collison. Harry Collison was the representative from England at the Christmas Conference.

Perhaps it is just this unavailability of the printed text for so many years which is the greatest indication that the Christmas Conference for the Foundation of the General Anthroposophical Society and the Laying of the Foundation Stone can never be restricted merely to a printed document; rather here is a living testimony to a spiritual reality. This spiritual reality comes towards us from the future as it continues to work on in humanity's life on earth. This event was actually inaugurated rather than concluded on January 1, 1924. It is therefore vitally important that these proceedings are now available for the English-speaking world through a translation which captures in an accurate and a sensitive manner the directness, the depth and the subtleties of this most significant event.

August 1989 VIRGINIA SEASE
Goetheanum, Dornach

Preface to the 1985 German Edition

The lectures, addresses and contributions to discussions given by Rudolf Steiner at the Christmas Conference for the Founding of the General Anthroposophical Society in 1923/24 were first published by Marie Steiner twenty-one years later. She undertook the revision of the text and wrote the introductory and concluding words. The original form of Marie Steiner's presentation has been maintained in the present new edition within the framework of the *Complete Works*. Any changes made in the text after comparison with the existing records have been documented in the Notes. A Supplement has been added containing facsimile reproductions of documents in Rudolf Steiner's handwriting as well as of texts and diagrams made on the blackboard during the Conference.

The Conference was for members of the Anthroposophical Society only. This fact determined the tone of Rudolf Steiner's contributions, especially the lectures. 'I was permitted to speak in internal circles in a manner which would have had to be different had I spoken publicly from the start.' *(The Course of my Life)*

The records taken down in shorthand were originally not intended for publication, and Rudolf Steiner was unable to check them himself. Though for the greatest part they may be assumed to be verbatim, nevertheless, as with all his published lectures, account must be taken of his own proviso in this matter: 'There will be nothing for it but to accept that there may be mistakes in the records I have been unable to check myself. *A judgment on the content of these private publications* will in any event only be acceptable when it is based on that knowledge which is a prerequisite for such judgment. In the case of most of these publications this is *at least* the knowledge of man and the universe as given by Anthroposophy, and also what may be found under the heading "anthroposophical history" in the wisdom that has been received from the spiritual world.' (*The Course of my Life*)

PART ONE

INTRODUCTORY

The Close of the Year and The Turn of the Year 1923/1924

Foreword by Marie Steiner to the first German Edition in 1944

IN THE BOOK *Rudolf Steiner und die Zivilisationsaufgaben der Anthroposophie* (Rudolf Steiner and the Tasks of Anthroposophy for Civilization),[2] published at Christmas, an attempt was made to depict through Rudolf Steiner's words and through his work in Spiritual Science how immense was the energy and how selfless the sacrifice of his endeavour to give to mankind the new spiritual impetus for which there is such dire need at this turning point of time. His influence on the public at large had reached its climax in 1922 when Wolff's concert agency[3] had applied for the organization of his lectures within Germany and when even the largest auditorium in many towns was too small to contain the crowds wanting to attend. Köthener Strasse in Berlin, which leads to the philharmonic concert hall, had even had to be cordoned off by the police because the congestion was so great. People from all around stood there with their luggage, unable to enter. This externally visible success fanned the flames of the opposition's will for destruction. Circles connected with the Pan-German movement[4] at that time had no scruples about instigating riots or indeed resorting to ambush or murder, as is shown in the cases of Erzberger,[5] Rathenau[6] and a good many others. Groups otherwise at loggerheads with each other joined forces in order to do away with a growing spiritual movement which appeared to threaten their own goals. So it was not difficult to stir up rowdy scenes. These were particularly violent on the occasion of Dr Steiner's lectures in Munich and Elberfeld.[7] The Wolff Agency was confident that it possessed sufficient personnel to organize and implement, all the more energetically, the arrangements for the lectures, in which it had a financial interest. It considered itself capable of reconnoitring the situation beforehand and felt it could then take preventative measures sufficient to cope with any disturbances. However, after further investigation, it had to admit that the enemy organizations were so powerful that it would unfortunately not be possible to guarantee the safety of the lecturer or even to ensure the smooth running of the event. It advised cancellation. Thus Dr Steiner's public lecturing was cut short by force at the very moment when it was at its most effective. Feeble and insignificant, but all the more unscrupulous, General G von G[8] now took the stage as a disseminator of propaganda. His hatred was inflamed by private family quarrels and personal intrigues. The hate campaign set in motion by the opposition from far and wide was at its height in 1922, the year which culminated in the burning of the Goetheanum, and in 1923.

Rudolf Steiner strove all the more strongly to imbue the Anthroposophical Society with its task for mankind and for the culture of mankind, doing everything he could to make it morally sound. It was to become the instrument through which, despite immense efforts on the part of the opposing powers, the spiritual renewal of mankind would have to be attempted. The book *Rudolf Steiner und die Zivilisationsaufgabe der Anthroposophie* describes this through his words and deeds. It is also revealed in lectures given in 1923 and published in booklet form.[9] The events described in the book lead to the point when it became possible to re-constitute the Anthroposophical Society as the General Anthroposophical Society, with its centre in Dornach, resting on the foundation of the newly-founded national groups. Before this could take place, the old connections linking us with Berlin as the earlier centre of activity had to be dissolved. It was my destiny to carry this out.

As the year 1923 drew to a close, inflation in Germany reached its nadir. A billion Reichsmark were now worth one pre-war mark. Ever since 1920, the strain of keeping up with the increasing speed of this avalanche had been making devastating demands on the nervous energy of anyone who had a business to run, especially when not only material values but above all spiritual treasures were involved. Official regulations which could not be ignored were changed every few days to take account of the shifting situation, and merely keeping abreast of the requirements devoured time and strength. If in addition you had taken upon yourself the burden of other people's affairs and had to make sure their rent and taxes were paid, you found yourself drowning in noughts when trying to work out what they owed — for taxes included not only the usual things but in addition items for the war, for the army, for the Ruhr, and all kinds of special funds. And next day everything would have changed once more. To send out a bill required a postage stamp which within quite a short time came to be worth much more than the payment requested. There was no lack of comical incidents, and the gallows humour evolved in their recounting did a little to lighten the burden of the depressing situation. Thus when the multiplication factor was a 'mere' few hundred thousand, a dear old member was heard to exclaim: 'Good gracious me, when you are seventy thousand years old you can't be expected to understand these sums any longer!' And the urchins in the streets of Berlin adopted boastful attitudes: 'Did you say that star was four hundred billion miles away from that one? What's in a few billion? That's nothing!' Such concepts of dwindling values must have had a decidedly negative influence on the strength of morals of the rising generation.

All over Germany things were being dismantled! We, too, could no longer maintain our dwelling in Berlin. And the Philosophisch-Anthroposophischer Verlag had to be transferred to Dornach to ensure its continuing existence. Even Fräulein Johanna Mücke,[10] stubborn and resilient Berliner though she was, could see no other solution. She was driven almost to despair in her isolation. We were forever either on tour or working feverishly in Dornach, while she waited in vain for replies to urgent letters, often facing decisions for which she felt unable to shoulder the responsibility alone. Dr Steiner was overburdened to the limit of his strength and now had to make preparations for the Christmas Foundation Conference and settle all the arrangements for international understanding and the reconstitution of the Society. Yet Fräulein Mücke could not be left without help any longer. Our worries on her account and about the continuing existence of the publishing company meant that we would have to divide the work between us. It was now my duty to hasten to Berlin in order to wind up our work and our home there.

So immediately after the Dutch conference[11] I travelled directly to Berlin. We had already given notice of our intention to relinquish our apartment. Now I had to rescue from Dr Steiner's library whatever we wanted to keep for the future. It was necessary to sift through all his papers in order to extract the important items from among the mountains of old letters and also manuscripts and newspapers which had become worthless. The last night before every lecture tour had been devoted to this job and each time several baskets full of torn-up papers had been the result. And yet an endless amount still awaited destruction on an even larger scale. It became our evening occupation for several weeks. Fräulein Vreede, who had come to Berlin to help, joined me and Fräulein Mücke. Whatever we wanted to keep was sent to Stuttgart. Permits for the transfer of the publishing company to Dornach had to be applied for, and everything had to be packed in accordance with border and customs regulations. Dr Steiner had given Dr Wachsmuth the task of helping us in this. He came from Stuttgart to Berlin to inspect the crates, now packed, and to arrange for their dispatch across the border. His visit was short. On their return, both our guests gave Dr Steiner quite dramatic descriptions of their impressions of Berlin.

We completed our work. Finally homes had to be found for the paintings and pictures; and the furniture from the Berlin group room, the Stuttgart Eurythmeum and our apartment in the Landhausstrasse had to be distributed. A last word to friends and we bade farewell to this place where we had worked and with which we had been connected for twenty-one years. Five hundred crates of books together with all the cupboards and shelves were transported to Switzerland. Fräulein Mücke herself had had to show the packers how to tackle the task with verve. Now she stayed on in Berlin for a while. But at least she had been relieved of the great burden and had the comfort of knowing that she had saved the publishing company. We owe it to her exemplary loyalty that in Dornach it has been able to flourish once more.

Thus I did not return to Dornach until shortly before the Christmas Foundation Conference, once the task of winding up everything in Berlin had been fully completed. It was as a matter of course that this part of the work should have fallen on me. The old form had to be dissolved before the Society, newly constituted in Dornach, could find its own form, taking into account the growth of the Movement and also the fields of work which corresponded to its new cultural tasks. Dissolution is always tinged with sadness, though joyful anticipation of coming educational and artistic tasks was undiminished. The past that had to be dismantled was infinitely significant, and anchored in it was the guarantee of fruitful new development.

Therefore I was astonished when during his introductory lecture, at the opening of the Christmas Foundation Conference, Dr Steiner conjured up before our souls a deeply moving image of the ruins of the Goetheanum, and then extended this image to include the publishing company. For the crates, packed to the brim, had resembled ruins merely externally, and this picture created an inaccurate impression among the listeners. When I later pointed this out to Dr Steiner and asked what he had meant, it turned out that he had received a report which had given him the impression that the devaluation of currency in Germany had brought about too great a dissipation of resources. When some months later Fräulein Mücke was able to show him the account books herself, he was delighted and said: 'But this gives quite another picture and shows that everything is alright.' He congratulated her on having rescued the publishing company out of that complicated situation.

To give a description of the Christmas Foundation Conference is perhaps one of the most difficult tasks one can set oneself. It is barely possible, with our limited insight, to gain an overall view of the impulse and power behind that event. It represents the most mighty endeavour of a teacher of mankind to lift his contemporaries out of their own small selves and awaken in them a conscious will to be allowed to become tools serving the wise guides of the universe. Yet at the same time this Christmas Foundation Conference is also bound up with something infinitely tragic. For we cannot but admit: We were called, but we were not chosen. We were incapable of responding to the call, as further developments showed.

At first every participant was as though lifted above him or herself, inwardly warmed through and through and at the same time deeply moved. But a destiny held sway over the whole situation, a destiny which has had to run its course in other spheres of existence. The outcome revealed what it meant for Dr Steiner to take our karma upon himself.

Herein lies the deeply esoteric nature of that deed of sacrifice. This is not the usual interpretation of the designation 'esoteric Vorstand'. What could have been deeply esoteric would have been to bring diverging earlier spiritual streams to a harmonious balance in the persons of some of their present representatives. This would have been an esoteric task that could have been achieved together with Dr Steiner through his superior insight, strength and capacity for love. But our human karma and that of the Society burst upon him the very minute the Christmas Foundation Conference had been brought to a close. On that last day, 1 January 1924, he suddenly fell seriously ill. At the social gathering with tea and refreshments, described as a 'Rout' on the programme, he was struck down as though by a sword aimed at his very life. Yet he continued without intermission and with boundless energy to be active until 28 September, the day on which he spoke to us for the last time.[12] His failing physical forces were nourished by spiritual fire, indeed they were borne by this fire and grew beyond themselves. But at the last, after superhuman achievements during the month of September, the power of this inner flame finally devoured him too.

For those who have the possibility of viewing events as a whole, the Christmas Foundation Conference is bathed in this tragic light. We have no right to turn our thoughts away from the gravity and suffering of these events. For insight is born of suffering and of pain. This pain must lead us to take hold of our tasks with a will that is all the greater.

There is much to be learnt from the discussions and events of the Conference, which were recorded in shorthand. If we follow them day by day just as they took place, we arrive at a picture that at first remained unclear to us because the excessive burden of work, and the bombardment of wishes from the members arriving from every direction, made it impossible to realize straight away the totality of the prospect that had been given. With time, what Dr Steiner had sketched along general lines by way of intentions for the future would have gained clearer contours. And a gradual putting into practice of his intentions would have enabled us to gain a complete picture. For this, a period of time was needed. First the spiritual foundation had to be deepened and strengthened. This was done through the cycle of lectures on the Mystery centres of the Middle Ages[13] and also the cycle *Anthroposophy*[14] which led up to the moment when the first lesson of the First Class was given. At the same time, the lecture tours could not be allowed to cease. These took Dr Steiner to France, Holland and England, as well as German-speaking and eastern regions. Wherever he went, the demands made on his strength were immense. In September he would have been ready to begin the Second Class. But the throng of members coming to Dornach was such that account had to be taken of it, as well as of the spiritual needs and receptivity of the new arrivals. In addition to the four separate lecture courses running every day,[15] so many personal wishes had to be met that the total physical exhaustion of the teacher and bestower became inevitable. From 28 September onwards, Dr Steiner had to give up any further work amongst the members. He was confined to his atelier, which had been transformed into a sick-room, and as far as the lecture tours were concerned, he had to ask us to go in his place. On his sick-bed he continued to write further letters to the members[16] and also the essays on the course of his life.[17]

Now it is our task to let the Christmas Foundation Conference speak for itself through the talks and lectures given by Rudolf Steiner and preserved for us in shorthand reports. What was said by the different officials or individual members, if extant, would overburden the book. Their questions are revealed by the answers given. The meetings and discussions in their totality represent for us a path of training in how to conduct meetings and deal with problems within the Society. All this is bathed in the atmosphere of most lofty spirituality, an offering, to the higher powers, of supplication and gratitude. The dominant endeavour is to conduct matters of this world in a practical and sensible manner while yet ensuring that they remain subordinate to the will of a wise universal guidance. The details of daily life are thus raised up to the sphere of spiritual goals and higher necessity.

Members from all the national Societies had gathered in large numbers. The lecture room in the old carpentry workshop[18] had to be extended by opening up the adjoining rooms, and the walls leading to the foyer, which still served as a workshop or, during performances, as a cloakroom, had to be taken down. Outside, the scant remains of the burnt Goetheanum building stuck up out of the snow-covered landscape.

For those arriving and settling in on 23 December a eurythmy performance was offered at 4.30 in the afternoon. The words with which Dr Steiner greeted the guests and introduced the performance contained the first indication of some of the fundamental motifs which were to run through all the lectures of the Conference. That evening brought the final lecture in the pre-Christmas cycle on *Mystery Knowledge and Mystery Centres.*[19] The opening of the Conference itself took place on the morning of 24 December. There now follows the address with which Rudolf Steiner greeted the guests on the occasion of the eurythmy performance on 23 December.

Introduction to the Eurythmy Performance

23 DECEMBER 1923

My dear friends!

Today our guests from further afield who have already arrived make up the majority of those present at this opening performance of eurythmy. There is no need for me to speak particularly about the nature of eurythmy, for our friends know about this from various writings which have appeared in print. But especially since we are gathering once more for an anthroposophical undertaking I should like to introduce this performance with a few words.

In the first instance eurythmy is that art which has originated entirely from the soil of Anthroposophy. Of course it has always been the case that every artistic activity which was to bring something new into civilization originated in supersensible human endeavour. Whether you look at architecture, sculpture, painting, or the arts of music or poetry, you will always find that the impulses visible in the external course of human evolution are rooted in some way in occult, supersensible ground, ground we may seek in connection with the Mysteries. Art can only flow into human evolution if it contains within it forces and impulses of a supersensible kind. But the present-day view of art arises in the main from the entirely materialistic tendency in thinking which has seized hold of Europe and America since the fifteenth century. And though a certain kind of scientific knowledge can flourish in this materialism, anything genuinely artistic cannot. True art can only come forth out of spiritual life.

Therefore it is as a matter of course that a special art has arisen out of the spiritual life of the Anthroposophical Movement. It is necessary to understand that art must be born out of the supersensible realm through the mediation of the human being. Considering the descending scale stretching from the supersensible realm down to externally perceptible phenonema, you find the faculty of Intuition at the top, at the point where — if I may put it like this — the human being merges with the spirit. Inspiration has to do with the capacity of the human being to face the supersensible on his own, hearing it and letting it reveal itself. And when he is able to link what he receives through Inspiration so intensely with his own being that he becomes capable of moulding it, then Imagination comes about.

In speech we have something which makes its appearance in an external picture, though it is an external picture which is extraordinarily similar to Inspiration. We might say that what we bear in our soul when we speak resembles Intuition; and what lies on our tongue, in our palate, comes out between our teeth and settles on our lips when we speak is the sense-perceptible image of Inspiration.

But where is the origin of what we push outwards from our inner soul life in speech? It originates in the mobile shape of our body, or I could say in our bodily structure in movement. Our ability to move our legs as well as our arms and hands and fingers is what gives us as little children our first opportunity to sense our relationship with the outside world. The first experience capable of entering into the consciousness of our soul is what we have in the physical movement of arms, hands and legs. The other movements are more connected with the human being. But the limbs which we stretch out into the space around us are what gives us a sense of the world. And when we stretch out our legs in a stride or a leap, or our arms to grasp something, or our fingers to feel something, then whatever we experience in doing this streams back to us. And as it streams back, it seizes hold of tongue, palate and larynx and becomes speech.

Thus in his organism the human being is through movement an expression of man as a whole. When you begin to understand this you sense that what in speech resembles Inspiration can descend into Imagination. We can call back something that is a gift to our limbs, to our tongue, our larynx and our palate and so on, we can recall it and let it stream back, asking: What kind of feelings, what kind of sensations stream outwards in our organism in order to create the sound *Ah*? We shall always discover that an *Ah* arises through something which expresses itself in one way or another in the air, through a particular movement of our organs of speech; or an *Eh* in optical axes crossing over, and so on. Then we shall be able to take what has streamed out in this way and become a sound or element of speech, and send it back into our whole being, into our human being of limbs, thus receiving in place of what causes speech to resemble Inspiration something else instead, something which can be seen and shaped and which therefore resembles Imagination.

So actually eurythmy came into existence when what works unconsciously in the human being to transform his capacity for movement into speech is subsequently recalled from speech and returned to the capacity for movement. Thus an element which belongs to Inspiration becomes an element belonging to Imagination.

Therefore an understanding of eurythmy is closely linked with discovering through eurythmy how Intuition, Inspiration and Imagination are related. Of course we can only show this in pictures, but the pictures speak clearly.

Consider, dear friends, a poem living in your soul. When you have entirely identified yourself inwardly with this poem and have taken it into yourself to such an extent and so strongly that you no longer need any words but have only feelings and can experience these feelings in your soul, then you are living in Intuition. Then let us assume that you recite or declaim the poem. You endeavour, in the vowel sounds, in the harmonies, in the rhythm, in the movement of the consonants, in tempo, beat and so on, to express in speech through recitation or declamation what lies in those feelings. What you experience when doing this is Inspiration. The element of Inspiration takes what lives purely in the soul, where it is localized in the nervous system, and pushes it down into larynx, palate and so on.

Finally let this sink down into your human limbs, so that in your own creation of form through movement you express what lies in speech; then, in the poem brought into eurythmy, you have the third element, Imagination.

In the picture of the descent of world evolution down to man you have that scale which human beings have to reascend, from Imagination through Inspiration to Intuition. In the poem transformed into eurythmy you have Imagination; in the recitation and declamation you have Inspiration as a picture; and in the entirely inward experience of the poem, in which there is no need to open your mouth because your experience is totally inward and you are utterly identified with it and have become one with it, in this you have Intuition.

In a poem transformed into eurythmy, experienced inwardly and recited, you have before you the three stages, albeit in an external picture. In eurythmy we have to do with an element of art which had from inner necessity to emerge out of the Anthroposophical Movement. What you have to do is bring into consciousness what it means to achieve knowledge of the ascent from Imagination to Inspiration, and to Intuition.

The shorthand report ends here. The eurythmy performance began after a few more words on the actual programme.

The Christmas Foundation Conference was opened on 24 December. [See the facsimile of the Programme.] It had been preceded during the course of the year by a number of general meetings of the Anthroposophical Society in Switzerland at which the problems needing an early solution were discussed. The discussions had been particularly lively during the conference of delegates from the Swiss branches of 8 December 1923,[20] and preparatory meetings had also taken place on 22 April and 10 June. A good many representatives of non-Swiss groups had been present as early on as the general meeting of the *Verein des*

Goetheanum[21] on 17 June. These non-Swiss representatives had arrived in large numbers for the international meeting of delegates from 20 to 22 July,[22] which had been devoted to the problems of rebuilding the Goetheanum and establishing it on a firm financial footing.

Dr Steiner had agreed to be present at these consultations but was not prepared to take the chair. His opinion had been sought quite a number of times, and he had emphasized above all the need for a moral basis. *Rudolf Steiner und die Zivilisationsaufgabe der Anthroposophie* contains many of the contributions he gave on that occasion. In the minutes of the meeting of 22 April we find the following:

'Let me add a few words, not as a statement but simply in the realm of feeling, to what has been said so far today.

'What we would look forward to in the outcome of the recent meeting in Stuttgart,[23] and also of today's meeting — and I hope similar meetings in other countries will follow — is that they should take a definite positive course, so that something positive can genuinely emerge from the will of the meeting. Mention has been made of the way the Anthroposophical Society is organized. But you see it has to be said that what marks the Anthroposophical Society is the very fact that it is not organized in any way at all. Indeed, for the most part the membership has wanted to have nothing to do with any organizing whatever, even on a purely human level. This was manageable to a certain degree up to a particular moment. But in view of the conditions prevailing now it is impossible to carry on in this way. It is necessary now to bring about a situation in which at least the majority of the membership can represent the affairs of the Society in a positive way, or at least start by following them with interest.

'The other day I was asked what I myself expect from this meeting. I had to point out that it is now necessary for the Anthroposophical Society to set itself a genuine task, so that it can take its place as something, with its own identity, that exists beside the Anthroposophical Movement; the Society as such must set itself a task. Until this task has emerged, the situation we have been speaking about today will never change. On the contrary, it will grow worse and worse. The organization of the opposition exists and is a reality. But for the majority of members the Anthroposophical Society is not a reality because it lacks a positive task which could arise out of a positive decision in the will. This was the reason for calling the meetings in Stuttgart and here. In Stuttgart the delegates meeting could not decide on a task for the Society. Instead it sought a way out in the suggestion that the membership of the Anthroposophical Society in Germany should be divided into two parts in the hope that out of the mutual relationship between these two Societies something might gradually develop of a kind that was not forthcoming from the delegates meeting. Today's meeting should have the great and beautiful aim of showing how the Anthroposophical Society can be set a positive and effective task which can also win the respect of those on the outside. Something great could come about today if those present would not merely sit back and listen to what individuals are putting forward so very well, as has happened so far, but if indeed out of the Society itself, out of the totality of the Society a common will could arise. If it does not, this meeting, too, will have run its course to no purpose and without result.

'I beg you, my dear friends, not to break up today without a result. Come to the point of setting a task for the Anthroposophical Society which can win a certain degree of respect from other people.'

The Christmas Foundation Conference for the founding of the General Anthroposophical Society was opened at 10 o'clock on the morning of 24 December. Dr Steiner greeted those present and introduced the lecture by Herr Albert Steffen on the history and destiny of the Goetheanum.

PART TWO

THE PROCEEDINGS OF THE CONFERENCE

The Opening of the Christmas Foundation Conference

by Rudolf Steiner

24 DECEMBER 1923, 10 O'CLOCK IN THE MORNING

My dear friends!

Allow me to announce the commencement of our Christmas Conference for the Founding of the General Anthroposophical Society. We shall in future always be of the heartfelt opinion —you will come to feel the definite rightness of this — that it will be significant for the development of the Anthroposophical Society to find its centre and its home here on Swiss soil in the manner expressed in the Statutes which I shall be suggesting to you.

The Society will in no way manifest any kind of a national character, but we shall always remain aware that we have been accepted here by our dear Swiss friends as a kind of guest in the realm of ideals, and we shall forever know how to respect this in a suitable way. Both privately and also in various public statements to our friends, I have often sought to show the importance of the fact that we have taken our place here on Swiss soil with our Goetheanum and with everything that seeks to be an Anthroposophical Society. This alone, my friends, is sufficient justification for the appearance of our dear friend Albert Steffen as the first speaker during our Christmas Foundation Conference. Of course he will speak here as a member and fellow founder of this Anthroposophical Society. But everything we feel especially in connection with the fact that the Goetheanum, as the central point of the Anthroposophical Society, stands here on Swiss soil, will be expressed symbolically when you now permit me to request Herr Albert Steffen — our dear and much respected friend, the distinguished poet whose presence among us may be counted as such great good fortune — to speak the first words of this our gathering.

Albert Steffen's lecture on the history and destiny of the Anthroposophical Society is published in the Supplement to *Das Goetheanum 1924*, Nos 2, 3 and 6.

DR STEINER:

My dear Herr Steffen!

With your words that are so warm and so filled with beautiful love you have given us a wonderful prelude to our gathering here. We could not have had a more beautiful prelude than the words you have spoken to us out of an anthroposophical heart of such warmth. I am quite sure that your kind words will shine over all our gatherings and meetings like a radiant star, and that we shall owe you most cordial gratitude for the feeling in our hearts which will endure throughout the period of our gathering, engendered by the words you have spoken to us on this first morning. We may be certain of ever feeling warmly enveloped within the marvellous land of Switzerland if an attitude of mind so truly Swiss continues to surround us with an atmosphere as beautiful as that now moving among us. Your words are founded indeed on a truly Swiss attitude of mind. I know that I speak from the bottom of every heart, now that our discussions are about to begin, when I offer you, dear friend Steffen, the most cordial thanks for the wonderful way in which you have provided the prelude for what is to take place over the next few days. To you come the warmest thanks from the heart of every one here present.

Rudolf Steiner's Opening Lecture and Reading of the Statutes

24 DECEMBER, 11.15 IN THE MORNING

My dear friends!

We begin our Christmas Conference for the founding of the Anthroposophical Society in a new form with a view of a stark contrast. We have had to invite you, dear friends, to pay a visit to a heap of ruins. As you climbed up the Goetheanum hill here in Dornach your eyes fell on our place of work, but what you saw were the ruins of the Goetheanum which perished a year ago. In the truest sense of the word this sight is a symbol that speaks profoundly to our hearts, a symbol not only of the external manifestation of our work and endeavour on anthroposophical ground both here and in the world, but also of many symptoms manifesting in the world as a whole.

Over the last few days, a smaller group of us have also had to take stock of another heap of ruins. This too, dear friends, you should regard as something resembling the ruins of the Goetheanum, which had become so very dear to us during the preceding ten years. We could say that a large proportion of the impulses, the anthroposophical impulses, which have spread out into the world over the course of the last twenty years made their initial appearance in the books — perhaps there were too many of them — of our publishing company, the *Philosophisch-Anthroposophischer Verlag* in Berlin. You will understand, since twenty years of work are indeed tied up in all that can be gathered under the heading '*Philosophisch-Anthroposophischer Verlag*', that all those who toiled to found and carry on the work of this publishing company gave of the substance of their hearts. As in the case of the Goetheanum, so also as far as the external aspect of this *Philosophisch-Anthroposophischer Verlag* is concerned, we are faced with a heap of ruins.[24] In this case it came about as a consequence of the terrible economic situation prevailing in the country where it has hitherto had its home. All possible work was prevented by a tax situation which exceeded any measures which might have been taken and by the rolling waves — quite literally — of current events which simply engulfed the publishing company.

Frau Dr Steiner has been busy over the last few weeks preparing everything anchored in this *Philosophisch-Anthroposophischer Verlag* for its journey here to the Goetheanum in Dornach. You can already see a small building[25] coming into being lower down the hill between the Boiler House and the Glass House. This will become the home of the *Philosophisch-Anthroposophischer Verlag*, or rather of its stock of books, which in itself externally also resembles a heap of ruins.

What can we do, dear friends, but link the causes of these heaps of rubble with world events which are currently running their course? The picture we see at first seems grim. It can surely be said that the flames which our physical eyes saw a year ago on New Year's Eve blazed heavenwards before the eyes of our soul. And in spirit we see that in fact these flames glow over much of what we have been building up during the last twenty years.

This, at first, is the picture with which our souls are faced. But it has to be said that nothing else at present can so clearly show us the truth of the ancient oriental view that the external world is maya and illusion. We shall, dear friends, establish a mood of soul appropriate for this our Christmas Foundation Conference if we can bring to life in our hearts the sense that the heap of ruins with which we are faced is maya and illusion, and that much of what immediately surrounds us here is maya and illusion.

Let us take our start from the immediate situation here. We have had to invite you to take your places in this wooden shed.[26] It is a temporary structure we have hurriedly put up over the last two days after it became clear how very many of our friends were expected to arrive. Temporary wooden partitions had to be put up next door. I have no hesitation in saying that the outer shelter for our gathering resembles nothing more than a shack erected amongst the ruins, a poor, a terribly poor shack of a home. Our initial introduction to these circumstances showed us yesterday that our friends felt the cold dreadfully in this shed, which is the best we can offer. But dear friends, let us count this frost, too, among the many other things which may be regarded as maya and illusion in what has come to meet you here. The more we can find our way into a mood which feels the external circumstances surrounding us to be maya and illusion, the more shall we develop that mood of active doing which we shall need here over the next few days, a mood which may not be negative in any way, a mood which must be positive in every detail. Now, a year after the moment when the flames of fire blazed skywards out of the dome of our Goetheanum, now everything which has been built up in the spiritual realm in the twenty years of the Anthroposophical Movement may appear before our hearts and before the eyes of our soul not as devouring flames but as creative flames. For everywhere out of the spiritual content of the Anthroposophical Movement warmth comes to give us courage, warmth which can be capable of bringing to life countless seeds for the spiritual life of the future which lie hidden here in the very soil of Dornach and all that belongs to it. Countless seeds for the future can begin to unfold their ripeness through this warmth which can surround us here, so that one day they may stand before the world as fully matured fruits as a result of what we want to do for them.

Now more than ever before we may call to mind that a spiritual movement such as that encompassed by the name of Anthroposophy, with which we have endowed it, is not born out of any earthly or arbitrary consideration. At the very beginning of our Conference I therefore want to start by reminding you that it was in the last third of the nineteenth century that on the one hand the waves of materialism were rising while out of the other side of the world a great revelation struck down into these waves, a revelation of the spirit which those whose mind and soul are in a receptive state can receive from the powers of spiritual life. A revelation of the spirit was opened up for mankind. Not from any arbitrary earthly consideration, but in obedience to a call resounding from the spiritual world; not from any arbitrary earthly consideration, but through a vision of the sublime pictures given out of the spiritual world as a modern revelation for the spiritual life of mankind, from this flowed the impulse for the Anthroposophical Movement.[27] This Anthroposophical Movement is not an act of service to the earth. This Anthroposophical Movement in its totality and in all its details is a service to the divine beings, a service to God. We create the right mood for it when we see it in all its wholeness as a service to God. As a service to God let us take it into our hearts at the beginning of our Conference. Let us inscribe deeply within our hearts the knowledge that this Anthroposophical Movement desires to link the soul of every individual devoted to it with the primeval sources of all that is human in the spiritual world, that this Anthroposophical Movement desires to lead the human being to that final enlightenment — that enlightenment which meanwhile in human earthly evolution is the last which gives satisfaction to man —which can clothe the newly beginning revelation in the words: Yes, this am I as a human being, as a God-willed human being on the earth, as a God-willed human being in the universe.

We shall take our starting point today from something we would so gladly have seen as our starting point years ago in 1913.[28] This is where we take up the thread, my dear friends, inscribing into our souls the foremost principle of the Anthroposophical Movement, which is to find its home in the Anthroposophical Society, namely, that everything in it is willed by the spirit, that this Movement desires to be a fulfilment of what the signs of the times speak in a shining script to the hearts of human beings.

The Anthroposophical Society will only endure if within ourselves we make of the Anthroposophical Movement the profoundest concern of our hearts. If we fail, the Society will not endure. The most important deed to be accomplished during the coming days must be accomplished within all your hearts, my dear friends. Whatever we say and hear will only become a starting point for the cause of Anthroposophy in the right way if our heart's blood is capable of beating for it. My friends, for this reason we have brought you all together here: to call forth a harmony of hearts in a truly anthroposophical sense. And we allow ourselves to hope that this is an appeal which can be rightly understood.

My dear friends, call to mind the manner in which the Anthroposophical Movement came into being. In many and varied ways there worked in it what was to be a revelation of the spirit for the approaching twentieth century. In contrast to so much that is negative, it is surely permissible to point emphatically here to the positive side: to the way in which the many and varied forms of spiritual life, which flowed in one way or another into the inner circles of outer society, genuinely entered into the hearts of our dear anthroposophical friends. Thus at a certain point we were able to advance far enough to show in the Mystery Dramas how intimate affairs of the human heart and soul are linked to the grand sweep of historical events in human evolution. I do believe that during those four or five years — a time much loved and dear to our hearts — when the Mystery Dramas were performed in Munich,[29] a good deal of all that is involved in this link between the individual human soul and the divine working of the cosmos in the realms of soul and spirit did indeed make its way through the souls of our friends.

Then came something of which the horrific consequences are known to every one of you: the event we call the World War. During those difficult times, all efforts had to be concentrated on conducting the affairs of Anthroposophy in a way which would bring it unscathed through all the difficulties and obstacles which were necessarily the consequence of that World War.

It cannot be denied that some of the things which had necessarily to be done out of the situation arising at the time were misunderstood, even in the circles of our anthroposophical friends. Not until some future time will it be possible for more than a few people to form a judgment on those moods which caused mankind to be split into so many groups over the last decade, on those moods which led to the World War. As yet there exists no proper judgment about the enormity which lives among us all as a consequence of that World War. Thus it can be said that the Anthroposophical Society — not the Movement — has emerged riven from the War.

Our dear friend Herr Steffen has already pointed out a number of matters which then entered into our Anthroposophical Society and in no less a manner also led to misunderstandings. Today, however, I want to dwell mainly on all that is positive. I want to tell you that if this gathering runs its course in the right way, if this gathering really reaches an awareness of how something spiritual and esoteric must be the foundation for all our work and existence, then those spiritual seeds which are everywhere present will be enabled to germinate through being warmed by your mood and your enthusiasm. Today we want to generate a mood which can accept in full earnestness that external things are maya and illusion but that out of this maya and illusion there germinates to our great joy — not a joy for our weakness but a joy for our strength and for the will we now want to unfold — something that can live invisibly among us, something that can live in innumerable seeds invisibly among us. Prepare your souls, dear friends, so that they may receive these seeds; for your souls are the true ground and soil in which these seeds of the spirit may germinate, unfold and develop. They are the truth. They shine forth as though with the shining of the sun, bathing in light all the seeming ruins encountered by our external eyes. Today, of all days, let us allow the profoundest call of Anthroposophy, indeed of everything spiritual, to shine into our souls: Outwardly all is maya and illusion; inwardly there unfolds the fullness of truth, the fullness of divine and spiritual life. Anthroposophy shall bring into life all that is recognized as truth within it.

Where do we bring into life the teaching of maya and of the light of truth? Let us bring it into life above all during this our Christmas Conference. Let us during this our Christmas Conference make the shining forth of the universal light — as it shone before the shepherds, who bore within them only the simplicity of their hearts, and before the kingly magi, who bore within them the wisdom of all the universe — let us make this flaming Christmas light, this universal light of Christmas into a symbol for what is to come to pass through our own hearts and souls!

All else that is to be said I shall say tomorrow when what we shall call the laying of the Foundation Stone of the Anthroposophical Society takes place. Now I wish to say this, my dear friends. In recent weeks I have pondered deeply in my soul the question: What should be the starting point for this Christmas Conference, and what lessons have we learnt from the experiences of the past ten years since the founding of the Anthroposophical Society?

Out of all this, my dear friends, two alternative questions arose. In 1912, 1913 I said for good reasons that the Anthroposophical Society would now have to run itself, that it would have to manage its own affairs, and that I would have to withdraw into a position of an adviser who did not participate directly in any actions. Since then things have changed. After grave efforts in the past weeks to overcome my inner resistance I have now reached the realization that it would become impossible for me to continue to lead the Anthroposophical Movement within the Anthroposophical Society if this Christmas Conference were not to agree that I should once more take on in every way the leadership, that is the presidency, of the Anthroposophical Society to be founded here in Dornach at the Goetheanum.

As you know, during a conference in Stuttgart[30] it became necessary for me to make the difficult decision to advise the Society in Germany to split into two Societies, one which would be the continuation of the old Society and one in which the young members would chiefly be represented, the Free Anthroposophical Society.

Let me tell you, my dear friends, that the decision to give this advice was difficult indeed. It was so grave because fundamentally such advice was a contradiction of the very foundations of the Anthroposophical Society. For if this was not the Society in which today's youth could feel fully at home, then what other association of human beings in the earthly world of today was there that could give them this feeling! Such advice was an anomaly. This occasion was perhaps one of the most important symptoms contributing to my decision to tell you here that I can only continue to lead the Anthroposophical Movement within the Anthroposophical Society if I myself can take on the presidency of the Anthroposophical Society, which is to be newly founded. You see, at the turn of the century something took place very deeply indeed within spiritual events, and the effects of this are showing in the external events in the midst of which human beings stand here on earth.

One of the greatest possible changes took place in the spiritual realm. Preparation for it began at the end of the 1870s, and it reached its culmination just at the turn of the century. Ancient Indian wisdom pointed to it, calling it the end of Kali Yuga. Much, very much, my dear friends, is meant by this. And when in recent times I have met in all kinds of ways with young people in all the countries of the world accessible to me, I have had to say to myself over and over again: Everything that beats in these youthful hearts, everything which glows towards spiritual activity in such a beautiful and often such an indeterminate way, this is the external expression for what came to completion in the depths of spiritual world-weaving during the last third of the nineteenth century leading up to the twentieth century. My dear friends, what I now want to say is not something negative but something positive so far as I am concerned: I have frequently found, when I have gone to meet young people, that their endeavours to join one organization or another encountered difficulties because again and again the form of the association did not fit whatever it was that they themselves wanted. There was always some condition or other as to what sort of a person you had to be or what you had to do if you wanted to join any of these organizations.

This is the kind of thing that was involved in the feeling that the chief disadvantage of the Theosophical Society — out of which the Anthroposophical Society grew, as you know — lay in the formulation of its three tenets.[31] You had to profess something. The way in which you had to sign a form, which made it look as though you had to make some dogmatic assertion, is something which nowadays simply no longer agrees with the fundamental mood of human souls. The human soul today feels that anything dogmatic is foreign to it; to carry on in any kind of a sectarian way is fundamentally foreign to it. And it cannot be denied that within the Anthroposophical Society it is proving difficult to cast off this sectarian way of carrying on. But cast it off we must. Not a shred must be allowed to remain within the new Anthroposophical Society which shall be founded. This must become a true world society. Anyone joining it must feel: Yes, here I have found what moves me. An old person must feel: Here I have found something for which I have striven all my life together with other people. The young person must feel: Here I have found something which comes out to meet my youth. When the Free Anthroposophical Society was founded I longed dearly to reply to young people who enquired after the conditions for joining it with the answer which I now want to give: The only condition is to be truly young in the sense that one is young when one's youthful soul is filled with all the impulses of the present time.

And, dear friends, how do you go about being old in the proper sense in the Anthroposophical Society? You are old in the proper sense if you have a heart for what is welling up into mankind today both for young and old out of spiritual depths by way of a universal youthfulness, renewing every aspect of our lives.

By hinting at moods of soul I am indicating what it was that moved me to take on the task of being President of the Anthroposophical Society myself. This Anthroposophical Society — such things can often happen — has been called by a good many names. Thus, for example, it has been called the 'International Anthroposophical Society'. Dear friends, it is to be neither an international nor a national society. I beg you heartily never to use the word 'international society' but always to speak simply of a 'General Anthroposophical Society' which wants to have its centre here at the Goetheanum in Dornach.

You will see that the Statutes are formulated in a way that excludes anything administrative, anything that could ever of its own accord turn into bureaucracy. These Statutes are tuned to whatever is purely human. They are not tuned to principles or to dogmas. What these Statutes say is taken from what is actual and what is human. These Statutes say: Here in Dornach is the Goetheanum. This Goetheanum is run in a particular way. In this Goetheanum work of this kind and of that kind is undertaken. In this Goetheanum endeavours are made to promote human evolution in this way or in that way. Whether these things are 'right' or 'not right' is something that must not be stated in statutes which are intended to be truly modern. All that is stated is the fact that a Goetheanum exists, that human beings are connected with this Goetheanum, and that these human beings do certain things in this Goetheanum in the belief that through doing so they are working for human evolution.

Those who wish to join this Society are not expected to adhere to any principle. No religious confession, no scientific conviction, no artistic intention is set up in any dogmatic way. The only thing that is required is that those who join should feel at home in being linked to what is going on at the Goetheanum.

In the formulation of these Statutes the endeavour has been made to avoid establishing principles, so that what is here founded may rest on all that is purely human. Look carefully at the people who will make suggestions with regard to what is to be founded here over the next few days. Ask yourselves whether you can trust them or not. And if at this Foundation Meeting you declare yourselves satisfied with what wants to be brought about in Dornach, then you will have declared yourselves for something that is a fact; then you will have declared yourselves to be in tune with something that is a fact. If this is possible, everything else will follow on. Yes, everything will run its course. Then it will not be necessary for the centre at Dornach to designate or nominate a whole host of trustees; then the Anthroposophical Society will be what I have often pointed to when to my deep satisfaction I have been permitted to be present at the founding of the individual national Societies.[32] Then the Anthroposophical Society will be something that can arise independently on the foundation of all that has come into being in these national Societies. If this can come about, then these national Societies will be truly autonomous too. Then every group which comes into being within this Anthroposophical Society will be truly autonomous.

In order to reach this truly human standpoint, my dear friends, we must realize that especially in the case of a Society which is built on spiritual foundations, in the way I have described, we shall come up against two difficulties. We must overcome these difficulties here, so that in future they will no longer exist in the way they existed in the past history of the Anthroposophical Society.

One of these difficulties is the following: Everyone who understands the consciousness of today will, I believe, agree that this present-day consciousness demands that whatever takes place should do so in full public view. A Society built on firm foundations must above all else not offend this demand of our time. It is not at all difficult to prefer secrecy, even in the external form, in one case or another. But whenever a Society like ours, built on a foundation of truth, seriously desires secrecy, it will surely find itself in conflict with contemporary consciousness, and the most dire obstacles for its continuing existence will ensue. Therefore, dear friends, for the General Anthroposophical Society which is to be founded we cannot but lay claim to absolute openness.

As I pointed out in one of my very first essays in *Luzifer-Gnosis*,[33] the Anthroposophical Society must stand before the world just like any other society that may be founded for, let us say, scientific or similar purposes. It must differ from all these other societies solely on account of the content that flows through its veins. The form in which people come together in it can, in future, no longer be different from that of any other society. Picture to yourselves what we can shovel out of the way if we declare from the start that the Anthroposophical Society is to be entirely open.

It is essential for us to stand firmly on a foundation of reality, that is on the foundation of present-day consciousness. This will mean, dear friends, that in future we shall have to handle our lecture cycles in a manner that differs greatly from that to which we have been accustomed in the past. The history of these lecture cycles represents a tragic chapter within the development of our Anthroposophical Society. They were first published in the belief that they could be retained within a given circle; they were printed for the members of the Anthroposophical Society. But we have long been in a situation in which our opponents, so far as the public declaration of the content is concerned, are far more interested in the cycles than are the members of the Society themselves. Do not misunderstand me; I do not mean that the members of our Society do not work inwardly with the lecture cycles, for they do. But their work is inward, it remains egoistic, a nice Society egoism. The interest which sends its waves out into the world, the interest which gives our Society its particular stamp in the world, this interest comes towards the cycles from our opponents. It has been known to happen that as little as three weeks after its publication a lecture cycle is already being quoted in the worst kind of publication brought out by the opposition. To continue in our old ways as regards the lecture cycles would be to hide our head in the sand, believing that because everything is dark for us everything must be dark in the outside world too.

That is why I have been asking myself for years what can be done about the cycles. We now have no alternative but to put up a moral barrier in place of the physical barrier we tried to erect earlier on, which has meanwhile been breached at all manner of points.

In the draft of the Statutes I have endeavoured to do just this. In future all the cycles, without exception, are to be sold publicly, just like any other books. But suppose, dear friends, there was a book about the integration of partial differential equations. For a great many people such a book is very esoteric indeed. I am probably not wrong in assuming that among those of you gathered here in these two rooms today there is only an extremely small esoteric circle of individuals who might fruitfully concern themselves with the integration of partial differential equations, or of linear differential equations. The book, however, may be sold to anybody. But supposing someone who knows nothing of partial differential equations and is incapable of differentiating or integrating anything at all, someone who knows nothing about logarithms, were to find a textbook on the subject belonging to one of his sons. He would look inside it, see rows and rows of figures but not understand a thing. Then suppose his sons were to tell him that all these figures were the street numbers of the houses in every city in the world. He might well think to himself: What a useful thing to learn; now if I go to Paris I shall know the street number of all the different houses.

As you see, there is no harm in the judgment of someone who understands nothing of the matter, for he is a dilettante, an amateur. In this instance life itself draws the line between the capacity to judge and the lack of capacity to judge.

Thus as regards anthroposophical knowledge we can at least try to draw the line morally and no longer physically. We sell the cycles to all who wish to have them but declare from the start who can be considered competent to form a valid judgment on them, a judgment by which we can set some store. Everybody else is an amateur as far as the cycles are concerned. And we also declare that in future we shall no longer take any account of judgments passed on the cycles by those who are amateurs. This is the only moral protection available to us. If only we carry it out properly, we shall bring about a situation in which the matters with which we are concerned are treated just as are books about the integration of partial differential equations. People will gradually come to agree that it is just as absurd for someone, however learned in other spheres, to pass a judgment about a lecture cycle as it is for someone who knows nothing of logarithms to say: This book about partial differential equations is stuff and nonsense! We must bring about a situation in which the distinction between an amateur and an expert can be drawn in the right way.

Another very great difficulty, dear friends, is the fact that the impulses of the Anthroposophical Movement are not everywhere thoroughly assessed in the right way. Judgments are heard here and there which absolutely deny the Anthroposophical Movement by seeing it as something that is parallel to the very things it is supposed to replace in human evolution. Only a few days ago somebody once again said to me: If you speak to such and such a group of people about what Anthroposophy has to offer, even those who work only in the practical realm accept it so long as you don't mention Anthroposophy or the threefold social order by name; you have to disown them. This is something that has been done by a great many people for many years, and it could not be more false. Whatever the realm, we must stand in the world under the sign of the full truth as representatives of the essence of Anthroposophy. We must be aware that if we are incapable of doing so we cannot actually further the aims of the Anthroposophical Movement. Any veiled representation of the Anthroposophical Movement leads in the end to no good.

Of course everything is individual in such matters. Not everything can be made to conform to a single pattern. Let me give you a few examples of what I mean.

Take eurythmy. As I said yesterday before the performance, eurythmy is drawn and cultivated from the very depths of Anthroposophy. We have to be aware that, imperfect though it still is, it places something in the world which is entirely new, something original which can in no way be compared with anything else that may seem to resemble it in the world today. We have to muster enough enthusiasm for our cause to enable us to exclude any external, superficial comparisons. I know how a sentence like this can be misunderstood, but nevertheless I say it to you in this circle, my dear friends, for it expresses one of the fundamental conditions required for the prospering of the Anthroposophical Movement within the Anthroposophical Society.

Similarly, I have sweated much blood lately — I speak symbolically, of course — over the new form of recitation and declamation which Frau Dr Steiner has developed in our Society. As with eurythmy, the nerve-centre of this form of declaiming or reciting is what is drawn and cultivated from the very depths of Anthroposophy, and it is with this nerve-centre that we must concern ourselves. This nerve-centre is what we have to recognize and there is no point in believing that the result can be improved by taking on board any bits and pieces which might also be good, or even better, belonging to similar methods elsewhere. It is of this absolutely new, this primary quality that we must be aware in all the realms of Anthroposophy.

Now a third example: A realm in which Anthroposophy can be especially fruitful is that of medicine. Yet Anthroposophy will quite definitely remain unfruitful in the realm of medicine, especially therapy, if the tendency persists to represent matters within the field of medicine in the Anthroposophical Movement in a manner which meets with the approval of those who represent medicine in the ordinary way today. We must carry Anthroposophy courageously into every realm, including medicine. Only then will we make progress in what eurythmy ought to be, in what recitation and declamation ought to be, in what medicine ought to be, not to mention many other different fields living within our Anthroposophical Society, just as we must make progress with Anthroposophy itself in the strict sense of the term.

Herewith I have at least hinted at the fundamental conditions which must be placed before our hearts at the beginning of our Conference for the founding of the General Anthroposophical Society. In the manner indicated it must become a Society of attitudes and not a Society of statutes. The Statutes are to express externally what is alive within every soul.

So now I would like to proceed to the reading[34] of the draft of the Statutes* which go in the direction I have thus far mentioned in brief.

'STATUTES OF THE ANTHROPOSOPHICAL SOCIETY'

'1. The Anthroposophical Society is to be an association of people whose will it is to nurture the life of the soul, both in the individual and in human society, on the basis of a true knowledge of the spiritual world.'

'2. The persons gathered at the Goetheanum in Dornach at Christmas, 1923, both the individuals and the groups represented, form the nucleus of the Society. They are convinced that there exists in our time a genuine science of the spiritual world and that the civilization of today is lacking the cultivation of such a science. This cultivation is to be the task of the Anthroposophical Society. It will endeavour to fulfil this task by making the anthroposophical spiritual science cultivated at the Goetheanum in Dornach the centre of its activities, together with all that results from this for brotherhood in human relationships and for the moral and religious as well as the artistic and cultural life in the human being.'

*See facsimiles of the manuscript draft and also the printed Statutes given to each participant, pages II – IX.

Note, my dear friends, how we are thus building not on principles but on human beings, on those human beings who are gathered together here. And what will those who join later declare? That they are essentially in agreement with these people as regards what is stated here. So all abstractions are avoided and the Anthroposophical Society is built on human beings.

'3. The persons gathered in Dornach as the nucleus of the Society' — you see how it is the individual people who are important — 'recognize and endorse the view of the leadership at the Goetheanum: "Anthroposophy, as fostered at the Goetheanum, leads to results which can serve every human being as a stimulus to spiritual life, whatever his nation, social standing or religion. They can lead to a social life genuinely built on brotherly love. No special degree of academic learning is required to make them one's own and to found one's life upon them, but only an open-minded human nature." '

This means that the results can be understood by all human beings who approach with an open-minded soul.

The matter is different — this is expressed next — as regards the research which leads to the results in question. A strict distinction must be made as regards this research. So the text continues:

' "Research into these results, however, as well as competent evaluation of them, depends upon spiritual-scientific training, which is to be acquired step by step. These results are in their own way as exact as the results of genuine natural science. When they attain general recognition in the same way as these, they will bring about comparable progress in all spheres of life, not only in the spiritual but also in the practical realm." '

'4. The Anthroposophical Society is in no sense a secret society, but is entirely public. Anyone can become a member, without regard to nationality, social standing, religion, scientific or artistic conviction, who considers as justified the existence of an institution such as the Goetheanum in Dornach, in its capacity as a School of Spiritual Science.'

As you see, even here, where the requirements for becoming a member are exactly defined, we have been careful to make it clear that someone desiring to become a member must consider as justified the existence not of the Goetheanum, but merely 'of an institution such as the Goetheanum in Dornach, in its capacity as a School of Spiritual Science.' You must thoroughly consider every turn of phrase in these draft Statutes. They are brief. Statutes ought to be brief, and not fill a whole tome. But you will see that the effort has been made to phrase every sentence in a manner which speaks out of direct consciousness.

'The Anthroposophical Society rejects any kind of sectarian activity. Party politics it considers not to be within its task.'

We need this sentence because numerous misunderstandings were brought about during the years when we were promoting the idea of the threefold social order. The misunderstandings arose out of a lack of clarity in the attitude of many of our members. The impression was frequently given that Anthroposophy wanted to become involved in the political affairs of the world — something that has never been and never can be the case — because many of our friends approached the political parties regarding the threefold idea. This was an error on their part right from the start.

'5. The Anthroposophical Society sees the School of Spiritual Science in Dornach as a centre for its activity. The School will be composed of three classes.'

Please do not be alarmed by these three classes, my dear friends. These three classes existed originally in the Anthroposophical Society,[35] though in a different form, up to the year 1914.

'Members of the Society will be admitted to the School on their own application after a period of membership to be determined by the leadership at the Goetheanum. They enter in this way the First Class of the School of Spiritual Science. Admission to the Second or Third Class takes place when the person requesting this is deemed eligible by the leadership at the Goetheanum.'

'6. Every member of the Anthroposophical Society has the right to attend all lectures, performances and meetings arranged by the Society, under conditions to be announced by the Vorstand.'

'7. The organizing of the School of Spiritual Science is, to begin with, the responsibility of Rudolf Steiner, who will appoint his collaborators and his possible successor.'

I can tell you now that I intend in future to divide this School of Spiritual Science into separate Sections under the leadership of suitable persons whom I shall appoint. These suitable persons, who will be the leaders of the Sections of the School of Spiritual Science, will at the same time be advisory members of the Vorstand which is to be formed and about which I shall be speaking shortly.

'8. All publications of the Society shall be public, in the same sense as are those of other public societies. The publications of the School of Spiritual Science will form no exception as regards this public character;' — in future, the lecture cycles will be entitled: Publications of the School of Spiritual Science — 'however, the leadership of the School reserves the right to deny in advance the validity of any judgment on *these* publications which is not based on the same training from which they have been derived. Consequently they will regard as justified no judgment which is not based on an appropriate preliminary training, as is also the common practice in the recognized scientific world. Thus the publications of the School of Spiritual Science' — this is what the cycles will be in future — 'will bear the following note: "Printed as manuscript for members of the School of Spiritual Science, Goetheanum, . . . Class." No one is considered competent to judge the content, who has not acquired — through the School itself or in a manner recognized by the School as equivalent — the requisite preliminary knowledge. Other opinions will be disregarded, to the extent that the authors of such works will not enter into a discussion about them.'

Everyone can buy the works. But valid judgments can only be made by those who belong to the Class mentioned in the note 'Printed as manuscript for members of the School of Spiritual Science, Goetheanum, . . . Class'.

'9. The purpose of the Anthroposophical Society will be the furtherance of spiritual research; that of the School of Spiritual Science will be this research itself. A dogmatic stand in any field whatsoever is to be excluded from the Anthroposophical Society.'

'10. The Anthroposophical Society shall hold a regular General Meeting at the Goetheanum at the beginning of each year, at which time the Vorstand shall present a full report with accounting. The agenda for this meeting shall be communicated by the Vorstand to all members, together with the invitation, three weeks before the meeting.'

Resolutions can of course be made about this.

'The Vorstand may call special meetings and fix the agenda for them. Invitations to such meetings shall be sent to members three weeks in advance. Motions proposed by individual members or groups of members shall be submitted one week before the General Meeting.'

We shall have to add a passage here stating that special meetings may also be called at the request of the membership.

'11. Members may join together in smaller or larger groups on any basis of locality or subject.'

From the point of view of the General Society this paragraph encompasses every group, including each national group. The General Society is neither international nor national but simply human in the widest sense; all the subdivisions are therefore groups. By this means we can bring into the Anthroposophical Society a life that is genuinely based on freedom, and also, wherever it wants to come into being, a life that is autonomous. We cannot make progress in any other way.

'The headquarters of the Anthroposophical Society is at the Goetheanum. From there the Vorstand shall bring to the attention of the members or groups of members what it considers to be the task of the Society.'

My dear friends, this sentence is especially important because it expresses what the Vorstand considers itself to be. It does not consider itself to be an elected body. It considers itself to be a group of people which says: Here at the Goetheanum we want to do something and we shall communicate about the different things we do with those who so wish, either individuals or groups; we shall recognize as a member every individual or every group who can accept these Statutes and be in agreement with them.

In doing this, the Vorstand declares that it places itself within the Society in the freest manner possible: it wants nothing else but to be a group of people with initiative for the cause of Anthroposophy. To live fully in initiative for the cause of Anthroposophy will have to be the heart's blood of this Vorstand. It is not a representative of people in the abstract; it is a representative of the anthroposophical cause here at the Goetheanum. Its task is to represent the cause of Anthroposophy here at the Goetheanum. And to declare one's membership of a society for which this Vorstand wants to have meaning means to join in the promotion of the cause of Anthroposophy. The membership and the Vorstand, and their relationship with one another, is thought of as being quite generally human in an entirely free way in the future. We have not achieved this as yet; we must make it obvious to all the world. Then there will be no more criticisms like that expressed by Leisegang[36] to the effect that a self-appointed Vorstand, not accountable to anybody, not elected anywhere, has been in existence for the last ten years. From the start we must stress forcefully that an election as such is impossible in the Anthroposophical Society and that only initiative is possible. Let us return to the Vorstand:

'The Vorstand communicates with officials elected or appointed by the various groups.'

How these come into being is a matter for the statutes of the different groups. For us here it will merely be a matter that on a basis we shall create we shall want to communicate with trust with these officials.

'Admission of members will be the concern of the individual groups; the certificate of membership shall, however, be placed before the Vorstand in Dornach, and shall be signed by them out of their confidence in the officials of the groups. In general, every member should join a group. Only those for whom it is quite impossible to find entry to a group should apply directly to Dornach for membership.'

'12. Membership dues shall be fixed by the individual groups; each group shall, however, submit . . . for each of its members to the central leadership of the Society at the Goetheanum.'

I have put dots here, though I already have an opinion which I may well voice if it comes to it. But for the moment I have put dots so that the matter may be as broadly considered as possible before tomorrow's discussions. For money is something we shall need here too. I have often indicated that idealism cannot take the form of saying: Oh, horrible ahrimanic money; let us not contaminate our ideals with it; our ideals should be as free from it as they possibly can be! The left fist clutches the purse-strings while the right hand is raised on high for the ideals. Alas, the uncomfortable gesture of putting that right hand into the left pocket is sometimes necessary; if the ideals are to be upheld, small sacrifices are necessary.

'13. Each working group formulates its own statutes, but these must not be incompatible with the Statutes of the Anthroposophical Society.'

'14. The organ of the Society is *Das Goetheanum,* which for this purpose is provided with a Supplement containing the official communications of the Society. This enlarged edition of *Das Goetheanum* will be supplied to members of the Anthroposophical Society only.'

This paragraph is of particular concern to me because wherever I go members with a good capacity to judge have been saying to me: We never seem to hear what is going on in the Anthroposophical Society. By instituting this journal we shall be able to conduct a careful correspondence which will more and more come to be a correspondence belonging to each one of you, and through it you will be able to live right in the midst of the Anthroposophical Society.

Now, my dear friends, in case after due consideration you should indeed come to agree with my appointment as President of the Anthroposophical Society, I still have to make my suggestions as to the membership of the Vorstand with whom I should actually be able to fulfil the tasks which I have indicated very briefly here.

So that the affairs of Anthroposophy can be truly and properly administered, members of the Vorstand must be people who reside here in Dornach. So far as my estimation of the Society is concerned, the Vorstand cannot consist of individuals who are situated all over the place. This will not prevent the individual groups from electing their own officials autonomously. And when these officials come to Dornach, they will be taken into the meetings of the Vorstand as advisory members while they are here. We must make the whole thing come to life. Instead of a bureaucratic Vorstand scattered all over the world there will be officials responsible for the individual groups, officials arising from amongst the membership of the groups; they will always have the opportunity to feel themselves equal members of the Vorstand which, however, will be located in Dornach. The work itself will have to be taken care of by the Vorstand in Dornach.

Moreover, the members of the Vorstand must without question be people who have devoted their lives entirely, both outwardly and inwardly, to the cause of Anthroposophy. So now after long deliberations over the past weeks I shall take the liberty of presenting to you my suggestions for the membership of the Vorstand:

I believe there will nowhere arise even the faintest hint of dissension but that on the contrary there will be in all your hearts the most unanimous and fullest agreement to the suggestion that *Herr Albert Steffen* be appointed as Vice-president. (Lively applause)

This being the case, we have in the Vorstand itself an expression of something I have already mentioned today: our links, as the Anthroposophical Society, with Switzerland. I cannot express my conviction more emphatically than by saying to you: If it is a matter of having a Swiss citizen who will give all his strength as a member of the Vorstand and as Vice-president, then there is no better Swiss citizen to be found.

Next we shall have in the Vorstand an individual who has been united with the Anthroposophical Society from the very beginning, who has for the greater part built up the Anthroposophical Society and who is today active in an anthroposophical way in one of the most important fields: *Frau Dr Steiner*. (Lively applause)

With your applause you have said everything and clearly

shown that we need have no fear that our choice in this direction might not have been quite appropriate.

A further member of the Vorstand I have to suggest on the basis of facts arising here over recent weeks. This is the person with whom I at present have the opportunity to test anthroposophical enthusiasm to its limits in the right way by working with her on the elaboration of the anthroposophical system of medicine: *Frau Dr Ita Wegman.* (Lively applause)

Through her work — and especially through her understanding of her work — she has shown that in this specialized field she can assert the effectiveness of Anthroposophy in the right way. I know that the effects of this work will be beneficial. That is why I have taken it upon myself to work immediately with Frau Dr Wegman on developing the anthroposophical system of medicine.[37] It will appear before the eyes of the world and then we shall see that particularly in members who work in this way we have the real friends of the Anthroposophical Society.

Another member I have to suggest is one who has been tried and tested in the utmost degree for the work in Dornach both in general and down to the very last detail, one who has ever proved herself to be a faithful member. I do believe — without intending to sound boastful — that the members of the Vorstand have indeed been rightly selected. Albert Steffen was an anthroposophist before he was even born, and this ought to be duly recognized. Frau Dr Steiner has of course always been an anthroposophist ever since an Anthroposophical Society has existed. Frau Dr Wegman was one of the very first members who joined in the work just after we did in the very early days. She has been a member of the Anthroposophical Movement for over twenty years. Apart from us, she is the longest standing member in this room. And another member of very long standing is the person I now mean, who has been tried and tested down to the very last detail as a most faithful colleague; you may indeed be satisfied with her down to the very last detail: *Fräulein Dr Lili Vreede.* (Applause)

We need furthermore in the anthroposophical Vorstand an individual who will take many cares off our shoulders, cares which cannot all be borne by us because of course the initiatives have to be kept separate. This is someone who will have to think on everyone's behalf, for this is necessary even when the others — again without intending to sound boastful — also make the effort to use their heads intelligently in anthroposophical matters. What is needed is someone who, so to speak, does not knock heads together but does hold them together. This is an individual who many will feel still needs to be tried and tested, but I believe that he will master every trial. This will be our dear *Dr Guenther Wachsmuth* who in everything he is obliged to do for us here has already shown his mastery of a good many trials which have made it obvious that he is capable of working with others in a most harmonious manner. As time goes on we shall find ourselves much satisfied with him. I hope, then, that you will agree to the appointment of Dr Guenther Wachsmuth, not as the cashier — which he does not want to be — but as the secretary and treasurer. (Applause)

The Vorstand must be kept small, and so my list is now exhausted, my dear friends. And the time allotted for our morning meeting has also run out. I just want to call once more on all our efforts to bring into this gathering above all the appropriate mood of soul, more and yet more mood of soul. Out of this anthroposophical mood of soul will arise what we need for the next few days. And if we have it for the next few days we shall also have it for the future times we are about to enter for the Anthroposophical Society. I have appealed to your hearts; I have appealed to the wisdom in you which your hearts can fill with glowing warmth and enthusiasm. May we sustain this glowing warmth and this enthusiasm throughout the coming meetings and thus achieve something truly fruitful over the next few days.

There are two more announcements to be made: This afternoon there will be two performances of one of the Christmas Plays, the Paradise Play. The first will take place at 4.30. Those who cannot find a seat then will be able to see it at 6 o'clock. Everybody will have a chance to see this play today.

Our next meeting is at 8 o'clock this evening when my first

lecture on world history in the light of Anthroposophy will take place.

Tomorrow, Tuesday, at 10 o'clock we shall gather here for the laying of the Foundation Stone of the Anthroposophical Society, and following straight on from that will be the Foundation Meeting of the Anthroposophical Society.

The meeting of General Secretaries and delegates planned for this afternoon will not take place because it will be better to hold it after the Foundation Meeting has taken place. It will be tomorrow at 2.30 in the Glass House lower down the hill, in the Architects' Office. That will be the meeting of the Vorstand, the General Secretaries and those who are their secretaries.

If Herr Abels could now come up here, I would request you to collect your meal tickets from him. To avoid chaos down at the canteen there will be different sittings and we hope that everything will proceed in an orderly fashion.

The Laying of the Foundation Stone of the General Anthroposophical Society

through Rudolf Steiner

25 DECEMBER, 10 O'CLOCK IN THE MORNING

DR STEINER greets those present with the words:

My dear friends!

Let the first words to resound through this room today be those which sum up the essence of what may stand before your souls as the most important findings of recent years.*

Later there will be more to be said about these words which are, as they stand, a summary. But first let our ears be touched by them, so that out of the signs of the present time we may renew, in keeping with our way of thinking, the ancient word of the Mysteries: 'Know thyself.'

Soul of Man!
Thou livest in the limbs
Which bear thee through the world of space

*In the 1985 German edition, from which this translation is made, the verses spoken here and in the subsequent sessions are given as shown in the shorthand report. See the Note on the Verses.

In the spirit's ocean-being.
Practise spirit-recalling
In depths of soul,
Where in the wielding will
Of world-creating
Thine own I
Comes to being
Within God's I.
And thou wilt truly live
In the World-Being of Man.

Soul of Man!
Thou livest in the beat of heart and lung
Which leads thee through the rhythm of time
Into the realm of thine own soul's feeling.
Practise spirit-awareness
In balance of the soul,
Where the surging deeds
Of the world's becoming
Thine own I
Unite
With the World-I.
And thou wilt truly feel
In the Soul-Weaving of Man.

Soul of Man!
Thou livest in the resting head
Which from the grounds of eternity
Opens to thee the world-thoughts.
Practise spirit-beholding
In stillness of thought,
Where the eternal aims of Gods
World-Being's Light
On thine own I
Bestow
For thy free willing.
And thou wilt truly think
In the Spirit-Foundations of Man.

My dear friends! Today when I look back specifically to what it was possible to bring from the spiritual worlds while the terrible storms of war were surging across the earth, I find it all expressed as though in a paradigm in the trio of verses your ears have just heard.*

For decades it has been possible to perceive this threefoldness of man which enables him in the wholeness of his being of spirit, soul and body to revive for himself once more in a new form the call 'Know thyself'. For decades it has been possible to perceive this threefoldness. But only in the last decade have I myself been able to bring it to full maturity while the storms of war were raging.[38] I sought to indicate how man lives in the physical realm in his system of metabolism and limbs, in his system of heart and rhythm, in his system of thinking and perceiving with his head. Yesterday I indicated how this threefoldness can be rightly taken up when our hearts are enlivened through and through by Anthroposophia.

We may be sure that if man learns to know in his feeling and in his will what he is actually doing when, as the spirits of the universe enliven him, he lets his limbs place him in the world of space, that then — not in a suffering, passive grasping of the universe but in an active grasping of the world in which he fulfils his duties, his tasks, his mission on the earth — that then in this active grasping of the world he will know the being of all-wielding love of man and universe which is one member of the all-world-being.

We may be sure that if man understands the miraculous mystery holding sway between lung and heart — expressing inwardly the beat of universal rhythms working across millennia, across the aeons of time to ensoul him with the universe through the rhythms of pulse and blood — we may hope that, grasping this in wisdom with a heart that has become a sense organ, man can experience the divinely given universal images as out of themselves they actively reveal the cosmos. Just as in active

*At this point, and again in the final words of this meeting at which the Foundation Stone was laid in members' hearts, Rudolf Steiner changed for a moment from the formal mode of address to the more intimate 'Du'. (Tr.)

movement we grasp the all-wielding love of worlds, so shall we grasp the archetypal images of world existence when we sense in ourselves the mysterious interplay between universal rhythm and heart rhythm, and through this the human rhythm that takes place mysteriously in soul and spirit realms in the interplay between lung and heart.

And when, in feeling, the human being rightly perceives what is revealed in the system of his head, which is at rest on his shoulders even when he walks along, then, feeling himself within the system of his head and pouring warmth of heart into this system of his head, he will experience the ruling, working, weaving thoughts of the universe within his own being.

Thus he becomes the threefoldness of all existence: universal love reigning in human love; universal Imagination reigning in the forms of the human organism; universal thoughts reigning mysteriously below the surface in human thoughts. He will grasp this threefoldness and he will recognize himself as an individually free human being within the reigning work of the gods in the cosmos, as a cosmic human being, an individual human being within the cosmic human being, working for the future of the universe as an individual human being within the cosmic human being. Out of the signs of the present time he will re-enliven the ancient words: 'Know thou thyself!'

The Greeks were still permitted to omit the final word, since for them the human self was not yet as abstract as it is for us now that it has become concentrated in the abstract ego-point or at most in thinking, feeling and willing. For them human nature comprised the totality of spirit, soul and body. Thus the ancient Greeks were permitted to believe that they spoke of the total human being, spirit, soul and body, when they let resound the ancient word of the Sun, the word of Apollo: 'Know thou thyself!'

Today, re-enlivening these words in the right way out of the signs of our times, we have to say: Soul of man, know thou thyself in the weaving existence of spirit, soul and body. When we say this, we have understood what lies at the foundation of all aspects of the being of man. In the substance of the universe there works and is and lives the spirit which streams from the heights and reveals itself in the human head; the force of Christ working in the circumference, weaving in the air, encircling the earth, works and lives in the system of our breath; and from the inmost depths of the earth rise up the forces which work in our limbs. When now, at this moment, we unite these three forces, the forces of the heights, the forces of the circumference, the forces of the depths, in a substance that gives form, then in the understanding of our soul we can bring face to face the universal dodecahedron with the human dodecahedron. Out of these three forces: out of the spirit of the heights, out of the force of Christ in the circumference, out of the working of the Father, the creative activity of the Father that streams out of the depths, let us at this moment give form in our souls to the dodecahedral Foundation Stone which we lower into the soil of our souls so that it may remain there a powerful sign in the strong foundations of our soul existence and so that in the future working of the Anthroposophical Society we may stand on this firm Foundation Stone.

Let us ever remain aware of this Foundation Stone for the Anthroposophical Society, formed today. In all that we shall do, in the outer world and here, to further, to develop and to fully unfold the Anthroposophical Society, let us preserve the remembrance of the Foundation Stone which we have today lowered into the soil of our hearts. Let us seek in the threefold being of man, which teaches us love, which teaches us the universal Imagination, which teaches us the universal thoughts; let us seek, in this threefold being, the substance of universal love which we lay as the foundation, let us seek in this threefold being the archetype of the Imagination according to which we shape the universal love within our hearts, let us seek the power of thoughts from the heights which enable us to let shine forth in fitting manner this dodecahedral Imagination which has received its form through love! Then shall we carry away with us from here what we need. Then shall the Foundation Stone shine forth before the eyes of our soul, that Foundation Stone which has received its substance from universal love and human love, its picture image, its form, from universal Imagination and human Imagination, and its brilliant radiance from universal thoughts and human thoughts, its brilliant radiance which whenever we recollect this moment can shine towards us with warm light, with light that spurs on our deeds, our thinking, our feeling and our willing.

The proper soil into which we must lower the Foundation Stone of today, the proper soil consists of our hearts in their harmonious collaboration, in their good, love-filled desire to bear together the will of Anthroposophy through the world. This will cast its light on us like a reminder of the light of thought that can ever shine towards us from the dodecahedral Stone of love which today we will lower into our hearts.

Dear friends, let us take this deeply into our souls. With it let us warm our souls, and with it let us enlighten our souls. Let us cherish this warmth of soul and this light of soul which out of good will we have planted in our hearts today.

We plant it, my dear friends, at a moment when human memory that truly understands the universe looks back to the point in human evolution, at the turning point of time, when out of the darkness of night and out of the darkness of human moral feeling, shooting like light from heaven, was born the divine being who had become the Christ, the spirit being who had entered into humankind.

We can best bring strength to that warmth of soul and that light of soul which we need, if we enliven them with the warmth and the light that shone forth at the turning point of time as the Light of Christ in the darkness of the universe. In our hearts, in our thoughts and in our will let us bring to life that original consecrated night of Christmas which took place two thousand years ago, so that it may help us when we carry forth into the world what shines towards us through the light of thought of that dodecahedral Foundation Stone of love which is shaped in accordance with the universe and has been laid into the human realm.

So let the feelings of our heart be turned back towards the original consecrated night of Christmas in ancient Palestine.

At the turning of the time
The Spirit-Light of the world
Entered the stream of earthly being.
Darkness of night
Had held its sway,
Day-radiant light
Streamed into souls of men.
Light that gives warmth
To simple shepherds' hearts,
Light that enlightens
The wise heads of kings.

Light Divine
Christ-Sun!
Warm thou our hearts,
Enlighten thou our heads,
That good may become
What we from our hearts would found
What we from our heads would direct
In conscious
Willing.

This turning of our feelings back to the original consecrated night of Christmas can give us the strength for the warming of our hearts and the enlightening of our heads which we need if we are to practise rightly, working anthroposophically, what can arise from the knowledge of the threefold human being coming to harmony in unity.

So let us once more gather before our souls all that follows from a true understanding of the words 'Know thou thyself in spirit, soul and body'. Let us gather it as it works in the cosmos so that to our Stone, which we have now laid in the soil of our hearts, there may speak from everywhere into human existence and into human life and into human work everything that the universe has to say to this human existence and to this human life and to this human work.

25 DECEMBER, 10 O'CLOCK IN THE MORNING

Soul of Man!
Thou livest in the limbs
Which bear thee through the world of space
In the spirit's ocean-being.
Practise spirit-recalling
In depths of soul,
Where in the wielding will
Of world-creating
Thine own I
Comes to being
Within God's I.
And thou wilt truly live
In the World-Being of Man.

For the Father-Spirit of the heights holds sway
In depths of worlds begetting being:
Seraphim, Cherubim, Thrones!
Let there ring out from the heights
What in the depths is echoed
And in the echo of the depths
The secret of the heights, resounding
Speaks:
Ex Deo nascimur.
The spirits of the elements hear it
In East, West, North, South:
May human beings hear it.

Soul of Man!
Thou livest in the beat of heart and lung
Which leads thee through the rhythm of time
Into the realm of thine own soul's feeling.
Practise spirit-awareness
In balance of the soul,
Where the surging deeds
Of the world's becoming
Thine own I
Unite
With the World-I.
And thou wilt truly feel
In the Soul-Weaving of Man.

For the Christ-Will in the encircling round holds sway
In the rhythms of the worlds, bestowing grace on the soul:
Through the spirits: Kyriotetes, Dynamis, Exusiai,
Let there be fired, ye spirits, from the East
What through the West is formed,
And the fire of the East,
As it receives form from the West
Speaks:
In Christo morimur.
The spirits of the elements hear it
In East, West, North, South:
May human beings hear it.

Soul of Man!
Thou livest in the resting head
Which from the grounds of eternity
Opens to thee the world-thoughts.
Practise spirit-beholding
In stillness of thought,
Where the eternal aims of Gods
World-Being's Light
On thine own I
Bestow
For thy free willing.
And thou wilt truly think
In the Spirit-Foundations of Man.

For the world-thoughts of the Spirit hold sway
In the being of worlds, craving for light:
Archai, Archangeloi, Angeloi!
Let there be prayed from the depths
What in the heights will be granted,
And when it is rightly understood
How it rings forth from Archai, Archangeloi, Angeloi,
When from the depths is prayed
What in the heights can be answered,
Then speaks it through the world:
Per Spiritum Sanctum reviviscimus.
The spirits of the elements hear it
In East, West, North, South:
May human beings hear it.

My dear friends, hear it as it resounds in your own hearts! Then will you found here a true community of human beings for Anthroposophia; and then will you carry the spirit that rules in the shining light of thoughts around the dodecahedral Stone of love out into the world wherever it should give of its light and of its warmth for the progress of human souls, for the progress of the universe.

The Foundation Meeting of the General Anthroposophical Society

25 DECEMBER, 11.15 IN THE MORNING

DR STEINER greets those present with the words:

My dear friends!

Allow me forthwith to open the Foundation Meeting of the Anthroposophical Society. My first task is to announce the names of the General Secretaries who will speak on behalf of the national Societies:

America, the United States: Mr Monges.
Austria: On behalf of the Council: Count Polzer.
Belgium: Madame Muntz.
Czechoslovakia: Dr Eiselt, Dr Krkavec.
Denmark: Herr Hohlenberg.
England: Mr Collison.
Finland: Herr Donner.
France: Mademoiselle Sauerwein.
Germany:
on behalf of the Council: Dr Unger.
on behalf of the Free Anthroposophical Society:
Dr Büchenbacher.
Holland: Dr Zeylmans van Emmichoven.
Honolulu: Madame Ferreri.

Italy: On behalf of the Council:
Baroness de Renzis, Rome,
The Duke of Cesaro, Fräulein Schwarz, Milan.
Norway: Herr Ingerö.
Sweden: Fräulein Henström.
Switzerland: Herr Steffen.

Secondly I have to read to you a telegram which has arrived: 'Please convey to the gathering our cordial greetings and best wishes for a good outcome, in the name of Sweden's anthroposophists.'

Before coming to the first point on the agenda I wish to ask whether in accordance with the rules of procedure anyone wishes to comment on the agenda?

No-one.

Then let us take the first point on the agenda. I call on Herr Steffen, who will also be speaking as the General Secretary of the Society in Switzerland, within whose boundaries we are guests here.

Albert Steffen speaks.

He concludes by reading a resolution of the Swiss delegates:

The delegates of the Swiss branches have decided to announce publicly today, on the occasion of the Foundation Meeting, the following resolution:

'Today, on the occasion of the Foundation Meeting of the General Anthroposophical World Society in Dornach, the Anthroposophical Society in Switzerland wishes to express its gratitude and enthusiasm for the fact that the Goetheanum, which serves the cultural life of all mankind, is to be built once again in Switzerland. The Swiss Society sees in this both good fortune and great honour for its country. It wishes to verify that it will do everything in its power to ensure that the inexhaustible abundance of spiritual impulses given to the world through the works of Rudolf Steiner can continue to flow out from here. In collaboration with the other national Societies it wants to hope that the pure and beneficial source may become accessible to all human beings who seek it.'

DR STEINER: My dear friends, in the interest of a proper continuation of the Meeting it seems to me sensible to postpone the discussion on announcements such as that we have just heard to a time which will arise naturally out of the proceedings.

For the second point on the agenda I now wish to call for the reports to be given by the various Secretaries of the various national Societies. If anyone does not agree with this arrangement of the agenda, please raise your hand.

It seems that no-one disagrees, so let us continue with the agenda. Will the different General Secretaries please come to the platform to speak to our friends. I first call on the General Secretary for the United States of America, Mr Monges, to speak.

Mr Monges gives his report.

DR STEINER: I would now like to call on the General Secretary for Belgium, Madame Muntz, to speak.

Madame Muntz expresses her thanks for this honour, declares herself in agreement with all the statements that have been made and wishes the Meeting all the best.

DR STEINER: I now call on the General Secretary for Denmark, Herr Hohlenberg, to speak.

Herr Hohlenberg reports.

DR STEINER: I now call on the representative of the Council in Germany, Dr Unger, to speak.

Dr Unger reports on the work of the German national Society. He concludes with words which have been recorded in the shorthand report:

At present we require in some aspects a rather comprehensive structure to accommodate this Society. This will have to be brought into full conformity with the Statutes presented here by Dr Steiner for the founding of the General Society. We declare that the Anthroposophical Society in Germany will incorporate every point of these Statutes into its own Statutes and that these Statutes as a whole will be given precedence over the Statutes or Rules of the Anthroposophical Society in Germany. In addition I have also been especially called upon to express deep gratitude to Dr Steiner for taking on the heavy obligations arising out of the founding of the General Anthroposophical Society. Out of all the impressions gained from this Conference, the question will have to be asked whether every aspect of the work done in a large Society such as that in Germany can participate in and wants to participate in what is wanted by Dornach. Ever since Dr Steiner took up residence in Dornach, ever since there has been work going on in Dornach, it has always gone without saying that what took place in Dornach was seen as the central point of all our work. Whatever else needs to be said about the work of the Society in Germany will be better brought forward during the further course of our gatherings. Let me just say, however, that in recent months we have begun a very intensive public programme. Hundreds of lectures of all kinds, but particularly also those arising out of a purely anthroposophical intention, have been given, especially in the southwestern part of Germany, even in the smallest places. All those who have participated, and there are many, agree without reservation that even in the smallest places there is a genuine interest in Anthroposophy, that everywhere hearts are waiting for Anthroposophy, and that wherever it is clearly and openly stated that the speaker stands on the soil of the spiritual research given to the world by Dr Steiner it is really so that people feel: I am reminded that I have a soul and that this soul is beginning to be aware of itself once more. This is the case in all human souls, even those found in the smallest places, so we may look with confidence towards continuing our work in future.

DR STEINER: I now call on the representative of the Free Anthroposophical Society in Germany, Dr Büchenbacher, to speak.

Dr Büchenbacher reports and concludes with the words: I would like to express our feeling of deepest gratitude to Dr Steiner for taking upon himself the leadership of the Anthroposophical Society. This gives us the will and the courage to work with what strength we have on the general stream of forces of the Anthroposophical Society. We express our profoundest thanks to him for having done this deed. And we request that the Free Anthroposophical Society for its part may be permitted to work according to its capacity towards the fulfilment of the tasks which Dr Steiner has set it.

DR STEINER: May I now call on the General Secretary of the English Anthroposophical Society, Mr Collison, to speak.

Mr Collison reports.

DR STEINER: I now call on the General Secretary of the Anthroposophical Society in Finland, Herr Donner, to speak.

Herr Donner reports.

DR STEINER: I now call on the General Secretary of the Anthroposophical Society in France, Mademoiselle Sauerwein, to speak.

Mademoiselle Sauerwein reports.

DR STEINER: I now call on the Dutch General Secretary of the Anthroposophical Society, Dr Zeylmans van Emmichoven, to speak.

Dr Zeylmans van Emmichoven reports.

DR STEINER: May I ask you to remain in your seats for a few more moments, dear friends. First of all, even during this Conference forgetfulness has led to the accumulation of a number of items of lost property. These have been gathered together and may be collected by the losers from Herr Kellermüller on their way out.

Secondly, the programme for the remainder of today will be as follows: At 2.30 there will be a meeting of the Vorstand with the General Secretaries, and any secretaries they may have brought with them, down in the Glass House, in the Architects' Office. This meeting will be for the Vorstand, the General Secretaries, and possibly their secretaries, only.

At 4.30 there will be a performance of the Nativity Play here.

Because of a eurythmy rehearsal my evening lecture will begin at 8.30.

I now adjourn today's meeting of members till tomorrow morning at 10 o'clock. I shall then have the pleasure of calling on the representative of Honolulu, Madame Ferreri, to speak, and representatives of other groups who did not speak today. The meeting is now adjourned till tomorrow morning at 10 o'clock.

Meeting of the Vorstand and the General Secretaries of the National Societies and their Secretaries

25 DECEMBER, 2.30 IN THE

AFTERNOON IN THE GLASS HOUSE

DR STEINER answers questions from the officials of the Societies on the various Paragraphs of the Statutes.

To a question on Paragraph 11 regarding the admission of individual members who do not wish to join a particular group he answers as follows:

This Paragraph would only come into consideration if it proves entirely impossible to bring these efforts to a satisfactory conclusion. Only then should individuals or groups apply for membership direct to Dornach. Efforts must first be made to join the relevant national Society and only if this fails for some reason would we admit an individual or a group here in Dornach.

Herr Hohlenberg asks what is meant by: 'Only for those for whom it is quite impossible to find entry to a group.'

DR STEINER: The Statutes are phrased in such a way as to include everything in as few words as possible. Perhaps it is necessary to clarify the sentence 'Only those for whom it is quite impossible to find entry to a group should apply directly to Dornach for membership' by adding that this refers not only to the group not agreeing to admit the individual but also to the individual finding it inwardly impossible to join the group. Thus for instance a person who is convinced that he cannot thrive in a particular group can, if all efforts fail, become a member in Dornach. Here in Dornach we for our part shall of course endeavour to convince the individual to join a group. When I was writing down this sentence I was thinking not only of external obstacles coming from the group but also of obstacles arising out of an individual's convictions.

HERR HOHLENBERG: Are all those who are already members to have their membership confirmed?

DR STEINER: This will be desirable if only for the reason that we are having proper membership cards printed to replace the old, not very beautiful membership cards, and every member will enjoy seeing a membership card which is somewhat larger and which commands a certain degree of respect. Therefore it would be good to send a circular to the individual groups letting them know that all the old membership cards can be exchanged for new ones.

MADEMOISELLE SAUERWEIN asks: If a number of members in a particular country want to form themselves into a group and elect a new officer who is not an officer of the national group, would they be allowed to do this or not?

DR STEINER: Of course nobody can be denied this right. All that can be done is to make efforts to prevent it, but nobody can be denied the right to form groups which would, of course, not be the national group but simply a private group. It would not be possible for it to be the national group because, of course, the national group already exists, does it not? But this cannot be included in the Statutes. The Statutes must contain the principles. But it can be included in By-Laws which we shall still have to elaborate.

Herr Donner wants to ask whether a group which does not want to be affiliated with the national Society in its own country can instead be affiliated with the Society of another country.

DR STEINER: In principle this would not be impossible. To exclude this on principle would be too great an infringement of the freedom of the individual members. We cannot exclude this possibility, but we would have to make efforts not to let such a situation arise in which a group in one country joins the Society of another country; if such a group were not to join the national Society, then it would join directly in Dornach. This could come about as a matter of usage. It cannot be excluded on principle. For instance it would not be possible to prevent a group coming into being in France and registering with the German Society. We would not be able to prevent this.

MADAME MUNTZ: Should we make efforts to bring it about that individuals who do not live in Belgium and yet do belong to our group apply for membership in their own countries, or not?

DR STEINER: In cases where they have done this from sympathy, this is all right. Cases where those in question have sympathies in a particular direction might as well be allowed to remain. But for the future it would be preferable for this not to happen. We need not take up a pedantic position; there is no need for this, but we do need something that can give us a certain degree of support.

DR UNGER: There are quite a number of people in South America who are members of the German Society and who have expressed their wish to remain so. Arrangements are, however, being made for a Society to be formed among the different groups. I have been asked to bring to this meeting the need expressed there that a South American Society should be planned. For the moment they wish to remain attached to Germany, and the method of transferring these groups will gradually come about.

DR STEINER: The configuration of the Society being what it is, it is of course the case that from the administrative point of view everything will have to be taken into consideration not in a bureaucratic way but in a way that is necessitated by human factors. Take Paragraph 14 of the Statutes: 'The organ of the Society is *Das Goetheanum*, which for this purpose is provided with a Supplement containing the official communications of the Society. This enlarged edition of *Das Goetheanum* will be supplied to members of the Anthroposophical Society only.' Would you not agree that this implies that if the South American groups belong to Germany they would be supplied with *Das Goetheanum* not by us here but that it would be sent to them from Germany? Similar situations are still likely to arise. Here we are of the opinion that things should not remain confined to paper. The things that are written in the Members' Supplement are things which every member wants to know as quickly as possible. So I think it would be a good thing for groups which exist outside their national groups to join directly in Dornach so that anthroposophical life can flourish as much as possible without having to make all kinds of detours.

Dr Wachsmuth informs the meeting that the South American Society had written a letter just before Christmas, having heard about the new decisions. He reads a statement from them.

HERR LEINHAS: I have had a similar letter. It arrived only a few days ago, and I have been asked for the moment to represent the national Society, which is to have its seat in Rio.

DR ZEYLMANS VAN EMMICHOVEN: In point 5 mention is made of the three Classes of the School of Spiritual Science in Dornach: 'Members of the Society will be admitted to the School on their own application.' I should like to ask whether the national Societies have anything to do with this or whether this is a purely personal matter for each member.

DR STEINER: What is contained in point 5 will be a matter for the Goetheanum in Dornach as far as the overall leadership is concerned. Everything that belongs to the configuration of this

School of Spiritual Science will have to be taken in hand by the leadership at the Goetheanum in Dornach. Among the things that will have to be dealt with will of course be the matter of making contact not only with officers but also with members who are doing certain work in one place or another. Members of the First, Second and Third Class of the Goetheanum will be everywhere, having been nominated by the Goetheanum. How they are chosen will depend entirely on the individual case, for it will be essentially an esoteric matter, but an esoteric matter which is handled in a modern way. Once things have got going it will become apparent that there will be members in the different national Societies who belong to one of the Classes of the Goetheanum. For these the Goetheanum will nominate their own leadership in the different countries, so that matters are territorially delimited and do not expand boundlessly. This matter, then, will be handled essentially by the leadership at the Goetheanum; I shall describe it in more detail as our Conference progresses. Point 7 also refers to this matter: 'The organizing of the School of Spiritual Science is, to begin with, the responsibility of Rudolf Steiner, who will appoint his collaborators and his possible successor.'

To begin with, I intend to set up, in addition to the three Classes, Sections which will be in charge of the different fields of research. For example there will be a Section for General Anthroposophy, another for what used to be called in France *Belles-Lettres*, a Section for Natural Science, for Education, for Art, for the various realms of art. Each Section will have a Section Leader and together these will constitute the leadership of the School of Spiritual Science. The members of the different Classes will be scattered all over the place; they will be members, for their pupilship is their own private affair. This is an independent institution which the national Societies will undertake to protect and guard as a matter of course.

FRÄULEIN HENSTRÖM: In Sweden, as far as I know, more than a third of the members have not joined a branch. In small villages this is natural, but there are a good many in Stockholm who do not wish to belong to the groups. They believe that they can work more freely if they stand by themselves and study the lectures alone. There are a good many of us who understand how important it is to stand firmly together and that it is therefore necessary for members to get to know one another personally. I think it is quite impossible if members refuse to conform to the groups and I wondered whether some encouragement could not be given from Dornach to bring about an improvement in this direction.

DR STEINER: We shall make every effort towards encouraging members in the different countries to join the main groups, which in most countries will mean the national Society. But we do not want to exert any pressure by means of some statute or other. We do not want to exert any pressure from Dornach in any direction, but we shall make every effort to help people understand, so that for instance in Sweden any members who live in an isolated situation, even if they want to remain isolated as far as their way of living is concerned, can nevertheless join the Stockholm Society or the national Society.

FRÄULEIN HENSTRÖM: I too would not want any compulsion to be brought to bear.

DR STEINER: We shall certainly endeavour to bring about an understanding of this matter.

Mr Monges enquires about the point of view and the manner in which the General Secretaries in the different countries are selected and whether this shall be a democratic procedure or what else?

DR STEINER: This is a further matter which I would not wish to lay down in any way by means of statutes for the various groups all over the world. I can well imagine, for example, that there are national Societies who will most certainly want to employ democratic procedures. I can also imagine that there will be others who will want to be thoroughly aristocratic in their approach, agreeing with the wishes of a particular individual upon whom they confer the task of nominating the other officers and so on. Thus I rather assume that the, shall I say, somewhat aristocratic method I have adopted with regard to appointing the Vorstand may well be imitated. In some quarters, however, this method may be regarded as highly undesirable, and in those quarters the democratic method could be used. An election is naturally all the easier the smaller the group in question, whereas I consider elections in a gathering as large as ours today to be totally meaningless. It is impossible to nominate and elect anybody in a situation where there is to start with so little mutual recognition. So in this gathering such a procedure would not be possible. But I can well imagine that a democratic institution of some kind might come into being in one place or another. In a general way, however, I do not find this question to be of paramount importance as a matter of principle. If on the one hand the selection is made by means of an election that is thoughtless, then the Societies will not flourish. They will come to nought if someone is simply nominated so that the election may be settled in a hurry, as is the case with political elections. Nothing can come of this in our circles.

The matter will be different, though, if consideration is given to those who have already earned some merit, or done certain work, or if their way of working has been observed. In such cases a majority is likely to come about quite naturally. But if the antecedents are all set for some kind of election, I do not believe that amongst us, since our main concern is for the work, some kind of democracy could prevent this work. In other words, in practice there will be little difference between democracy and aristocracy. We might try this out over the next few days. We could ask whether the Vorstand I have suggested would be elected or not. This would give us a democratic basis, for I do consider their election to be a necessary condition, otherwise I myself would also have to withdraw! Freedom must reign, of course. But, dear friends, I too must have freedom. I cannot allow anything to be imposed on me. Anyone who is expected to carry out a function must have freedom above all else. Is this not so? Thus I rather assume that what I have just said will be born out everywhere, for the most part. Whether democracy or aristocracy is the method, the Society will not look much different.

MR MONGES: We in America are very political.

DR STEINER: If Dornach is permitted to have its say to a certain extent, then everything will work out satisfactorily.

FRÄULEIN SCHWARZ: It was said some time ago that members of the old Theosophical Society cannot become anthroposophists, that is they cannot belong to the Anthroposophical Society. Will this continue to be the case or not?

DR STEINER: Who said that? I certainly never said such a thing! Never. The decision as to whether a person shall be admitted or not has to be taken individually in each case. I have always expressly stated that it matters not a jot whether someone belongs to a carpenters' club, or an insurance company, or a scientific research society, or the Theosophical Society. The only thing that matters is the human being. I have never said that the stamp of membership of any other society presents an obstacle for joining the Anthroposophical Society. Of course there might be individual cases in which membership of the Theosophical Society could present an obstacle. It is naturally questionable whether Mrs Besant[39] or Mr Leadbeater,[40] should they apply for membership of the Anthroposophical Society, would be admitted or not. So the question might arise in individual cases. But as a matter of principle it can have no validity whatsoever; otherwise we would come down to principles which would not be in keeping with a society that is to be formed in the modern style.

The Duke of Cesaro brings up a question regarding the number of votes allotted to members. There was once some unpleasantness in a national section of the old Theosophical Society, for example; and the solution had been to break up the whole group in order to gain more votes. Such things ought no longer to be possible.

DR STEINER: As you say, Your Grace, it is desirable that such things should not happen. But on the other hand there are certain difficulties involved in fixing the number of members at the lower end. There you come up against the question: How many members should there be in a group? So far we have had quite a definite view on this. But problems might now arise in this connection: Should we perhaps put everything pertaining to matters of modern usage into Paragraph 3, so that everything esoteric is contained in Paragraph 3, or should we name the number of members a group ought to contain? In the latter case the minimum number would be seven, because only seven can yield a true majority. In the case of three and five there can of course be a seeming majority. But those who understand the nature of the human being know that with a majority of two to one arrived at amongst three members, or of three to two arrived at when there are five members, the one who makes the seeming majority does not count properly. Not until you can have four to three can you arrive at a possible majority, which results if on the one side you have three and on the other side one third more. This then makes a true majority possible. So the minimum number would be seven members. I would not object to including this number here, but I did consider that these Statutes are more likely to be respected in the eyes of the world if we refrain from including things like the number seven. I therefore think, Your Grace, that your suggestion would be better included in the By-Laws, which would mean that in practice this is how the matter would be handled. This is probably the solution for us in this case.

PROFESSOR DR MAURER: I want to ask whether it might not be possible to curtail the other Paragraph as well, as regards the Classes. Perhaps it would be preferable not to launch this aspect on the public. I rather fear that all kinds of historical and other parallels might once again be dredged up and possibly used against us.

DR STEINER: Take Paragraph 5 as it is formulated here and ask yourself whether it could not be applied to any university just as it stands. As it stands it is applicable to any university and cannot possibly cause any offence. Everything else will be a matter of how we handle it.

PROFESSOR DR MAURER: Yes, I agree it is applicable, but there are other points which are open to attack. Taken in its usual sense it could remind people of something which did exist historically.

DR STEINER: Historically it was never the custom to speak of 'Classes', only of 'Degrees'.

PROFESSOR DR MAURER: Nevertheless people will immediately jump to the wrong conclusion and I merely wanted to prevent the incidence of such mistaken and warped conclusions.

DR STEINER: It would be the greatest possible mistake to include anything in our Statutes arising from any conclusion. We cannot avoid having misunderstandings attached to what we do. But anyone interpreting Paragraph 5 wrongly must really want to do so. We cannot prevent this. Paragraph 5 is phrased in such a way that absolutely nobody can say anything other than that in this School of Spiritual Science in Dornach there are three Classes, just as if in Freiburg there were a university with four medical classes, a four-year course. The description in Paragraph 5 accords exactly with the pattern of universities in the outside world, so there is not the smallest opportunity for objection that could be seized with any even seeming justification. The same applies to the way the affairs of the School are conducted. You know that at a university it is the leadership who decide whether a student is ready to move on to the next year or not.

PROFESSOR DR MAURER: This has not always been the case. In the faculties of philosophy it was never a matter of moving up to the next class; this did not happen at Strasbourg under Professor Windelband[41] or anywhere else for that matter. You simply presented yourself and were accepted. Naturally what you gained from the lectures depended on your abilities. Nowadays I agree that in the interest of the students a certain amount of grading has been introduced. I only wanted to draw attention to this matter because our opponents will immediately point it out.

DR STEINER: It is certainly not the case that a medical student who has just arrived at the university will be allowed to attend the special classes on anatomical medicine. There are proper classes for this, are there not. I do not believe that he would be allowed to attend immediately.

PROFESSOR DR MAURER: No, of course not.

DR STEINER: In the case of the philosophical faculty there are good reasons which have come about historically. A justification can certainly always be found for these things. Originally there was no such thing as a philosophical faculty at the universities. The three faculties were those of theology, medicine, and jurisprudence. These three faculties were always graded into classes. The philosophical department was at the basis of all three. First you attended the faculty of philosophy. This is where you started, whether you wanted to study theology, jurisprudence or medicine. Then you moved up from this faculty of philosophy into the different faculties. From then on you moved up in classes. I do not believe that it is any different in other countries. So if you take our Constitution to be the general anthroposophical and philosophical faculty, then advancing on from there you have the three Classes. The set-up is absolutely identical with that of a university. I have taken the utmost care to ensure that it shall be absolutely indisputable. In universities, though, the faculty of philosophy gradually developed into a faculty in its own right. More and more lectures were given till the whole situation degenerated into anarchy and chaos. No one entering the faculty of philosophy has any idea what lectures he ought to attend, indeed he can go to lectures he cannot understand at all. This is a chaotic situation that has arisen at the universities.

What we have written down here corresponds exactly to what was customary at universities, in Vienna for instance, up to the year 1848. This is entirely indisputable. And I believe that this is the case to this day in Paris; and also in Italy there are universities which still conduct matters in this way. At German universities there are certain things which have developed chaotically. But what we have written down here is absolutely indisputable. If we were to do these things without including them in our Statutes — and do them we must, otherwise Paragraph 8 about the lecture cycles would also have to be modified — we would immediately find ourselves in another situation which would not serve our purposes at all. This Paragraph must stand as it is and so must Paragraph 8. Of course we can consider requests for changes regarding details, but a complete suppression of the School with its three Classes would not be acceptable.

PROFESSOR DR MAURER: I quite see that it will be necessary to move up Class by Class. I was merely concerned that it might give our opponents something on which they could seize.

DR STEINER: The only change that could be considered would be to say: 'The Anthroposophical Society sees the School of Spiritual Science in Dornach as the centre for its activity. The School will be composed of three classes after the manner of other universities.' If you wish to include this we can certainly do so.

BARONESS DE RENZIS: Should the report on our work in Italy and the direction it is taking be given now, or are we to discuss the Statutes only?

DR STEINER: I would request you to speak tomorrow about the work in Italy.

Baroness de Renzis wishes to ask a question about the direction the work is taking in general.

DR STEINER: I would ask you to give your report tomorrow.

BARONESS DE RENZIS: Ought we to announce the anthroposophical character of any undertaking or initiative arising out of our Movement from the start, thus provoking the danger of having it rejected, or should we endeavour to disseminate an anthroposophical understanding within public opinion without throwing down the challenge of it being judged and rejected? It is necessary to decide this so that we know what is to determine the attitude of our groups in the future.

DR STEINER: It is of course not the word 'Anthroposophy' itself that matters but there are other things that do matter. Take the following example. Medicine is a case in point. It is today not possible to take medicine beyond the point it has now reached, which is not far enough, without starting to speak of the etheric body of the human being, and also of the astral body and the ego-organization, for it is here that the real causes of illness lie. So it is necessary simply to place before the world the substance of what Anthroposophy contains. We have gained some extremely instructive experience in this matter. Frau Dr Wegman has run courses with me in London, Vienna and The Hague.[42] One of these took place at Dr Zeylmans' Dutch institute. I have given lectures to doctors in which I spoke quite directly of anthroposophical matters. At appropriate moments I have spoken about the astral body, the etheric body and so on. In doing this it is barely relevant what terminology is used. In some instances one feels it is more appropriate to name the etheric body and in others it is better to use different words in describing it. For example when you want to speak of the etheric body you can say: The effects on the physical substances which come not from the centre of the earth but from the periphery of the universe. Only those who have not fully come to grips with their subject matter are tied to a specific terminology, is this not so? We have found that when we speak in this way people can make something of what we say. They know that this is something new making its appearance in the world. If you avoid speaking clearly, all people can say is: Well, here is another opinion about the effect of this or that medicament on the human organism; it has been held before and was then replaced by another; now here is yet another opinion. They cannot distinguish whether a clinical report or a clinical dissertation comes from some external source or from us. But if we want to bring what can really lead us to the centre of the illness, then we cannot avoid speaking about the etheric body and so on, even if we use different terminology. Then people know what is what. We go furthest when we act in this way. It is not in the first instance a matter of the actual name of Anthroposophy; what matters is nowhere to shy away from whatever is necessary to explain something properly. If you try to dress Anthroposophy up in 'this is what the parson says too', then people have no idea what you are getting at. I myself once proved this point. I gave a course of twelve lectures in Vienna[43] ranging over every aspect of Anthroposophy including its practical applications. If you read this cycle today you will not find a single mention of the word Anthroposophy. It is perfectly possible for there to be occasions when it is inappropriate to use the word Anthroposophy. This is for sure. For me what matters is the actual subject itself, the spirit of the subject. You have no idea how many well-meaning people have come to me saying: People dread the expression 'etheric body'; could we not say 'the functional element in the human organism'? But this is a meaningless expression. To speak of the etheric body you have to distinguish between the physical body in which all the forces are related to gravity, the mechanical pull of gravity, and the etheric body in which all the forces can be related to the periphery, to all that is ever in weaving movement. This is the difference. The 'functional element in the human organism' refers to the function and not to this fundamental contrast. So these well-meant suggestions that come, often from outsiders, cannot be taken into account.

BARONESS DE RENZIS: Is it sufficient to speak of the 'essence' of things?

DR STEINER: It is not necessary to throw the actual word 'Anthroposophy' at people, but if asked whether you are an anthroposophist it would be quite a good thing if you did not say: No!

We shall continue this meeting tomorrow. We must try to make sure that we have enough breathing space during this Conference.

Continuation of the Foundation Meeting

26 DECEMBER, 10 O'CLOCK IN THE MORNING

DR STEINER:

My dear friends!

We are in the middle of the reports by the General Secretaries and the representatives of the groups working in all kinds of places outside Dornach. In a moment we shall continue with these reports. But first I would like to speak a few words in the midst of these reports, words to which I am moved by what has been said in such a satisfactory way by these speakers. From what we have been told we may gather how very devoted is the work being carried on out there. We may add what we were told yesterday to the names I allowed myself to mention the day before. There, too, despite the ruins on which we stand, we may see what can encourage us during this Conference not to be pessimistic in any way but rather to strive actively for a genuine optimism.

During this Conference we must everywhere, in every realm, consider the activity of building-up rather than the activity of dismantling. So today, early on in the Conference, I want to suggest that we give it a certain definite direction. During the meetings of members over the next few days there will of course be opportunities for discussing various matters. But today, early on, I want to say the following: As we saw in the necessary content of the Statutes, we have to connect total openness with the Anthroposophical Society. Anything less, dear friends, is not permitted by the signs of the times. The present age can no longer tolerate any tendency towards secrecy. This presents us with a fundamental problem which we shall have to solve.

By this I do not mean that we shall have to discuss it a great deal during the Conference, for it is in our hearts that this fundamental problem will have to be solved. We must be absolutely clear about the fact that our Society, before all others, will be given the task of combining the greatest conceivable openness with true and genuine esotericism.

At first under the obstacles and hindrances of those terrible years of the war, but then also through all kinds of inner difficulties, we have indeed experienced the establishment of this problem in every direction. Indeed lately no meeting within the Anthroposophical Society has taken place which lacked, as it were, the backdrop — though unnoticed by many — of this problem: How can we combine full openness with the profoundest, most serious and inward esotericism? To achieve this it will be necessary to banish from our gatherings in the future anything which smacks in any way of the atmosphere of a clique. Anthroposophy does not need the atmosphere of a clique. When hearts truly understand Anthroposophy they will beat in unison without the need for heads to knock together. If we solve this purely human problem of letting our hearts sound in harmony with one another without the need for our heads to knock together, then from the human side we shall have done everything necessary, also in the leadership of the Anthroposophical Society, to prepare for the achievement of the things that have been depicted.

We must achieve these things; we must reach the point at which we can feel in all our deeds that we are connected with the spiritual world. This is the very aspect which must be different in the Anthroposophical Society from any other possible association in the present time. The difference must be that out of the strength of Anthroposophy itself it is possible to combine the greatest conceivable openness with the most genuine and inward esotericism. And in future this esotericism must not be lacking even in the most external of our deeds. There is in this field still a lot to learn from the past ten years.

What I am saying is also related to our responsibilities. Consider the following, my dear friends: We stand in the world as a small Society, and this Society has a peculiar destiny at present. Even if it wanted to, it could not reject this characteristic of openness which I have been emphasizing so strongly. It would be unable to reject it. For if out of some leaning of sympathy we were to decide today to work only inwardly with our groups, which would of course be very nice, if we were not to concern ourselves with the public at large, we would discover that there would soon be an increasingly inimical concern for us on the part of the public. The more we fail to concern ourselves with the signs of the times, the more will be the inimical concern for us on the part of everything that can possibly be against us. Only if we find the path, only if with courage we find the straight path to what we should do shall we succeed in navigating the ship of the Anthroposophical Society through the exceedingly stormy waves which surge and break around it. What we should do is the following: As a small Society we face the world, a world — you know the one I mean — which actually does not love us. It does not love us. This is a fact we cannot alter. But on the other hand there is no need to do anything on purpose to make ourselves unpopular. I do not mean this in a superficial sense but in a deeper sense of which I speak from the foundations of occult life. If we ask ourselves over and over again what we must do to make ourselves better liked by this circle or by that circle in the world, by any circle which does not like us today; if we keep asking ourselves how we should behave in this field or in that field so as to be taken seriously here or there; if we do this, we shall most certainly not be taken seriously. We shall only be taken seriously if at every moment in whatever we do we feel responsible towards the spiritual world. We must know that the spiritual world wants to achieve a certain thing with mankind at this particular moment in historical evolution; it wants to achieve this in the most varied realms of life, and it is up to us clearly and truly to follow the impulses that come from the spiritual world. Though this might give offence initially, in the long run it is the only beneficial way. Therefore we shall also only come to terms among ourselves if at every opportunity we steep ourselves in whatever impulses can come out of the spiritual world.

So now, having given these indications, which I shall bring to completion over the next few days, I once more want to repeat before you at least a part of those words which were spoken to you yesterday in accordance with the will of the spiritual world. May they stand as an introduction in our souls again today as we enter into our discussions.

Soul of Man!
Thou livest in the limbs
Which bear thee through the world of space
In the spirit's ocean-being.
Practise spirit-recalling
In depths of soul,
Where in the wielding will
Of world-creating
Thine own I
Comes to being
Within God's I.
And thou wilt truly live
In the World-Being of Man.

Soul of Man!
Thou livest in the beat of heart and lung
Which leads thee through the rhythm of time
Into the realm of thine own soul's feeling.
Practise spirit-awareness
In balance of the soul,
Where the surging deeds
Of the world's becoming
Thine own I
Unite
With the World-I.
And thou wilt truly feel
In the Soul-Weaving of Man.

Soul of Man!
Thou livest in the resting head
Which from the grounds of eternity
Opens to thee the world-thoughts.
Practise spirit-beholding
In stillness of thought,
Where the eternal aims of Gods
World-Being's Light
On thine own I
Bestow
For thy free willing.
And thou wilt truly think
In the Spirit-Foundations of Man.

We can work rightly with words such as these, which are heard coming from the Cosmic Word, if we arrange them in our own soul in such a way that they cannot depart from us again. And it will be possible for them to be so arranged if, amongst all that has resounded, you first highlight that part which can give you the rhythm. Dear friends, let me write down here first of all the part that can indicate the rhythm:

In the first verse:

[Rudolf Steiner writes on the blackboard as he speaks. See Facsimile 4, Page XV, top.]

Spirit-recalling,

in the second verse:

Spirit-awareness,

in the third verse:

Spirit-beholding.

Contemplate this in its rhythmical connection with what is brought about in the human soul which is called upon, the human soul which is called upon by itself, through the words:

Thine own I
Comes to being
Within God's I —,

consider the rhythm linked with 'spirit-awareness' when you hear:

Thine own I
Unite
With the World-I —,

and the rhythm linked with 'spirit-beholding' when you hear:

On thine own I
Bestow
For thy free willing —.

[As shown on the blackboard]

Spirit-recalling	*Spirit-awareness*	*Spirit-beholding*
•	•	•
Thine own I	*Thine own I*	*On thine own I*
Comes to being	*Unite*	*Bestow*
Within God's I —	*With the World-I —*	*For thy free willing*

Take in this way each phrase so that it can only stand as I have written it here. Take what comes rhythmically out of the Cosmic Rhythm: 'own I within God's I', 'own I in the World-I', 'own I in free willing'. And take what rises up from 'comes to being' to 'unite' to 'bestow', where there is the transition to moral feeling. Feel the connection with 'spirit-recalling', 'spirit-awareness' and 'spirit-beholding'. Then you will have in the inner rhythm what it is during these few days that the spiritual world is bringing to us to raise our hearts, to illumine our thinking, to give wings and enthusiasm to our willing.

I now have a telegram to read to you: 'Christmas greetings, best wishes, Ethel Morgenstierne.' And now may I ask the representative of Honolulu, Madame Ferreri, to speak.

Madame Ferreri reports.

DR STEINER: May I now ask the representative of Italy, Baroness de Renzis, to speak.

Baroness de Renzis reports.

DR STEINER: May I perhaps suggest that certain questions raised here, such as that of accepting applications for membership on the basis of correspondence only, and similar matters, shall be discussed later when we consider the Statutes.

DR STEINER: The Duke of Cesaro will also give a report concerning Italy on behalf of the Novalis Group in Rome.

The Duke of Cesaro reports.

DR STEINER: Now may I ask Fräulein Schwarz to speak on behalf of the other Italian group.

Fräulein Schwarz reports on behalf of the group in Milan.

DR STEINER: Now would the representative of the work in Yugoslavia, Herr Hahl, please speak.

Herr Hahl reports.

DR STEINER: May I ask the representative of the Norwegian Society, Herr Ingerö, to speak.

Herr Ingerö speaks.

DR STEINER: Now may I ask the representative of the Council of the Austrian Society, Count Polzer, to speak.

26 DECEMBER, 10 O'CLOCK IN THE MORNING

Count Polzer speaks.

DR STEINER: Now may I ask the representative of the group in Porto Alegre in Brazil, Dr Unger, to speak.

DR UNGER: Allow me in a few words to carry out a commission which I was most delighted to accept. For quite some time we have been corresponding with friends over there, mostly from Germany, who had emigrated and had begun to work there anthroposophically. Herr Brandtner in particular has been writing lately. He has made great efforts to get something going in Porto Alegre. And connected with this, work is also going on in other South American towns which will gradually be co-ordinated so that independent centres from which to work may be set up there too. For this purpose Herr Mayen from Breslau was asked by the friends over there to go out, first of all to Rio. He will gradually take on work in a number of towns. I have been particularly asked to give voice to the sympathetic interest of the friends over there. Everything that comes to us from over there expresses the most intimate interest in all that has to do with Dornach and whatever continues to come from Dornach. As often as possible someone comes to Europe and we hope most fervently that anthroposophical life may soon start to blossom there in the most intensive way. Just as I bring greetings from our friends over there, so I hope that when I report back to Porto Alegre I may also be permitted to send them from here our good wishes for the prospering of the work in Porto Alegre.

DR STEINER: May I now ask the representative of the Swedish Anthroposophical Society, Fräulein Henström, to speak.

Fräulein Henström reports.

DR STEINER: May I now ask the representative of the Swiss Anthroposophical Society, Herr Aeppli, to speak.

Herr Aeppli reports.

DR STEINER: May I now ask the representative of the Council in Czechoslovakia, Dr Krkavec, to speak.

Dr Krkavec reports.

DR STEINER: May I now ask the other representative of the Council in Czechoslovakia, Dr Eiselt, to speak.

Dr Eiselt reports.

DR STEINER: This brings the reports to a close. I believe I may be allowed to say that you are all, with me, exceedingly grateful to those who have given them. For they enable us to see that we have a foundation on which to base our new work, since now we know how much truly great, devoted and varied work is being done and has already been done in the Anthroposophical Society.

Now I should like to move on to the third point on our agenda, consideration of the Statutes. First the Statutes must be read out. Though you all have a copy, I would nevertheless like to ask that they be read out once more, so that we can then commence the discussion of each point. Would Dr Wachsmuth now please read the Statutes in accordance with point three of our agenda.

Dr Wachsmuth reads out the Statutes of the Anthroposophical Society.

DR STEINER: As you will have gathered from various remarks I have made, it would be really good if on the one hand our meeting could be allowed to run as freely as possible amongst its individual members. However, on the other hand, if a proper discussion is to take place, it is necessary for us to be quite strict in conducting the debate. So please take this not as pedantry but as a necessity applicable to any gathering. Today we have run out of time, so I would ask you that we continue this meeting tomorrow after Dr Wachsmuth's lecture. Tomorrow morning at 10 o'clock Dr Wachsmuth will give his lecture. Then we shall break for a quarter of an hour before continuing the meeting. At this meeting I should like to conduct the proceedings as follows. Not in order to be pedantic but so that we can be as efficient as possible there will first be a kind of general debate on the Statutes, a debate in which first of all the whole attitude, meaning and spirit of the Statutes in general is discussed.

Then I shall ask you to agree to the Statutes in general, after which we shall open a detailed debate in which we take one Paragraph at a time, when contributors will be asked to speak only to the Paragraph under consideration. There will then be a concluding debate leading to the final adoption of the Statutes. This is how I would ask you to proceed tomorrow when we discuss the Statutes.

Now I have to announce that our Conference continues this afternoon with a eurythmy performance at 4.30 and my lecture at 8 o'clock this evening. Tomorrow at 10 o'clock we shall hear Dr Guenther Wachsmuth's lecture in the field of natural science about the face of the earth and the destiny of man. Then after a quarter of an hour's break we shall continue with this meeting.

I also have several more announcements to make. As I had to stress earlier, before we began our meeting, it is quite difficult, because there are so many of us — and it is of course wonderful that there are so many dear friends here — to hold this gathering together. You cannot tell, just by coming to the meetings, how difficult it is. Of course we are deeply sorry that the primitive quarters here are causing such discomfort and so many problems for our dear friends. Nevertheless, I have to ask that in future not more than three seats are held by any one person. I have to say this because it has happened that whole rows of seats have been held by a single person, and this has led to innumerable discussions with those who have come in later.

Then I should like to remind you of the wish we expressed earlier that the two front rows be reserved for those dear friends who are either disabled or deaf or need special consideration for any other reason. If there are any seats left in these two rows, which is sure to be the case, then please leave them free for the General Secretaries of the different countries and for the secretaries who might be accompanying them. It will become necessary in the next few days to have the General Secretaries together here where they can be seen rather than scattered all over the hall.

Thirdly I would perhaps like once more to ask our Dornach friends — truly I have nothing personal against them — to take their seats next door in the 'summer villa'.[44] I know it is most inhospitable in this rainy and snowy weather, but all we can do is ask our Dornach friends to put up with the rain so that the friends from further afield can sit here in the hall away from the rain.

Also I would like to mention that from today the upper canteen will be open in the evening for those friends who are quartered in the dormitories or other inhospitable places, so that they may have somewhere to go that is heated. Food and drink will not be served then, but I hope that the conversations that can take place there will be all the more stimulating and encouraging. So although it will not be possible to quench hunger and thirst, it will be possible to keep as warm as may be in the evenings after my lecture until 11 o'clock at night.

Furthermore I want to draw your attention to the following: Mr Pyle in the most admirable way has modelled a very fine money-box[45] which he has had produced. You will find these money-boxes outside the doors. If you look at them carefully you will find that the beautiful forms tempt you to want to own such a money-box yourselves. They are for sale, so you can buy one and take it home and put something in it every day. When it is full you can use what you have collected to put towards the re-building of the Goetheanum, or for any other purposes related to the Goetheanum. Let me point out that even if you only put in 10 Rappen every day — think what you might spend this on each day — by the end of the year you will have saved quite a tidy sum. I can see my respected friends here are already working out how much! You will find that it will be a worthwhile amount. But I don't want to encourage you to put in only 10 Rappen. I would rather you put in whatever amount you consider proper, or whatever you feel obliged to put in even if you don't think it proper.

Those who find it difficult for one reason or another to take a money-box home with them will see that similar money-boxes have been set out here into which they may put something. Naturally if you do not have your own money-box to take home, it would be a good thing if you could delve deeply into your purse while you are here, so that these money-boxes may be filled. We shall have no trouble in seeing to it that they are rapidly emptied.

Finally I would please ask that spectators at the Christmas Plays refrain from booking their seats for the evening lectures.

You see, without all these many wishes — let us not call them prohibitions — we shall be unable to keep the Conference going in an orderly manner.

Now, my dear friends, I adjourn this meeting until the appointed hour tomorrow.

Continuation of the Foundation Meeting

27 DECEMBER, 10 O'CLOCK IN THE MORNING

Lecture by Dr Guenther Wachsmuth on anthroposophy and the destiny of the earth

11.15

The Words of the Foundation Stone, then discussion of the Statutes

---

DR STEINER:

My dear friends!

Once more let us fill our hearts with the words which out of the signs of the times are to give us in the right way the self knowledge we need:

Soul of Man!
Thou livest in the limbs
Which bear thee through the world of space
In the spirit's ocean-being.
Practise spirit-recalling
In depths of soul,

Where in the wielding will
Of world-creating
Thine own I
Comes to being
Within God's I.
And thou wilt truly live
In the World-Being of Man.

Soul of Man!
Thou livest in the beat of heart and lung
Which leads thee through the rhythm of time
Into the realm of thine own soul's feeling.
Practise spirit-awareness
In balance of the soul,
Where the surging deeds
Of the world's becoming
Thine own I
Unite
With the World-I.
And thou wilt truly feel
In the Soul-Weaving of Man.

Soul of Man!
Thou livest in the resting head
Which from the grounds of eternity
Opens to thee the world-thoughts.
Practise spirit-beholding
In stillness of thought,
Where the eternal aims of Gods
World-Being's Light
On thine own I
Bestow
For thy free willing.
And thou wilt truly think
In the Spirit-Foundations of Man.

Once more out of these cosmic verses let us write down before our souls a rhythm so that we may gradually press forward spiritually to their structure. From the first verse we take the words:

[Rudolf Steiner writes on the blackboard as he speaks. See Facsimile 4, Page XV bottom.]

Thine own I
Comes to being
Within God's I.

And from the second verse, which contains a second soul process, we take:

Thine own I
Unite
With the World-I.

And from the third verse we take:

On thine own I
Bestow
For thy free willing.

With these words, to form the corresponding rhythm, we now unite those words which always sound with them, having an inner soul connection with these that I have already written on the blackboard:

And thou wilt truly *live*
In the World-Being of Man.

And from the second verse:

And thou wilt truly *feel*
In the Soul-Weaving of Man.

The final harmony of the third verse is:

And thou wilt truly *think*
In the Spirit-Foundations of Man.

[As shown on the blackboard]

Thine own I	*Thine own I*	*On thine own I*
Comes to being	*Unite*	*Bestow*
Within God's I	*With the World-I*	*For thy free willing*
live	*feel*	*think*
World-Being	*Soul-Weaving*	*Spirit-Foundation*
of Man	*of Man*	*of Man*

You will find, my dear friends, that if you pay attention to the inner rhythms that lie in these verses, if you then present these inner rhythms to your soul and perform a suitable meditation within yourself, allowing your thoughts to come to rest upon them, then these sayings can be felt to be the speaking of cosmic secrets in so far as these cosmic secrets are resurrected in the human soul as human self knowledge.

Now, dear friends, let us prepare to have — if you will pardon the ugly expression — a general debate about the Statutes. To start with let me draw your attention to what kind of points come into question for this general debate. Later — if you will pardon an even uglier expression — we shall have a kind of detailed debate on special concerns about the individual Paragraphs.

The first thing to be considered would be the fact that in future the Vorstand-committee situated in Dornach is to be a true Vorstand which takes into account the central initiative necessary in every single case with respect to one thing or another. It will be less a matter of knowing that there is a Vorstand in such and such a place to which it is possible to turn in one matter or another — though this too is possible and necessary, of course. Rather it will be a matter of the Vorstand developing the capacity to have active initiatives of its own in the affairs of the Anthroposophical Movement, giving suggestions which are really necessary in the sense of the final point in the last Paragraph of the Statutes:

'The organ of the Society is *Das Goetheanum*, which for this purpose is provided with a Supplement containing the official communications of the Society. This enlarged edition of *Das Goetheanum* will be supplied to members of the Anthroposophical Society only.'

In this Supplement will be found everything the Vorstand thinks, would like to do and, on occasion, will be able to do. Thus especially through the Supplement to *Das Goetheanum* the Vorstand will constantly have the intention of working outwards in a living way. But as you know, for blood to circulate there have to be not only centrifugal forces but also centripetal forces that work inwards. Therefore arrangements will have to be made so that a number of members unite themselves closely in their soul with the Vorstand in everything that might concern not only the Anthroposophical Society in the narrower sense but also in the whole cultural life of the present day in relation to the working of the Anthroposophical Society. A number of members will be closely linked in their soul with the Vorstand in order to communicate back all that goes on outside in the world. By this means we shall achieve an entirely free constitution of the Anthroposophical Society, a constitution built on a free interchange. Then stimulus and suggestion will come from every direction. And these suggestions will bear fruit depending on the way in which things are recognized. So it will have to be arranged that there are correspondents for the Vorstand which is located in Dornach, where it works.

At the present moment of the Anthroposophical Society's development it is important that we make our arrangements on the basis of reality and not of principles. There is, is there not, a difference between the two. If you base your considerations on the structure of a society and arrange its affairs in accordance with this, then you have a theoretical structure of principles. We have had plenty of this kind of thing recently, and it was absolutely no use. Indeed in many ways it caused us serious difficulties. So I want to exert every effort to make arrangements in the future that arise out of the real forces of the Society, out of the forces that exist already and have already had their effect, and of which it can be seen from their context that they can work. So it seems to me that it would be a good thing to be clear at least in spirit about the establishment of correspondents of the Vorstand, people who would take on the voluntary duty of writing to us every week about what they consider noteworthy in cultural life outside in the world and about what might be interesting for the Anthroposophical Society. A number of people, which could always of course be extended, ought to take on this obligation here and now. I for my part should like to suggest several people straight away to constitute an externally supporting Vorstand that is exactly equivalent to the central Vorstand which, as I have already said, is located here in Dornach, which means that it cannot have any members who do not live here in Dornach. In this way we would achieve a genuine circulation of blood. So I want to suggest that certain persons of the following kind — forgive me for generalizing; we can certainly discuss this further — keep in regular contact with the Vorstand on a weekly basis. The kind of person I mean is someone who has already resolved to work very actively out there in the periphery for our anthroposophical cause: Herr van Leer. Secondly I am thinking of the following people: Mr Monges, Mr Collison, Mrs Mackenzie, Herr Ingerö, Herr Zeylmans, Mademoiselle Sauerwein, Baroness de Renzis, Madame Ferreri, Fräulein Schwarz, Count Polzer, Dr Unger, Herr Leinhas, Dr Büchenbacher.

I have started by naming these people because I am of the opinion that if they would commit themselves voluntarily to report in a letter every week to the editors of *Das Goetheanum*, not only on what is going on in the anthroposophical field but on anything that might be interesting for Anthroposophy in the cultural life of the world and indeed life in general, this would give us a good opportunity to shape this Supplement to *Das Goetheanum* very fruitfully.

The second thing to consider in the general debate about the Statutes is the fact that the establishment of a Vorstand in the way I have suggested to you means that the Anthroposophical Society will be properly represented, so that other associations or organizations which exist for the promotion of the cause of Anthroposophy, wherever they happen to be, can refer back to this central Vorstand. The central Vorstand will have to consider its task to be solely whatever lies in the direction of fulfilling the Statutes. It will have to do everything that lies in the direction of fulfilling the Statutes. This gives it great freedom. But at the same time we shall all know what this central Vorstand represents, since from the Statutes we can gain a complete picture of what it will be doing. As a result, wherever other organizations arise, for instance the *Goetheanum Bauverein*, it will be possible for them to stand on realistic ground. Over the next few days there will be the task of creating a suitable relationship between the Vorstand that has come into being and the *Goetheanum Bauverein.*[46] But today in the general debate about the Statutes we can discuss anything of this kind which might be worrying you about them.

The third thing to consider will be a matter raised in a meeting of delegates of the Anthroposophical Society in Switzerland, namely how to organize the relationship between the members of the Anthroposophical Society who live here close to the Goetheanum either permanently or on a temporary basis on the one hand and the members of the Swiss Anthroposophical Society on the other. It was quite justifiably stated here the other day at a delegates' meeting of our Swiss friends[47] that if people who happen to be present by coincidence, or perhaps not by coincidence but only temporarily, for a short while, interfere too much in the affairs of the Swiss Society, then the Swiss friends might feel pressured in their meetings. We need to ensure that the Goetheanum branch — though for obvious reasons it should and must be a part of the Swiss Anthroposophical Society — is given a position which prevents it, even if it has non-Swiss members, from ever becoming an instrument for persuasion or for creating a majority. This is what was particularly bothering the Swiss members at their delegates' meeting recently. This situation has become somewhat awkward for the following reasons:

The suggestion had been made by me to found national Societies on the basis of which the General Anthroposophical Society would be founded here at Christmas. These national Societies have indeed come into being almost without exception in every country where there are anthroposophists. At all these anthroposophical foundation meetings it was said in one way or another that a national Society would be founded like the one already in existence in Switzerland. So national Societies were founded everywhere along the lines of the Swiss Anthroposophical Society. However, it is important to base whatever happens on clear statements. If this had been done there would have been no misunderstanding which led to people saying that since national Societies were being founded everywhere a Swiss national Society ought to be formed too. After all, it was the Swiss Society on which the others were modelled. However, the situation was that the Swiss Society did not have a proper Council, since its Council was made up of the chairmen of the different branches. This therefore remains an elastic but rather indeterminate body. For things to appear in a more orderly fashion in the future, it will be necessary for the Swiss Anthroposophical Society to form itself with a Council and perhaps also a General Secretary like those of the other national Anthroposophical Societies. Then it will be possible to regularize the relationship with the Goetheanum branch. This is merely a suggestion. But in connection with it I want to say something else.

The whole way in which I consider that the central Vorstand, working here at the Goetheanum, should carry out its duties means that of necessity there is an incompatibility between the offices of this Vorstand and any other offices of the Anthroposophical Society. Thus a member of the Vorstand I have suggested to you here ought not to occupy any other position within the Anthroposophical Society. Indeed, dear friends, proper work cannot be done when offices are heaped one on top of another. Above all else let us in future avoid piling offices one on top of the other. So it will be necessary for our dear Swiss friends to concern themselves with choosing a General Secretary, since Herr Steffen, as the representative of the Swiss, whose guests we are in a certain way as a worldwide Society, will in future be taking up the function of Vice-president of the central Society. You were justifiably immensely pleased to agree with this. I do not mean to say that this is incompatible with any other offices but only with other offices within the Anthroposophical Society.

Another thing I want to say is that I intend to carry out point 5 by arranging the School of Spiritual Science in Dornach in Sections as follows. These will be different from the Classes.[48] The Classes will encompass all the Sections. Let me make a drawing similar to that made by Dr Wachsmuth; not the same, but I hope it encompasses the whole earth in the same way. The Classes will be like this: General Anthroposophical Society, First Class, Second Class, Third Class of the School of Spiritual Science. [See Facsimile 5, Page XVIII bottom.]

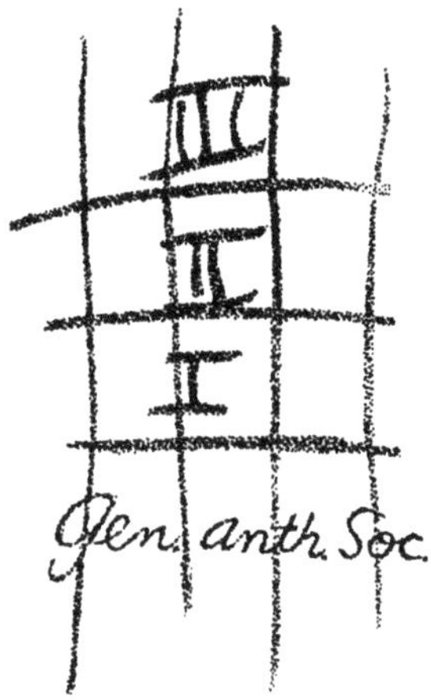

The Sections will reach from top to bottom, so that within each Section it will be possible to be a member of whichever Class has been attained. The Sections I would like to found are:

First of all a General Anthroposophical Section, which will to start with be combined with the Pedagogical Section. I myself should like to take this on in addition to the overall leadership of the School of Spiritual Science. Then I want to arrange the School in such a way that each Section has a Section Leader who is responsible for it; I believe these must be people residing here. One Section will encompass what in France is called '*belles-lettres*'. Another will encompass the spoken arts and music together with eurythmy. A third Section will encompass the plastic arts. A fourth Section is to encompass medicine. A fifth is to encompass mathematics and astronomy. And the last, for the moment, is to be for the natural sciences. So suitable representatives will be found here for these Sections which are those which for the time being can responsibly be included within the general anthroposophical sphere which I myself shall lead. The Section Leaders must, of course, be resident here.

These, then, are the main points on which I would like the general debate to be based. I now ask whether the applications to speak, already handed in, refer to these points. Applications to speak have been handed in by Herr Leinhas, Dr Kolisko, Dr Stein, Dr Palmer, Herr Werbeck, Miss Cross, Mademoiselle Rihouët, Frau Hart-Nibbrig, Herr de Haan, Herr Stibbe, Herr Tymstra, Herr Zagwijn, Frau Ljungquist. On behalf of Switzerland, the working committee. On behalf of Czechoslovakia, Dr Krkavec, Herr Pollak, Dr Reichel, Frau Freund. Do these speakers wish to refer to the debate which is about to begin? (From various quarters the answer is: No!)

DR STEINER: Then may I ask those wishing to speak to raise their hands and to come up here to the platform. Who would like to speak to the general debate?

DR ZEYLMANS: Ladies and gentlemen, I merely want to say that I shall be very happy to take on the task allotted to me by Dr Steiner and shall endeavour to send news about the work in Holland to Dornach each week.

DR STEINER: Perhaps we can settle this matter by asking all those I have so far mentioned — the list is not necessarily complete — to be so good as to raise their hands. (All those mentioned do so.)

Is there anyone who does not want to take on this task? Please raise your hand. (Nobody does so.) You see what a good example has been set in dealing with this first point. All those requested to do so have declared themselves prepared to send a report each week to the editors of *Das Goetheanum*. This will certainly amount to quite a task for Herr Steffen, but it has to be done, for of course the reports must be read here once they arrive.

Does anyone else wish to speak to the general debate? If not, may I now ask those friends who agree in principle with the Statutes as Statutes of the General Anthroposophical Society to raise their hands. In the second reading we shall discuss each Paragraph separately. But will those who agree in principle please raise their hands. (They do.)

Will those who do not wish to accept these Statutes in principle please raise their hands. (Nobody does.)

The draft Statutes have thus been accepted in their first reading. (Lively applause.)

We now come to the detailed debate, the second reading, and I shall ask Dr Wachsmuth to read the Statutes Paragraph by Paragraph for this debate in detail.

Dr Wachsmuth reads Paragraph 1 of the Statutes:

'1. The Anthroposophical Society is to be an association of people whose will it is to nurture the life of the soul, both in the individual and in human society, on the basis of a true knowledge of the spiritual world.'

DR STEINER: Would anyone now like to speak to the content or style and phrasing of this first Paragraph of the Statutes? Dear friends, you have been in possession of the Statutes for more than three days. I am quite sure that you have thought deeply about them.

HERR KAISER: With reference to the expression 'the life of the soul' I wondered whether people might not ask: Why not life as a whole? This is one of the things I wanted to say. Perhaps an expression that is more general than 'of the soul' could be used.

DR STEINER: Would you like to make a suggestion to help us understand better what you mean?

HERR KAISER: I have only just noticed this expression. I shall have to rely on your help as I can't think of anything better at the moment. I just wanted to point out that the general public might be offended by the idea that we seem to want to go and hide away with our soul in a vague kind of way.

DR STEINER: Paragraph 1 is concerned with the following: Its phrasing is such that it points to a certain nurturing of the life of the soul without saying in detail what the content of the activity of the Anthroposophical Society is to be. I believe that especially at the present time it is of paramount importance to point out that in the Anthroposophical Society the life of the soul is of central concern. That is why it says that the Anthroposophical Society is to be an association of people who cultivate the life of the soul in this way. We can talk about the other words later. The other things it does are stated in the subsequent points. We shall speak more about this. This is the first Paragraph. Even the first Paragraph should say something as concrete as possible. If I am to ask: What is a writer? I shall have to say: A writer is a person who uses language in order to express his thoughts, or something similar. This does not mean to say that this encompasses the whole of his activity as a human being; it merely points out what he is with regard to being a writer. Similarly I think that the first point indicates that the Anthroposophical Society, among all kinds of other things which are expressed in the subsequent points, also cultivates the life of the soul in the individual and in human society in such a way that this cultivation is based on a true knowledge of the spiritual world. I think perhaps Herr Kaiser meant that this point ought to include a kind of survey of all the subsequent points. But this is not how we want to do it. We want to remain concrete all the time. The only thing to be stated in the first point is the manner in which the life of the soul is to be cultivated. After that is stated what else we do and do not want to do. Taken in this way, I don't think there is anything objectionable in this Paragraph. Or is there? If anyone has a better suggestion I am quite prepared to replace 'of the soul' with something else. But as you see, Herr Kaiser did think briefly about it and did not come up with any other expression. I have been thinking about it for quite a long time, several weeks, and have also not found any other expression for this Paragraph. It will indeed be very difficult to find a different expression to indicate the general activity of the Anthroposophical Society. For the life of the soul does, after all, encompass everything. On the one hand in practical life we want to cultivate the life of the soul in such a way that the human being can learn to master life at the practical level. On the other hand in scientific life we want to conduct science in such a way that the human soul finds it satisfying. Understood rightly, the expression 'the life of the soul' really does express something universal.

Does anyone else want to speak to Paragraph 1? If not, I shall put this point 1 of the Statutes to the vote. Please will those who are in favour of adopting this point raise their hands. This vote refers to this one point only, so you are not committing yourselves to anything else in the Statutes. (The vote is taken.)

If anyone objects to Paragraph 1, please raise your hand. (Nobody does.) Our point 1 is accepted. Please read point 2 of the Statutes.

Dr Wachsmuth reads Paragraph 2 of the Statutes:

'2. The persons gathered at the Goetheanum in Dornach at Christmas, 1923, both the individuals and the groups represented, form the nucleus of the Society. They are convinced that there exists in our time a genuine science of the spiritual world and that the civilizaton of today is lacking the cultivation of such a science. This cultivation is to be the task of the Anthroposophical Society. It will endeavour to fulfil this task by making the anthroposophical spiritual science cultivated at the Goetheanum in Dornach the centre of its activities, together with all that results from this for brotherhood in human relationships and for the moral and religious as well as the artistic and cultural life in the human being.'

DR STEINER: The first purpose of this Paragraph is to express what it is that unites the individual members of the Anthroposophical Society. As I said in a general discussion a few days ago, we want to build on facts, not on ideas and principles. The first fact to be considered is most gratifying, and that is that eight hundred people are gathered together here in Dornach who can make a declaration. They are not going to make a declaration of ideas and principles to which they intend to adhere. They are going to declare: At the Goetheanum in Dornach there exists a certain fundamental conviction. This fundamental conviction, which is expressed in this point, is essentially shared by all of us and we are therefore the nucleus of the Anthroposophical Society. Today we are not dealing with principles but with human beings. You see these people sitting here in front of you who first entertained this conviction; they are those who have been working out of this conviction for quite some time at the Goetheanum. You have come in order to found the Anthroposophical Society. You declare in the Statutes your agreement with what is being done at the Goetheanum. Thus the Society is formed, humanly formed. Human beings are joining other human beings. Human beings are not declaring their agreement with Paragraphs which can be interpreted in this way or in that way, and so on. Would anyone like to speak to Paragraph 2?

DR UNGER: My dear friends! Considering the very thing that has brought all these people together here we must see this point 2 as something which is expressed as a whole by all those members of the Anthroposophical Society gathered here. Acknowledgement of the very thing which has brought us together is what is important. That is why I wonder whether we might not find a stronger way of expressing the part which says 'are convinced that there exists in our time a genuine science of the spiritual world . . .' As it stands it sounds rather as though spiritual science just happens to exist, whereas what every one of us here knows, and what we have all committed ourselves to carry out into the world, has in fact been built up over many years. Would it not be possible to formulate something which expresses the years of work in wide-reaching circles? I am quite aware that Dr Steiner does not wish to see his name mentioned here because this could give a false impression. We ought to be capable of expressing through the Society that this science exists, given by the spiritual world, and that it has been put before all mankind in an extensive literature. This 'having been put before all mankind' ought to be more strongly expressed as the thing that unites the Society.

DR STEINER: Dear friends, you can imagine that the formulation of this sentence was quite a headache for me too. Or don't you believe me? Perhaps Dr Unger could make a suggestion.

DR UNGER suggests: *'represented by a body of literature that has been presented to all mankind over many years.'* This could simply be added to the sentence as it stands.

DR STEINER: Would your suggestion be met by the following formulation: 'are convinced that there exists in our time a genuine science of the spiritual world *elaborated for years past, and in important particulars already published*'?

DR UNGER: Yes.

DR STEINER: So we shall put 'elaborated for years past, and in important particulars already published . . .' Does anyone else wish to speak?

Dr Schmeidel wishes to put 'for decades past' instead of 'for years past'.

DR STEINER: Many people would be able to point out that actually two decades have passed since the appearance of *The Philosophy of Freedom.*[49] I do not think there is any need to make the formulation all that strong. If we are really to add anything more in this direction then I would suggest not 'for decades past' but 'for *many* years past'. Does anyone else wish to speak?

DR PEIPERS: I do not see why Dr Steiner's name should not be mentioned at this point. I should like to make an alternative suggestion: *'in the spiritual science founded by Dr Steiner.'*

DR STEINER: This is impossible, my dear friends. What has been done here must have the best possible form and it must be possible for us to stand for what we say. It would not do for the world to discover that the draft for these Statutes was written by me and then to find my name appearing here in full. Such a thing would provide the opportunity for the greatest possible misunderstandings and convenient points for attack. I think it is quite sufficient to leave this sentence as general as it is: 'elaborated for many years past, and in important particulars already published . . .' There is no doubt at all that all these proceedings will become public knowledge and therefore everything must be correct, inwardly as well.

Would anyone else like to speak?

HERR VAN LEER: The Goetheanum is mentioned here; but we have no Goetheanum.

DR STEINER: We are not of the opinion that we have no Goetheanum. My dear Herr van Leer, we are of the opinion that we have no building, but that as soon as possible we shall have one. We are of the opinion that the Goetheanum continues to exist. For this very reason, and also out of the deep needs of our heart, it was necessary last year, while the flames were still burning, to continue with the work here on the very next day, without, as Herr Steffen said, having slept. For we had to prove to the world that we stand here as a Goetheanum in the soul, as a Goetheanum of soul, which of course must receive an external building as soon as possible.

HERR VAN LEER: But in the outside world, or in twenty years' time, it will be said: In the year 1923 there was no Goetheanum in Dornach.

DR STEINER: I believe we really cannot speak like this. We can indeed say: The building remained in the soul. Is it not important, dear Herr van Leer, to make the point as strongly as possible that here, as everywhere else, we place spiritual things in the foreground? And that what we see with our physical eyes therefore does not prevent us from saying 'at the Goetheanum'? The Goetheanum does stand before our spiritual eyes!

HERR VAN LEER: Yes indeed.

DR STEINER: Does anyone else wish to speak to Paragraph 2?

HERR LEINHAS: I only want to ask whether it is advisable to leave in the words 'in important particulars already published'. Newspapers publish the fact that we do, actually, have some secret literature such as those cycles which have not yet been published. Keeping these things secret will now be made impossible by the Statutes. Is it right to indicate at this point the literature which has so far not been published?

DR STEINER: Actually, this is not even what is meant. All that is meant is that there are also other truths which are not included in the lecture cycles, that is they have never yet been made public, not even in the cycles. I think we can remedy this by saying: 'elaborated for years past and in important particulars *already* published' or '*also already* published.' This should take account of this. The 'already' will take account of this objection. Would anyone else like to speak to Paragraph 2 of the Statutes?

HERR INGERÖ: I have a purely practical question: There are individual members here as well as representatives of groups. Obviously the groups who have sent representatives will agree to these Statutes. But otherwise will the Statutes have to be formally ratified when we get home? Will the members have to be presented with all this once again after which we would write to you to say that the Statutes have been adopted?

DR STEINER: No. I have assumed that delegates from individual groups have arrived with a full mandate so that they can make valid decisions on behalf of their group. That is what is meant by this sentence. (Applause and agreement.) This was also my interpretation in regard to all the different foundation meetings of the national groups at which I was present. It will be quite sufficient if the delegates of the national groups give their agreement on the basis of the full mandate vested in them. Otherwise we should be unable to adopt the Statutes fully at this meeting.

DR KOLISKO: I would like to ask about the fact that an Anthroposophical Society did exist already, known publicly as the Anthroposophical Society, yet now it appears to be an entirely new inauguration; there is no mention in Paragraph 2 of what was, up till now, the Anthroposophical Society in a way which would show that this is now an entirely new foundation. I wonder whether people might not question why there is no mention of the Anthroposophical Society which has existed for the last ten years but only of something entirely new.

DR STEINER: I too have thought about this. While the Statutes were being printed I wondered whether a note might be added to this point: 'The General Anthroposophical Society founded here was preceded by the Anthroposophical Society founded in 1912.' Something like that. I shall suggest the full text of this note at the end of this detailed debate. For the moment let us stick to the Paragraph itself. I shall add this as a note to the Statutes. I believe very firmly that it is necessary to become strongly aware of what has become noticeable in the last few days and of what I mentioned a day or two ago when I said that we want to link up once again where we attempted to link up in the year 1912. It is necessary to become strongly aware of this, so a strong light does in fact need to be shed on the fact of the foundation of the Anthroposophical Society here and now during this present Christmas Conference. I therefore do not want to make a history lesson out of the Statutes by pointing out a historical fact, but would prefer to include this in a note, the text of which I shall suggest. I think this will be sufficient. Does anyone else wish to speak about the formulation of Paragraph 2? If not, please would those dear friends who are in favour of the adoption of this Paragraph 2 raise their hands. (They do.) Please would those who are not in favour raise their hands. Paragraph 2 is adopted herewith. Please now read Paragraph 3.

Dr Wachsmuth reads Paragraph 3:

'3. The persons gathered in Dornach as the nucleus of the Society recognize and endorse the view of the leadership at the Goetheanum: "Anthroposophy, as fostered at the Goetheanum, leads to results which can serve every human being as a stimulus to spiritual life, whatever his nation, social standing or religion. They can lead to a social life genuinely built on brotherly love. No special degree of academic learning is required to make them one's own and to found one's life upon them, but only an open-minded human nature. Research into these results, however, as well as competent evaluation of them, depends upon spiritual-scientific training, which is to be acquired step by step. These results are in their own way as exact as the results of genuine natural science. When they attain general recognition in the same way as these, they will bring about comparable progress in all spheres of life, not only in the spiritual but also in the practical realm." '

DR STEINER: Please note, dear friends, that something has been left out in the printed version. The Paragraph should read as follows: 'The persons gathered in Dornach as the nucleaus of the Society recognize and endorse the view of the leadership at the Goetheanum:' What now follows, right to the end of the Paragraph, should be within quotation marks. This is to do with my having said that here we ought to build on the purely human element. Consider the difference from what was said earlier. In the past it was said: The Anthroposophical Society is an association of people who recognize the brotherhood of man without regard to nationality — and so on, all the various points. This is an acceptance of principles and smacks strongly of a dogmatic confession. But a dogmatic confession such as this must be banned from a society of the most modern kind; and the Anthroposophical Society we are founding here is to be a society of the most modern kind. The passage shown here within quotation marks expresses the view of the leadership at the Goetheanum, and in Paragraph 3 one is reminded of one's attitude of agreement with the view of the leadership at the Goetheanum. We are not dealing with a principle. Instead we have before us human beings who hold this conviction and this view. And we wish to join with these people to form the Anthroposophical Society. The most important sentence is the one which states that the results, and that means all the results, of spiritual science can be equally understood by every human being and human soul but that, in contrast, for an evaluation of the research results a training is needed which is to be cultivated in the School of Spiritual Science within its three Classes. It is, then, not stated that people must accept brotherhood without regard to nation or race and so on, but it is stated that it is the conviction of those who up till now have been entrusted with the leadership at the Goetheanum that what is cultivated there leads to this; it leads to brotherhood and whatever else is mentioned here. So by agreeing to this Paragraph one is agreeing with this conviction. This is what I wanted to say by way of further interpretation.

DR TRIMLER: For the purpose of openness would it not be necessary here to state who constitutes the leadership at the Goetheanum? Otherwise 'the leadership at the Goetheanum' remains an abstract term.

DR STEINER: In a following Paragraph of the Statutes the leadership of the School of Spiritual Science is mentioned, and at another point in the Statutes the Vorstand will be mentioned; the names of the members of the Vorstand will be stated. Presumably this will be sufficient for what you mean? However, the naming of the Vorstand will probably be in the final point of the Statutes, where it will be stated that the Vorstand and the leadership at the Goetheanum are one and the same. So if you thought it would be more fitting, we could say:

'The persons gathered in Dornach as the nucleus of the Society recognize and endorse the view of the leadership at the Goetheanum which is *represented by the Vorstand nominated by this foundation gathering*. This could of course be added. So it would read: 'recognize and endorse the view of the leadership at the Goetheanum which is represented by the Vorstand nominated by this foundation gathering'. This will do. Who else would like to speak?

HERR LEINHAS: Does this constitute a contradiction with point 7 where it says that Rudolf Steiner organizes the School of Spiritual Science and appoints his collaborators and his possible successor? Supposing you were not to choose as your collaborators those who are in the Vorstand as it stands at the moment?

DR STEINER: Why should there be a contradiction? You see, it is like this, as I have already said: Here, as the leadership at the

Goetheanum, we shall have the Vorstand. And the Vorstand as it now stands will be joined, in the capacity of advisers, by the leaders of the different Sections of the School of Spiritual Science. In future, this will be the leadership of the Goetheanum. Do you still find this contradictory?

HERR LEINHAS: No.

HERR SCHMIDT: I have one worry: Someone reading the sentence 'Research into these results, however, as well as competent evaluation of them, depends upon spiritual-scientific training . . .' might gain the impression that something is being drummed into people.

DR STEINER: What is being drummed in?

HERR SCHMIDT: It is possible for people to gain this impression. Personally I would prefer it if we could say: 'depends upon spiritual-scientific training, which is to be acquired step by step, *and which is suggested in the published works of Dr Steiner*', so that the impression is not aroused of something that is not quite above-board or not quite comprehensible for outsiders.

DR STEINER: But this would eliminate the essential point which must be included because of the very manner in which the lecture cycles must be treated. What we have to achieve, as I have already said, is the following: We must bring it about that judgments can be justified, not in the sense of a logical justification but in the sense that they must be based on a solid foundation, so that a situation can arise — not as regards a recognition of the results but as regards an assessment of the research — in which there are people who are experts in the subject matter and others who are not. In the subsequent Paragraph we dissociate ourselves from those who are not experts in the sense that we refuse to enter into any discussion with them. As I said, we simply want to bring about this difference in the same way that it exists in the field of the integration of partial differential equations. In this way we can work at a moral level against the possibility of someone saying: I have read Dr Steiner's book *Knowledge of the Higher Worlds* and therefore I am fully competent to assess everything else that has been published. This is what must be avoided. Therefore the very point to be made is that on the basis of my published books it is not possible to form a judgment on all the other things that are discussed above and beyond these. It would be wrong if we were not to refuse such judgments.

Herr Schmidt feels that he has been misunderstood.

DR STEINER: It says here: 'Research into these results, however, as well as competent evaluation of them, depends upon spiritual-scientific training, which is to be acquired step by step.' Why is this not clear? It does not mean that anything is drummed into anybody but rather that as with everything in the world you have to learn something before you can allow yourself to form a judgment. What we are rejecting is the assumption that anthroposophical matters can be judged from other points of view. There is a history behind this too. Let me tell you about it, for all these formulations are based on the experience of decades, as I have already said. I once gave a cycle of lectures in Bremen[50] to a certain group of people who were permitted to attend not so much on the basis of their intellectual capacity as on that of their moral maturity. Now there was a very well-known philosopher, a Platonist, who reckoned that anyone who had read the whole of Plato ought to be able to form a judgment about Anthroposophy. On this basis he sent people to me about whom he said: These are good philosophers so they ought to be allowed to attend, since they are capable of forming judgments. Of course they were less capable of forming judgments than were some quite simple, humble people whose very mood of soul made them capable of forming judgments. I had to exclude them. So it is important that particularly in the case of this Paragraph we are extremely accurate. And it would not be accurate if we were to say that the necessary schooling can be attained on the basis of my published books. The interpretation of what constitutes the necessary schooling is stated in Paragraph 8: 'All publications of the Society shall be public, in the same sense as are those of other public societies. The publications of the School of Spiritual Science' — let us say in future the cycles — 'will form no exception as regards this public character; however, the leadership of the School reserves the right to deny in advance the validity of any judgment of *these* publications which is not based on the same training from which they have been derived. Consequently they will regard as justified no judgment which is not based on an appropriate preliminary training, as is also the common practice in the recognized scientific world. Thus' and so on. So you see, the requirement in Paragraph 3 must accord with that in Paragraph 8. If you have another suggestion, please go ahead. But the one you suggested just now is quite impossible.

HERR SCHMIDT: Perhaps there could be a reference to Paragraph 8 at this point, for instance in the form of a note which says that the published books reveal the principles of the schooling.

DR STEINER: This could certainly be pointed out in a note. But this note belongs at the point where it is stated that all publications shall be public, including the books about the conditions of the schooling. That is where such a note should be put. But I thought that saying that all books shall be public, all publications shall be public, would include the fact that all books about the schooling would be public.

FRÄULEIN X: Ought it not to say: *anthroposophical* spiritual science; 'as well as competent evaluation of them, depends upon *anthroposophical* spiritual-scientific training'?

DR STEINER: What you want to bring out here is made quite clear in Paragraph 8 by the reference to Dornach. If we say 'anthroposophical' we have once again an abstract word. I especially want to express here that everything is concrete. Thus the spiritual-scientific training meant — it is shown in this Statute — is that represented in Dornach. If we say *anthroposophical* spiritual science we are unprotected, for of course anyone can give the name of Anthroposophy to whatever he regards as spiritual science.

HERR VAN LEER: I would like the final sentence to be changed from 'not only in the spiritual but also in the practical realm' to: *'in the spiritual as well as in the practical realm'*.

DR STEINER: I formulated this sentence like this because I thought of it as being based on life. This is what I thought: It is easy for people to admit in what is said here that it can constitute the foundation for progress in the spiritual realm. This will meet with less contradiction — there will be some, but less — than that Anthroposophy can also lead to something in the practical realm. This is more likely to be contradicted. That is why I formulated this sentence in this way. Otherwise the two realms are placed side by side as being of equal value in such an abstract manner: 'in the spiritual as well as in the practical realm'. My formulation is based on life. Amongst anthroposophists there are very many who will easily admit that a very great deal can be achieved in the spiritual realm. But many people, also anthroposophists, do not agree that things can also be achieved in the practical realm. That is why I formulated the sentence in this way.

MR KAUFMANN: Please forgive me, but it seems to me that the contradiction between Paragraph 3 and Paragraph 7 pointed out by Herr Leinhas is still there. Paragraph 7 says: 'The organizing of the School of Spiritual Science is, to begin with, the responsibility of Rudolf Steiner, who will appoint his collaborators and his possible successor.' I was under the impression that the Vorstand suggested by Dr Steiner has been elected *en bloc* by the present gathering. But now if Paragraph 3 calls the Vorstand, elected at the foundation meeting, the leadership at the Goetheanum, this seems to contradict Paragraph 7. I had understood Paragraph 3 to mean the leadership at the Goetheanum to be Dr Steiner and such persons as he has already nominated or will nominate who, in their confidence in him as the leadership at the Goetheanum, in accordance with Paragraph 7, hold the views stated within quotation marks in Paragraph 3 which are recognized positively by those present at the meeting. But if this is carried out by the Vorstand of the Anthroposophical Society elected here, then this seems to me to be an apparent contradiction, at least in the way it is put.

DR STEINER: I should like to ask when was the Vorstand *elected*? When was the Vorstand *elected*?

MR KAUFMANN: I was under the impression that it was accepted when you proposed it; and the agreement of the meeting was expressed very clearly.

DR STEINER: You must understand that I do not regard this as an election, and that is why just now I did not suggest: 'the leadership at the Goetheanum which is represented by the Vorstand *elected* by this foundation gathering' but '*formed*'.

MR KAUFMANN: Is this Vorstand identical with that mentioned in Paragraph 7?

DR STEINER: Surely the Vorstand cannot be identical with my single person if it consists of five different members!

Mr Kaufmann asks once again.

DR STEINER: No, it is not identical. Paragraph 7 refers to the establishment of the School of Spiritual Science which I sketched earlier on. We shall name the Vorstand in a final Paragraph. But I regard this Vorstand as being absolutely bound up with the whole constitution of the Statutes. I have not suggested this Vorstand as a group of people who will merely do my bidding but, as I have said, as people of whom each one will bear the full responsibility for what he or she does. The significance for me of this particular formation of this Vorstand is that in future it will consist of the very people of whom I myself believe that work can be done with them in the right way. So the Vorstand is in the first place the Vorstand of the Society. What is mentioned in Paragraph 7 is the leadership of the School of Spiritual Science. These are *two* things. The School of Spiritual Science will function in the future with myself as its leader. And the leaders of the different Sections will be what might be called the Collegium of the School. And then there will be the Vorstand of the Anthroposophical Society which you now know and which will be complemented by those leaders of the different Sections of the School of Spiritual Science who are not anyway members of the Vorstand. Is this not comprehensible?

MR KAUFMANN: Yes, but in the way it is put it seems to me that the contradiction is still there.

DR STEINER: What is contradictory?

MR KAUFMANN: Reading the words, you gain the impression that the Vorstand has been nominated by you personally. This would contradict Paragraph 7.

DR STEINER: Yes, but why is this not sufficient? It has nothing to do with Paragraph 7. Paragraph 7 refers only to the preceding Paragraph 5, the School of Spiritual Science. What we are now settling has nothing to do with Paragraph 7. We are only concerned here with the fact that the Vorstand has been formed. It has been formed in the most free manner imaginable. I said that I would take on the leadership of the Society. But I shall only do so if the Society grants me this Vorstand. The Society has granted me this Vorstand, so it is now formed. The matter seems to me to be as accurate as it possibly can be. Of course the worst thing that could possibly happen would be for the Statutes to express that the Vorstand had been 'nominated' by me. And this is indeed not the case in view of the manner in which the whole Society expressed its agreement, as occurred here.

HERR KAISER: Please excuse me for being so immodest as to speak once again. As regards Paragraph 1,[51] the only thing I would suggest is that you simply say 'life' and nothing else; not 'intellectual life' and not 'life of the soul', but simply 'life'.

With regard to point 3, I would not want to alter a single word in the version which Dr Steiner has given with almost mathematical precision. But in order to meet the concern of our respected friend I would merely suggest the omission of the words 'which is to be acquired step by step'.

DR STEINER: Yes, but then we do not express what ought to be expressed, namely that the schooling is indeed to be acquired step by step. We shall print on the cycles: First Class, Second Class, Third Class. And apart from this it is necessary to express in some way that there are stages within the schooling. These stages are quite simply a fact of spiritual science. Otherwise, you will agree, we have no way of distinguishing between schooling and dilettantism. Someone who has only just achieved the first stage of the schooling is a dilettante for the second and third stage. So I am afraid we cannot avoid wording it in this way.

DR UNGER: I should like to suggest that we conclude the debate about this third point.

A SPEAKER: I believe we should agree to recognize the formulation of Paragraph 1 as it has emerged from the discussion.

ANOTHER: I should only like to make a small suggestion. A word that could be improved: the word 'the same'* in 'the same progress' in the last sentence of Paragraph 3. I would like to see it deleted and replaced by 'also progress'.

DR STEINER: We could do this, of course. But we would not be —what shall I say? — using language in as meaningful a way. 'Gleich' is such a beautiful word, and one which in the German language, just in this kind of context, has gradually come to be used increasingly sloppily. It would be better to express ourselves in a way which still gives a certain fragrance to what we want to say. Wherever we can it is better to use concrete expressions rather than abstract ones. You see, I do actually mean 'the same progress as in the other realms'. So that it reads: 'These results

*The German word in Paragraph 3 is 'gleich', which is translated as 'comparable' in the official translation into English of the Statutes. For the purpose of the present passage in the discussion, the word 'same' has been substituted. It is an equally appropriate rendering for 'gleich' and makes the discussion as translated here more comprehensible. (Tr.)

are in their own way as exact as the results of genuine natural science. When they attain general recognition in the same way as these, they will bring about the same progress in all spheres . . .'

Of course I do not want to insist on this. But I do think it is not at all a bad thing to retain, or bring back to recognition, a word in the German language which was originally so resonant, instead of replacing it by an abstract expression. We are anyway, unfortunately, even in language on the way to abstraction.

Now we are in the following situation: Since an application to close the debate has been made, I ought to adjourn any further debate, if people still want to speak about Paragraph 3, till tomorrow. We should then not be able to vote on this Paragraph today. Please understand that I am obliged to ask you to vote on the application to close the debate. In the interests of proper procedure, please would those friends who wish the conclusion of the debate indicate their agreement.

DR UNGER: I only meant the discussion on point 3. We are in the middle of the detailed debate.

DR STEINER: Will those who are opposed to closing the debate please raise their hands. I am sorry, that is not possible! We shall now vote on the acceptance or rejection of Paragraph 3. Will those respected friends who are in favour of adopting point 3 please raise their hands. (They do.)

Will those respected friends who are against it please raise their hands. (Nobody does.) Point 3 has thus been adopted at the second reading. Tomorrow we shall continue with the detailed debate, beginning with point 4.

We shall gather, as we did today, after the lecture by Herr Jan Stuten on the subject of music and the spiritual world. So the continuation of the detailed debate will take place in tomorrow's meeting, which will begin at the same time as today. This afternoon at 4.30 there will be a performance of the Three Kings play.

Continuation of the Foundation Meeting

28 DECEMBER, 10 O'CLOCK IN THE MORNING

BEFORE the lecture, Dr Steiner makes some announcements regarding arrangements:

My dear friends!

Before opening today's meeting I must ask your forgiveness for yesterday's unpleasantness about access to the hall and having to wait outside. I do beg your forgiveness for this most annoying incident which, however, was truly the consequence of a whole sequence of misunderstandings. From now on we shall make sure that our friends will find the doors open here half an hour before any meeting. I am also doing my best to have two more radiators put in tonight so that it will no longer be quite so cold in the outer room. It is really difficult in this primitive accommodation to create conditions which are satisfactory for everybody. Please believe me when I say that the conditions are the least satisfactory of all for the Vorstand and myself. Let us hope that we can avoid too much trouble in the coming days.

Now may I ask Herr Stuten to speak. He is going to give us the pleasure of a lecture about the element of music in spiritual life.

Herr Stuten gives his lecture on music and the spiritual world.

After a fifteen-minute break the debate on the Statutes continues. Dr Steiner opens with the following words:

28 DECEMBER, 10 O'CLOCK IN THE MORNING

My dear friends! Today once again I shall speak the words which are to give us the foundation for our present work as well as for our continued work outside:

Soul of Man!
Thou livest in the limbs
Which bear thee through the world of space
In the spirit's ocean-being.
Practise spirit-recalling
In depths of soul,
Where in the wielding will
Of world-creating
Thine own I
Comes to being
Within God's I.
And thou wilt truly live
In the World-Being of Man.

For the Father-Spirit of the heights holds sway
In depths of worlds begetting being.

Soul of Man!
Thou livest in the beat of heart and lung
Which leads thee through the rhythm of time
Into the realm of thine own soul's feeling.
Practise spirit-awareness
In balance of the soul,
Where the surging deeds
Of the world's becoming
Thine own I
Unite
With the World-I.
And thou wilt truly feel
In the Soul-Weaving of Man.

For the Christ-Will in the encircling round holds sway
In the rhythms of the worlds, bestowing grace on the soul.

Soul of Man!
Thou livest in the resting head
Which from the grounds of eternity
Opens to thee the world-thoughts.
Practise spirit-beholding
In stillness of thought,
Where the eternal aims of Gods
World-Being's Light
On thine own I
Bestow
For thy free willing.
And thou wilt truly think
In the Spirit-Foundations of Man.

For the world-thoughts of the Spirit hold sway
In the being of worlds, craving for light.

Now, dear friends, let us once more inscribe the inner rhythm into our souls, the rhythm that can show us closely how these very words resound out of the rhythm of the universe.

The first verse:

[Rudolf Steiner writes on the blackboard as he speaks. See Facsimile 4, Page XVI top.]

Practise spirit-recalling

This is the activity that can be accomplished within one's own soul. It corresponds to what out there in the great universe is expressed in the words:

For the Father-Spirit of the heights holds sway
In depths of worlds begetting being.

The second is:

Practise spirit-awareness

That is the process within, which is answered out there in the universe by:

For the Christ-Will in the encircling round holds sway
In the rhythms of the worlds, bestowing grace on the soul.

The third is:

Practise spirit-beholding

From out there comes the answer:

For the world-thoughts of the Spirit hold sway
In the being of worlds, craving for light.

[As shown on the blackboard]

1
Practise spirit-recalling

For the Father-Spirit of the heights holds sway
In depths of worlds begetting being.

2
Practise spirit-awareness

For the Christ-Will in the encircling round holds sway
In the rhythms of the worlds, bestowing grace on the soul.

3
Practise spirit-beholding

For the world-thoughts of the Spirit hold sway
In the being of worlds, craving for light.

DR STEINER: We shall now continue our meeting with a discussion of Paragraph 4 of the Statutes. Would Dr Wachsmuth please read Paragraph 4.

Paragraph 4 is read by Dr Wachsmuth:

'4. The Anthroposophical Society is in no sense a secret society, but is entirely public. Anyone can become a member, without regard to nationality, social standing, religion, scientific or artistic conviction, who considers as justified the existence of an institution such as the Goetheanum in Dornach, in its capacity as a School of Spiritual Science. The Anthroposophical Society rejects any kind of sectarian activity. Party politics it considers not to be within its task.'

DR STEINER: Mr Collison has applied to speak first.

MR COLLISON: Please pardon me, as a very old member, for saying a few words about the Statutes. We have now come to point 4. I believe that it cannot be our intention to improve on these Statutes. Dr Steiner has put so much effort into them and they are truly all-embracing. It seems to me that any debate on the various points should serve the purpose solely of asking any questions there might be about the meaning or the extent of any of them.

(Lengthy applause.)

DR STEINER: Who would like to speak about Paragraph 4?

The suggestion is made that the Statutes should be adopted by acclamation.

DR STEINER: Yes, but I still have to ask whether anybody would like to speak to Paragraph 4. This Paragraph is in the main concerned with the fact that quite soon we shall be presenting the Anthroposophical Society to the world as an entirely public society. And everything that can contain the esoteric element, despite this public character, will be ensured by Paragraph 5 and subsequent Paragraphs.

May I ask once more who would like to speak to Paragraph 4 of the Statutes? There seems to be nobody. So will those friends who are in favour of adopting Paragraph 4 please raise their hands. (They do.) Who is in favour of rejecting Paragraph 4? (No hands are raised.) Paragraph 4 is adopted at the second reading.

Would Herr Wachsmuth please read Paragraph 5 of the Statutes.

Paragraph 5 is read out:

'5. The Anthroposophical Society sees the School of Spiritual Science in Dornach as a centre for its activity. The School will be composed of three Classes. Members of the Society will be admitted to the School on their own application after a period of membership to be determined by the leadership at the Goetheanum. They enter in this way the First Class of the School of Spiritual Science. Admission to the Second or Third Class takes place when the person requesting this is deemed eligible by the leadership at the Goetheanum.'

DR STEINER: Now, my dear friends, the purpose of this Paragraph is to enable the soul which naturally belongs to the Anthroposophical Society and which can be given to it in the Goetheanum at Dornach, to be given to it indeed in the near future. This Paragraph of the Statutes is intended to make members, or those who still want to become members, conscious of the fact that in the Goetheanum we are given the soul of the Anthroposophical Movement. This will make it possible for the esoteric impulses that ought to be given to the Anthroposophical Society to actually be given to it. We shall make progress if you endeavour to penetrate to the spirit of this fifth Paragraph.

I would only like to say a few things about how I see the constitution of the School of Spiritual Science in Dornach, at the Goetheanum, in the future. Those who have sojourned and worked within the Anthroposophical Society for some time have had the opportunity of realizing quite well that in the matter of advancing in the schooling by stages it will more and more be a question not merely of intellectual capacities, least of all the type of intellectual and empirical schooling customary in the outside world except where absolutely necessary in respect of specialist knowledge. An important role will have to be played by the capacities that lie in the feelings and in those of direct perception of the esoteric and the occult, and by moral qualities and so on. The fundamental feature of what will be at work with regard to the three Classes, which are built on the foundation of the Anthroposophical Society, which in its turn is entirely public —this fundamental feature in the working of the three Classes will be, of course, the spiritual-scientific content. But for this very reason it will be necessary for us to present the working of the School of Spiritual Science before the world in a way that shows how it can inspire the various realms of civilization, of knowledge, of art and so on. Here, too, from the start, we must not allow ourselves to think along any given lines. What is meant by thinking along a given line? To think along a given line would be to say: The School of Spiritual Science must be divided up in accordance with a concept or an idea such as a logical division into the first Section, the second Section, the third, the fourth, the fifth Section and so on. This can be nicely thought out. [See Facsimile 5, Page XIX top.]

SCHOOL OF SPIRITUAL SCIENCE

What is usually the consequence of such a way of thinking? It is a structure that lies in the realm of Cloud-cuckoo-land. And on top of that, this structure has to be administered! So then you start hunting for suitable people, you look around all over the place for people who have to fit into the first, the second, the third Section, and finally they are somehow juggled in by means of some sort of election or something. Usually what then becomes apparent is that they settle as though into a chrysalis in their particular department in the scheme; they creep into their chrysalis, but no butterfly emerges. So let us not proceed in an abstract way. Let us start by taking the activities that are already going on and put together the Sections out of the existing facts. Let us take what is already there. You see, dear friends, the management of what has to be administered, including what has to be administered in the highest spiritual sense in the different realms, cannot be carried out by just anybody who might be called and who might not even live here permanently. Is it not so that if more is to be done than merely talking about work, if the work itself is actually to be done with full responsibility, then firstly each one doing the work must be constantly available for all the others, and secondly the leadership as a whole must be accessible at any time to those who are responsible. That is why simply out of spiritual empiricism I thought that the School of Spiritual Science at the Goetheanum in Dornach should be led by me with regard to all esoteric matters and that I should be supported in this leadership by those people who have shared spiritually in the work of bringing about the building of the Anthroposophical Movement.

What I am now going to say therefore arises naturally out of the situation in Dornach at the moment. First of all it will fall to me to maintain an overall view and to administer the School as a whole, while also taking on the leadership of the general anthroposophical and pedagogical aspects.

I would carry out the leadership of the other aspects by placing at the head of the different Sections those persons who are in a position, from what has gone before, to run a particular branch of the work of the Anthroposophical Movement.

Out of this there would arise: Firstly — I have mentioned it already — what in France is called *'belles-lettres'*. I don't know whether the expression is still used. No? What a pity! In Germany they spoke of *'schöne Wissenschaften'* up to the nineteenth century, and then the term lapsed. The 'beautiful sciences', sciences which brought beauty into human knowledge, aesthetics, art. How typical that even in France the expression '*belles-lettres*' is no longer used!

SOMEONE CALLS OUT: '*Académie des lettres!*'

Yes, but the '*belles*' has been left out! And it is just this aspect with which I am concerned. We have plenty of sciences, but where are the 'beautiful sciences'? I don't know what those of you gathered here, especially the younger members, intent on science, think about the matter, but here in Dornach we link up not only with more recent times but also with most ancient past times. Therefore we may, and indeed must, create a Section for the field that in France used to be called '*belles-lettres*' and in Germany is called '*schöne Wissenschaften*'. Perhaps we shall have to give it a less unaccustomed name for the world at large, but so far I haven't found one. And once again I have to say that it is perfectly obvious that there is a person here who could not be more suitable as the leader of this Section, and that is our dear friend *Albert Steffen* who will most certainly do nothing in this realm which is not most eminently suited to the spiritual-scientific Movement as it is intended to take its start here from Dornach. (Lively applause.)

Then there is the realm of the spoken arts together with music and eurythmy. Once again there is a person on whom the choice falls quite naturally, so there is no need for me to say a great deal. My leadership of this realm will be through *Frau Dr Steiner* as the Section Leader. (Lively applause.)

Another department to be created here is a Section for the natural sciences themselves. You know that our attitude to the natural sciences is such that we seek in them something extremely profound and that it is most urgent for us to metamorphose the way they are treated nowadays into something quite different. You will see from a work of literature which is almost ready at the printer that our dear friend, Dr Guenther Wachsmuth, has devoted himself enthusiastically to this metamorphosis of natural science. Therefore we shall most fruitfully be able to entrust the department for the natural sciences to *Dr Guenther Wachsmuth.* (Applause.)

In connection with this will be a department which must be cultivated especially carefully because always in times when true spiritual knowledge has been striven for its field has been not so much a chapter of spiritual science as rather something quite organically linked with spiritual science. It is impossible to imagine that in olden times the spiritual vision, the spiritual knowledge given to mankind could have been separated in any way from the medical element. It will be seen in the work which Frau Dr Wegman has been doing with me here, which is soon to be made public, how not only a synthesis but an organic development can arise for a true anthroposophical view of the world. Once more, therefore, it is as a matter of course that the administration of the medical department, the Medical Section, should be conducted through me with the help of the Section Leader *Frau Dr Wegman.* (Applause.)

Now my dear friends, if you call to mind the old Goetheanum, and if you call to mind the beautiful words spoken about it today by our friend Herr Stuten in his excellent lecture, then you will see that the sculptural or plastic arts, too, have played a great role here. They will have to go on playing this role in future, so we shall certainly need a Section for the Sculptural Arts. You know that for years Miss Maryon has been at my side in carrying out the sculptural arts for the Goetheanum. Most unfortunately she is unable to take part in this gathering as she is suffering from a long illness which has prevented her even from stepping over here to take part. But I hope that after a while, when she is well again, she will be able to devote herself to the work of which I am now speaking. I shall carry out all that needs to be done here by way of sculpture and in the realm of the sculptural arts through the leader of this Section, *Miss Maryon.* (Applause.)

And there is another person who has marked out her territory in the world so clearly that whenever advice or help is needed in the realm of mathematics and astronomy it comes from her. You, and especially those resident in Dornach, can see from the content of my most recent lectures, including those given here before the last cycle, how necessary it is, especially in the field of astronomy, to go back to the more ancient conceptions. If you consider a small note in my memoires which are now appearing in *Das Goetheanum* — just at the beginning of the article coming out this evening[52] — you will see how very profound are the reasons for the motto over Plato's Academy: 'God geometrizes'. And indeed it is only possible to penetrate Platonic instruction — I am speaking of Platonic instruction and not spiritual-scientific instruction — by means of mathematics. Everything which needs to be put straight in this field must be put straight. And I believe that you will be as enthusiastic as you were in the other cases when I tell you that in the future I shall let this area be tended through *Fräulein Dr Vreede* as the Section Leader. (Applause.)

My dear friends! If I had divided up these Sections according to ideas, no doubt there would have been others too, but the people would have been lacking here in Dornach who could have seen to what was necessary in accordance with all the fundamental conditions. You may believe me that whereas the Statutes are the fruit of four weeks' consideration, the announcements I have just made are based on the experience of years. So this is how things will have to stand.

Later on, when we come to include the Vorstand in the Statutes, I shall speak on this final point of the Statutes and tell you how I see the relationship between the Collegium of Section Leaders, who administer the School, and the Vorstand, which bears the initiative for the leadership of the Anthroposophical Society.

Now would anyone wishing to speak to Paragraph 5 of the Statutes please do so. (Nobody does.) Mr Collison's words appear to be having a remarkably muting effect!

HERR INGERÖ: Respected friends! Just a brief question: In Paragraph 5 does the statement 'a period of membership determined by the leadership at the Goetheanum' refer to an individual period or will it be general?

DR STEINER: It will be entirely individual. You must consider how it will arise. Of your own free will you become a member of the

Anthroposophical Society, or you are one already and have been for some time. For most of you sitting here the conditions are already fulfilled. But it also says here 'on their own application'. This means that you express your will to become a member of the School. And then the leadership of the Goetheanum decides whether this is possible at the present moment or not until some future moment. This is how this matter will be dealt with in practice.

Would anyone else like to speak to Paragraph 5? If not, will those who wish to adopt Paragraph 5 please raise their hands. (They do.) Will those who do not wish to accept it please raise their hands. (Nobody does.) Paragraph 5 is herewith adopted at the second reading.

Please would you now read Paragraph 6.

Dr Wachsmuth reads Paragraph 6 of the Statutes:

'6. Every member of the Anthroposophical Society has the right to attend all lectures, performances and meetings arranged by the Society, under conditions to be announced by the Vorstand.'

DR STEINER: My dear friends! You may perhaps be brought up short by the clause: 'under conditions to be announced by the Vorstand.' I considered it for a long time. I said to myself that the most natural formulation for this sentence would be: 'Every member of the Anthroposophical Society has the right to attend all lectures, performances and meetings arranged by the Society.' It could indeed have been left like this. But then in principle we should have been unable to do what unfortunately we do have to do. We would not, for example, have been able to fix the price of tickets for the different events. This is the kind of conditions meant. In fact the thought uppermost in my mind was the price of tickets. It is dreadful, is it not, to have this thought uppermost in one's mind. But it cannot be avoided. For just as human beings cannot live on air alone, so is it also not possible to exist with the Anthroposophical Movement if our idealism does not occasionally reach for our wallet. Other similar conditions might also arise.

But I cannot help finding it necessary to lay down in this Paragraph this matter of conditions of entry which refer to the public aspect of the Society. Does anyone wish to speak to Paragraph 6? (Nobody does.) Mr Collison really is a magician! Does anyone want to speak to Paragraph 6? If not, will those dear friends who are in favour of adopting Paragraph 6 at the second reading please raise their hands. (They do.)

Will those friends who do not wish to do so raise their hands. (Nobody does.) Paragraph 6 is adopted at the second reading. (Applause.)

Will Dr Wachsmuth now please read Paragraph 7.

Paragraph 7 is read:

'7. The organizing of the School of Spiritual Science is, to begin with, the responsibility of Rudolf Steiner, who will appoint his collaborators and his possible successor.'

DR STEINER: I have just been telling you how I see the leadership of the School. And I have nothing more in particular to say to this Paragraph. Will those respected friends who wish to speak to this Paragraph please do so. Does anyone want to speak to Paragraph 7? It seems not. So will those friends who wish to adopt Paragraph 7 at the second reading please raise their hands. (They do.) Will those who do not wish to adopt it please raise their hands. (Nobody does.) Paragraph 7 is adopted at the second reading.

Now will Dr Wachsmuth please read Paragraph 8.

Paragraph 8 is read:

'8. All publications of the Society shall be public, in the same sense as are those of other public societies. The publications of the School of Spiritual Science will form no exception as regards this public character; however, the leadership of the School reserves the right to deny in advance the validity of any judgment on *these* publications which is not based on the same training from which they have been derived. Consequently they will regard as justified no judgment which is not based on an appropriate preliminary training, as is also the common practice in the recognized scientific world. Thus the publications of the School of Spiritual Science will bear the following note: "Printed as manuscript for members of the School of Spiritual Science, Goetheanum, ... Class. No one is considered competent to judge the content, who has not acquired — through the School itself or in a manner recognized by the School as equivalent —the requisite preliminary knowledge. Other opinions will be disregarded, to the extent that the authors of such works will not enter into a discussion about them." '

DR STEINER: My dear friends! With this I have attempted to put into practice something about which I have been thinking — if you would like to know a definite point in time — since the year 1913 before the laying of the foundation stone of the Goetheanum. We must be clear about the fact that it is quite likely that a movement such as the Anthroposophical Movement will create a society to be its bearer which in some form smacks of sectarianism. You cannot really blame such people who take part in a society of that kind, for you know how great a tendency towards sectarianism coming from ancient atavistic impulses people still carry within them. Often they do not realize it, but people do bear sectarian impulses within themselves. Thus it has come about that amid what I might call the somewhat tumultuous arrangements for the printing of the cycles something has entered the Society, with regard to the way these matters are dealt with, which does make a sectarian impression. For it is incomprehensible to people in their modern consciousness that it is possible to print a number of copies of something, a number exceeding one hundred, and then to want to hide it within some sort of community. You just can't do this. In some fields it would indeed be fruitful to hide certain things, but it is not carried out. In the year 1888 I once spoke with the well-known philosopher, Eduard von Hartmann,[53] whose field concerned the unconscious, about how few people there are who read books about the theory of knowledge, even though 500 and even sometimes 1000 copies are printed. Eduard von Hartmann said that one ought to disseminate not more than 60-70 copies, for there were only 60-70 people who could really understand the theory of knowledge. I am referring to the theory of knowledge which Eduard von Hartmann was just preparing. I believe, though, that in my own little book on the theory of knowledge, *The Theory of Knowledge Implicit in Goethe's World Conception*[54] — it has just appeared in a new edition — that I have contributed something in this field which everybody can read. However, I do believe that it is not possible to carry out the principle of keeping something secret once it has been put into print. In practice it has proved impossible. After all, we now have a situation in which our enemies are far more quick to speak in public about a new publication than are the anthroposophists themselves. Facts such as these have to be taken into account. We can only make progress with our great aims if on the other hand we take into account this spirit of the age. This spirit of the age cannot tolerate external secrets, but it can quite well tolerate internal secrets. For the really esoteric anthroposophical writings will still remain a very, very great secret for people for a long time to come. And externally we do not need to keep things physically secret if we can keep them private morally by working towards a recognition on the part of the world at large that, as with any other field of knowledge, there are boundaries between experts and non-experts. In dealing with the non-experts it must always be possible for us to point out that their judgment is comparable to the judgment of a peasant on differential calculus. If we work on this basis, we shall after a while — not straight away — succeed in solving the matter of the cycles in appropriate fashion. As I said, I have been thinking about this question for ten years and now a solution had to be found. This moral solution is the only one I can think of. After 'All publications of the Society shall be public, in the same sense as are those of other public societies' I want to add 'The conditions under which one acquires a spiritual training have also been made public, and they shall continue to be presented publicly'. This is to be added in the form of a note in order to avoid the misunderstanding that was pointed out yesterday. I must of course reserve the possibility of perhaps improving the style of the imprint that is to go in the publications. Perhaps after

'Printed as manuscript for members of the School of Spiritual Science, Goetheanum, . . .' should be added 'but fully available to everyone' or something like that. We shall see. It will have to be finalized very soon because the stamp to be used on the cycles that have already been printed, or are about to be printed, will have to be made up so that we can put the whole thing into practice as soon as possible once we have brought the Anthroposophical Society into being through our Conference here. Now, may I ask who would like to speak to Paragraph 8?

DR BÜCHENBACHER: Instead of 'erkannt' in the penultimate sentence, should it not say 'anerkannt'?

DR STEINER: Yes, of course. It's a printer's error.*

DR BÜCHENBACHER: May I ask whether the cycles which have already been in the possession of members for years are to be treated as publications of the School of Spiritual Science?

DR STEINER: All the cycles. In confronting the consciousness of our time we can do no other than make these measures applicable to all the cycles. This matter will mean that there will have to be a certain amount of piety among members, too. It is not a suggestion that they should sell off the cycles in their possession as quickly as possible to a second-hand bookseller.

FRÄULEIN SIMON: Does this also apply to all the publications similar to the cycles? Will they also have this note imprinted or stamped in them?

DR STEINER: On the whole it will apply only to the cycles and those publications which are equal to the cycles.

HERR WERBECK: What about the national economy course given here? Does that count as a cycle?

DR STEINER: The matter is somewhat different regarding the few

*The difference has no bearing on the translation of this sentence into English. (Tr.)

works which have not actually been published by me or by the anthroposophical publishing company but which a particular circle has been given permission to print. In one way I am quite grateful to you for giving me the opportunity to speak about this rather vexed question. In the case of these papers it should be a matter of course that they are only to be used by those who have been permitted to do so. This national economy course is one, and the medical course is another, and so on. If they were to be published more widely, the author's rights would have to be returned to me. If we were planning to transform these papers into the form given to the cycles bearing this note, they would have to be returned to me, and they could only be brought out by the *Philosophisch-Anthroposophischer Verlag* as cycles published bearing this note. The customary author's rights would have to be considered in such a case. Does anyone else wish to speak to this Paragraph?

DR KOLISKO: Regarding what Dr Steiner has just said I should like to say the following: I would be very happy to give the specialist courses, the three scientific courses which Dr Steiner gave in Stuttgart, and also the medical course, back to the *Philosophisch-Anthroposophischer Verlag* because I am convinced that it would be better if all these publications were to be brought out by the School of Spiritual Science if Dr Steiner has this in mind. This is what I wanted to say about this vexed question.

DR STEINER: Does anyone else wish to speak to Paragraph 8?

HERR LEINHAS: It says here 'the authors of such works will not enter into a discussion about them'. Does this mean that the intention is that members of the School belonging to a particular Class shall not enter into a discussion with others?

DR STEINER: Yes, of course.

HERR GOYERT: I want to ask whether it is intended that the note to be put in the cycles is also to be put in the copies that are already in the possession of members?

DR STEINER: In the Supplement to *Das Goetheanum* we shall appeal to members who possess such copies to write this note in their copies themselves. And as regards the copies still in stock, they will all have the note stamped in them. Every cycle, regardless of whether it came into being in the past or is yet to come into being in the future, will bear this note.

DR PEIPERS: Would it not be desirable, in order to avoid misunderstandings, to state in a note that the specialist scientific courses are included among the publications?

DR STEINER: What kind of misunderstanding is likely to arise? You cannot include something ephemeral in a statute. I mean it is impossible to say in a statute: 'To avoid a misunderstanding' — about something that is obvious, and then expect it to refer, let us say for example, to the medical course. It is obvious that the medical course was given subject to certain conditions. And if it was given subject to these conditions, then, should it be published, it will be returned to me. I find this a matter of course. We should have to include an awful lot in the Statutes that does not belong there if we were to mention all kinds of things which are customary. I do not think this sort of thing belongs in the Statutes.

MR KAUFMANN: In future are we to advise new members to read the cycles even though they do not yet belong to the corresponding Class of the School?

DR STEINER: This is an entirely individual and personal matter. It is of course not possible to issue directives about it. There will be new members to whom it will be quite suitable to recommend the reading of the cycles, since they will be publicly available, and there will be others for whom this advice will not be suitable; the latter will then either abide by the advice or they will read them anyway. I think it is extremely difficult to give directives about this, and I have had some strange experiences in this connection. For instance I made the acquaintance of a branch[55] which even went to the extent of advising its members whether or not they should read this book or that book. Some people who were already members were not even allowed to read my book *Theosophy* because it was thought to be unsuitable for them. Well, it was up to these members themselves whether they found the leader of this group to be such an authority that they were prepared to stand to attention even in their souls! Or else they did not. You cannot issue generalized directives.

MADEMOISELLE SAUERWEIN: Will the cycles be published in the accustomed form or will they then be available from bookshops?

DR STEINER: The cycles will be published by the *Philosophisch-Anthroposophischer Verlag*, but the route by which they make their way to those who possess copies will of course depend on those people themselves. If they want to order them by some means through the book trade — we shall of course not offer terms for them, as the expression goes — if someone wants to order a cycle from a bookseller, we shall have no objection to fulfilling the order. That is quite customary.

FRAU MUNTZ: If outsiders ask us to give them a cycle, should we do so?

DR STEINER: This has hitherto gone on to such an extent that I would not know how it could be prevented. Only by strictly emphasising the public nature of everything can we get beyond what smacks of sectarianism. Is there anyone else who would like to speak to Paragraph 8 of the Statutes? If not, then I shall now put this Paragraph to the vote. Will those friends who are in favour of adopting Paragraph 8 at the second reading please raise their hands. (They do.) Now will those friends who are against it please raise their hands. (Nobody does.) Paragraph 8 has been adopted at the second reading.

Would Dr Wachsmuth now please read Paragraph 9.

Paragraph 9 is read out:

'9. The purpose of the Anthroposophical Society will be the

furtherance of spiritual research; that of the School of Spiritual Science will be this research itself. A dogmatic stand in any field whatsoever is to be excluded from the Anthroposophical Society.'

DR STEINER: It seems to me that the content of this Paragraph is easily understood. I would only like to point out that it is not a repetition of what has been said in earlier Paragraphs but that it is necessary because it states the purpose of the Anthroposophical Society, namely the furtherance of spiritual research, that is in so far as it is cultivated at the School of Spiritual Science in Dornach. And it has to be stressed that anything dogmatic is excluded from the administration of the Anthroposophical Society.

Does anyone wish to speak to this Paragraph 9? If not, will those friends who wish to adopt Paragraph 9 at the second reading please raise their hands. (They do.) Now will those friends who are against it raise their hands. (Nobody does.) Paragraph 9 is thus adopted at the second reading.

Now we come to Paragraph 10. Will Dr Wachsmuth please read out Paragraph 10.

Paragraph 10 is read out:

'10. The Anthroposophical Society shall hold a regular General Meeting at the beginning of the year at the Goetheanum, at which time the Vorstand shall present a full report with accounting. The agenda for this meeting shall be communicated by the Vorstand to all members, together with the invitation, three weeks before the meeting. The Vorstand may call special meetings and fix the agenda for them. Invitations to such meetings shall be sent to members three weeks in advance. Motions proposed by individual members or groups of members shall be submitted one week before the General Meeting.'

DR STEINER: Does anyone wish to speak to this Paragraph 10? My endeavour has been to say as much as is necessary in the Statutes.

HERR HOHLENBERG: I would like to ask whether this General Meeting has to take place at the beginning of the year or whether another time can be chosen?

DR STEINER: I am not capriciously attached to the beginning of the year if it is enough for you not to have the guarantee of being able to count on a particular time so that the meeting might sometimes be in January and sometimes in December. Would this suffice? We do not want to arrange any of these things in an abstract way and we will try to put out our feelers here and there. If you think it is enough, we can say: 'The Anthroposophical Society shall hold a regular General Meeting each year at the Goetheanum.' I only included it because I thought that not stating the time of the meeting would meet with contradiction.

DR KOLISKO: I am in favour of leaving it in.

DR STEINER: Why?

DR KOLISKO: Because after having had many conversations I have come to realize that very many friends attach great value to the meeting taking place at Christmas time when this Christmas Conference itself is taking place.

DR STEINER: Perhaps it would be better to state it as a general wish without including it in the Statutes. Such things can be arranged in a different way.
When we have finished the discussion on the Statutes I shall be announcing to you that the Vorstand — I hope it will still be possible during this Conference —will be presenting you with By-Laws as well. These will include a number of subsidiary points which do not belong in the Statutes. The Statutes should be composed in a way that makes it possible for anybody to read them in about a quarter of an hour, with five minutes to spare in which to think about them. So I am eager to make these Statutes as brief as possible. They must be so short that there is no room in them for any special points. So I think it will be quite alright to leave this out. Does anyone else wish to speak?

HERR DONNER: In connection with this point it would be good to consider whether the national Societies should hold their General Meetings first, before the General Meeting of the General Anthroposophical Society. Would it be practical for this to be done every time?

DR STEINER: It would indeed be quite practical if it could become customary for the national Societies to hold their meetings first, in which they would nominate their delegates for the meeting here, after which they would hold another meeting to report on what had gone on here. This would perhaps be the best custom if it comes about.

MRS MERRY: I do not think three weeks are enough for the invitation.

DR STEINER: Very well, let us say six weeks. I have already said in the Vorstand that it could be six weeks. There is also another sentence to be added. The sentence I want to add here is: 'A certain number of members, to be determined from time to time in the By-Laws, has the right to request a special General Meeting at any time.' The possibility for this must also be left open.

HERR LEINHAS: I only want to recommend that the time for calling a special meeting should remain at three weeks; for the General Meeting itself six weeks, for the special meeting a shorter period.

DR STEINER: Very well. Three weeks can be made to suffice for the special meeting. Would anyone else like to speak to Paragraph 10? It seems not. So may I ask those friends who are in favour of adopting Paragraph 10 to raise their hands. (They do.) Please will those who are against it raise their hands. (Nobody does.) Paragraph 10 is adopted.

Will Dr Wachsmuth please read Paragraph 11.

Paragraph 11 is read out:

'11. Members may join together in smaller or larger groups

on any basis of locality or subject. The headquarters of the Anthroposophical Society is at the Goetheanum. From there the Vorstand shall bring to the attention of the members or groups of members what it considers to be the task of the Society. The Vorstand communicates with officials elected or appointed by the various groups. Admission of members will be the concern of the individual groups; the certificate of membership shall, however, be placed before the Vorstand in Dornach, and shall be signed by them out of their confidence in the officials of the groups. In general, every member should join a group. Only those for whom it is quite impossible to find entry to a group should apply directly to Dornach for membership.'

DR STEINER: Does anyone wish to speak on this point? Naturally this point in particular can be explained further in the By-Laws. What is included here need not be said in general. This Paragraph shows how admissions are to be handled and everything else is a matter of general custom, which there is indeed no harm in changing from time to time.

Does anyone wish to speak to Paragraph 11? Seemingly not. So may I ask those friends who are in favour of adopting Paragraph 11 to raise their hands. (They do.) Now will those friends who are in favour of rejecting Paragraph 11 raise their hands. (Nobody does.) Paragraph 11 is thus adopted at the second reading.

Would Dr Wachsmuth now please read Paragraph 12.

Paragraph 12 is read out:

'12. Membership dues shall be fixed by the individual groups; each group shall, however, submit . . . for each of its members to the central leadership of the Society at the Goetheanum.'

DR STEINER: I would now ask you for the moment not to discuss the amount to be inserted here. It will be considered to start with after the Vorstand has made suggestions at the meeting of the General Secretaries tomorrow morning at 8.30. What the General Secretaries consider to be possible and necessary can then be reported at the subsequent meeting of members. I would ask you to accept this Paragraph in its overall sense. Does anyone wish to speak? If not, will those friends who accept Paragraph 12 in this sense please raise their hands. (They do.) Will those friends who wish to reject Paragraph 12 raise their hands. (Nobody does.) Paragraph 12 is adopted at the second reading.

Would Dr Wachsmuth now read Paragraph 13.

Paragraph 13 is read out:

'13. Each working group formulates its own statutes, but these must not be incompatible with the Statutes of the Anthroposophical Society.'

DR STEINER: Does anyone wish to speak to Paragraph 13?—I think it is as obvious as anything could be. May I then ask those friends who adopt Paragraph 13 to raise their hands. (They do.) Will those friends who wish to reject Paragraph 13 raise their hands. (Nobody does.) Paragraph 13 is adopted at the second reading.

Would Dr Wachsmuth now read Paragraph 14.

Paragraph 14 is read out:

'14. The organ of the Society is *Das Goetheanum*, which for this purpose is provided with a Supplement containing the official communications of the Society. This enlarged edition of *Das Goetheanum* will be supplied to members of the Anthroposophical Society only.'

DR STEINER: I have already spoken about this Paragraph 14 and would now ask those friends who wish to speak to it to do so. Does anyone wish to speak to Paragraph 14?

QUESTION: Will *Das Goetheanum* be available from Switzerland only?

DR STEINER: We will adopt as a custom whatever will be most practical in the circumstances. An arrangement has already been made with the German section, in whose case it will be distributed from Stuttgart. Obviously we shall do whatever is most practical in any given circumstances.

A SPEAKER: To make things quite clear it ought to say: 'The organ of the Society is *the weekly Das Goetheanum*'.

DR STEINER: The weekly. Very well. Does anyone else wish to speak?

HERR GOYERT: If the weekly is changed into a different kind of journal, then this will no longer be correct.

DR STEINER: Let us hope that this will not be the case. Perhaps it will be quite a good thing if we have a means of keeping the weekly journal as it is, and not changing it. Does anyone else wish to speak? If not, will those friends who are in favour of adopting Paragraph 14 please raise their hands. (They do.) Please would those not in favour raise their hands. (Nobody does.) Paragraph 14 is adopted at the second reading.

Now we have to add a fifteenth Paragraph:

'At the Foundation Meeting at Christmas 1923 the constitution of the Founding Vorstand will be:

Rudolf Steiner as President
Albert Steffen as Vice-president
Frau Dr Wegman as Recording Secretary
Dr Guenther Wachsmuth as Secretary and Treasurer
Frau Dr Steiner as a member
Fräulein Dr Vreede as a member.'

Now I still want to mention that this is to be the Vorstand responsible for the Society but that for all matters pertaining to the leadership of the soul of the Anthroposophical Society, namely the School of Spiritual Science at the Goetheanum, the relevant meetings and consultations shall also be attended by those Section Leaders who are not members of the Vorstand. At the moment all the Section Leaders except one are also members of the

Vorstand. Does anybody wish to speak to this point? It says: The total Vorstand is 'formed', which is an indication of the fact that it is neither elected nor nominated but that it is a self-evident Vorstand which is designated as a result of the reasons which have been given; it is a Vorstand designated by the facts themselves and receives the ground on which it stands at this Foundation Meeting.

QUESTION: Is it not possible for there to be an accumulation of offices?

DR STEINER: I expressly said yesterday that it will be incompatible for members of the Vorstand to hold other offices in the Anthroposophical Society. For example it is not desirable for one of the members of the Vorstand to be the General Secretary of some group, or for instance the leader of a branch or something similar. Then he can devote himself exclusively to his task. But for the leadership of the School it is naturally necessary to call those who are most suitable. And the leadership of the School is likely for the most part to consist of members of the Vorstand. Therefore in this instance there is an accumulation of offices whereby the Section Leaders will be advisory members of the Vorstand. Does anybody else wish to speak to Paragraph 15? No. Then I would now ask you to give your consent, not by voting in the sense of the votes conducted for the other Paragraphs but with the feeling that you acknowledge the justification of this fundamental manner of leadership of a true Anthroposophical Society. I would ask you to give your agreement that this Vorstand be constituted for the leadership of the Anthroposophical Society. (Long applause.)

DR STEINER: My dear friends, I believe I speak also on behalf of those who stand here beside me, the members of the Vorstand who are not unprepared but more than enough prepared, when I express the most cordial gratitude for your consent and when I give the promise that the leadership of the Anthroposophical Society will be conducted in the sense of its spiritual foundations and conditions.

We are now coming to the end of our meeting. Having completed the second reading, we now come to the adoption of the Statutes as a whole in the third reading. May I now ask, after the discussion of the individual Paragraphs in the detailed debate, whether anybody would like to speak once more about the Statutes as a whole? I only wish to say that I would like to add the following historical note, which was asked for yesterday, after Paragraph 2: 'The Anthroposophical Society is in continuity with the Society founded in 1912. It would like, however, to create an independent point of departure, in keeping with the true spirit of the present time, for the objectives established at that time.'

This is the note with which we can add what was said on this point yesterday. Now, would anyone still like to speak about the Statutes as a whole? If this is not the case, may I ask those respected friends who are in favour of adopting the Statutes at the third reading to raise their hands. (They do.) Will those who are not in favour please make this known by raising their hands. (Nobody does.)

My respected friends, the Statutes of the Anthroposophical Society are adopted herewith. We shall once again continue with this meeting of members tomorrow morning after Herr Werbeck's lecture. Would you please remain seated for a few more seconds as I have some announcements to make.

Firstly: The next gathering today will be for the eurythmy performance at 4.30 this afternoon. The programme will be entirely new. Secondly: The General Secretaries are requested to meet at 8.30 on Saturday morning, as they did last Tuesday at 2.30, down in the Glass House. I would also request the representatives of the various Swiss branches to be present, as the question already mentioned about the Swiss Anthroposophical Society will be discussed to start with in this smaller circle.

Further: Unfortunately the meeting of members of the school associations for free education in Switzerland cannot take place here in the hall because it is needed for eurythmy rehearsals. There is therefore no room large enough for all the members to participate as listeners at this meeting. The meeting will take place this afternoon down in the Glass House and in consequence I unfortunately have to ask for the attendance only of the members of the Swiss school association itself and of those friends from non-German speaking countries, that is America, England, France, Spain, Italy, Sweden, Norway, Holland and so on. Alas, the baby has to be chopped in half somewhere, and so, to start with for today's meeting, I would ask those from countries with really weak currencies not to attend. That means all the German members and also, if they cannot find any room, the members from Austria.

Also: It has been drawn to my attention — we never seem to get away from these things — that people should be more careful about what they say on the street, in the tram, or wherever they are staying. It is quite a good thing not to irritate other people by saying all sorts of peculiar things. This is all I am able to say just now. Other things can be said when the Vorstand presents you with some By-Laws. They can be said tomorrow in the members' meeting.

At 4.30 this afternoon is the eurythmy performance. This evening at 8.30 will be my lecture. It will be necessary to have the lecture at 8.30 every evening. And tomorrow morning at 8.30 is the meeting I have announced for the General Secretaries and the members of the Swiss councils. Then at 10 o'clock Herr Werbeck's lecture on the opposition to Anthroposophy, and after a short interval the continuation of this meeting.

Rudolf Steiner's Contribution During The Meeting of the Swiss School Association[56]

28 DECEMBER, IN THE AFTERNOON

IN THE GLASS HOUSE

TOWARDS the end of the meeting, Dr Steiner spoke the following words:

In addition to what I took the liberty of saying at the close of the last course which I was able to hold for the Swiss teachers, I have perhaps only a few more remarks to make in connection with the difficulties of the Swiss school movement. It seems to me that things do in part indeed depend on how the educational movement connected with Anthroposophy is run here in Switzerland.

The Waldorf School in Germany has remained essentially in a position of isolation. Though there have been one or two further foundations, in Hamburg, Cologne and so on, the Waldorf School in Germany, in other words in a relatively extensive area, has remained a solitary example. It will remain to be seen, therefore, whether what is to be started in England as a kind of Waldorf school, and also the school with three classes that already exists in Holland, will also to begin with remain as solitary examples.

Apart from everything else it has to be said that the reason why these schools are still only isolated examples, and also why it can be expected that they will remain so for a long time, is simply that the present social circumstances really do make it impossible for an attitude to come about that could lead to the financing of a larger number of such schools. Experience over the years has shown this quite clearly. And this challenges us to think carefully about the whole direction we should take with our educational movement.

This is especially necessary with regard to Switzerland. For Switzerland is pervaded by a very strong sense for everything represented by the state. And now that the Swiss school association for independent education has been founded, I do believe that the chief difficulties will arise from this Swiss sense of statehood. Even less than anywhere else will it be possible here in Switzerland to find an opening for the belief that a truly independent school could be an example for a model method of education, or that schools such as this could be founded on a larger scale. We should not allow ourselves to be under any illusion in this respect. Aversion to a system of education that is independent of the state is very great here.

Of course what Herr Gnädiger has just said is right, namely that there will be interest in how things are done in a model school.

Least of all here in Switzerland can you expect the president of the *Schweizerischer Schulverein*, of whom you have spoken, to have any interest in the school other than that pertaining to its status as a model. Perhaps his interest will turn out to be such that he would like to influence Swiss state schools to take up certain methodological aspects from this model school. But this seems to me to be the only aspect that can be counted on to attract interest here in Switzerland. That is why it seems to me to be important to take up these two things wherever educational associations of the kind you have mentioned are founded; and also that many such associations should be founded, more and more of them!

Another aspect is that the crux of anthroposophical education is its method. The schools apply a certain method. It is not a question of any particular political direction but purely and simply of method. It is also not a question of any particular religious creed, or of seeing Anthroposophy somehow as a religious creed. It is simply a question of method.

In the discussion that followed my lecture cycle[57] my answer to questions on this was simply that the educational method represented here can be applied anywhere, wherever there is the good will to introduce it.

If this is done on the one hand, and if on the other hand —in order to create an understanding in wider circles — it is clearly emphasized that this is the proper method and that it is being applied in a school that can serve as a model, if these two points are given the main emphasis in the programme, if it is stressed that every school could use these methods and that a model school could demonstrate how fruitful they are, and if things are worked out neatly, then I believe that something could be achieved even in Switzerland. And then on the basis of these two points educational associations ought to be founded everywhere. But it would have to be made clear to everyone that the aim was not to found as many private schools as possible to compete with the state schools. In Switzerland such a thing would be regarded as something very peculiar and it would never be understood. But there would be an understanding for a model school which could be a source of inspiration for a method of education. Progress cannot be made in any other way. It is important to present these things to people in principle again and again and wherever the opportunity arises.

I believe it would be a good thing if you could always give the greatest prominence to these two aspects. They are perfectly true, and much damage has been done to us by the constant repetition of the view that Waldorf education can only be carried out in schools apart from the main stream, whereas I have constantly repeated that the methods can be applied in any school.

This is what I wanted to say, for everything else is linked to this. I also believe that a financial basis will only be won when there can be an understanding of these things. There will be very little understanding in Switzerland for independent schools if they are not linked to what I have just been saying. But if this is done, I believe that our efforts could lead to a greater degree of success than has been the case hitherto. So far the existing financial situation is not sufficient basis for the founding of a school in Basel.

Meeting of the Vorstand of the General Anthroposophical Society and of the General Secretaries of the National Societies together with their Secretaries and the Swiss Branches

29 DECEMBER, 8.30 IN THE MORNING

IN THE GLASS HOUSE

DR STEINER:

My dear friends!

I would now like to open the meeting of the General Secretaries and the representatives of the Swiss branches. The best thing to do will be to include in the agenda our discussion about rearranging the affairs of the Swiss Anthroposophical Society. Wishes concerning this were expressed during the last meeting of delegates[58] and in the course of our further discussions about the General Anthroposophical Society it will be a good thing to take these various wishes into account in the hope that a satisfactory arrangement can be found concerning the relationship of the branch at the Goetheanum and indeed of the General Anthroposophical Society as a whole. Would you now please speak to this point on the agenda. Suggestions at the other meeting were voiced very energetically indeed.

Dr Hugentobler speaks on this point and asks questions.

DR STEINER: With regard to these matters we must take into account that basically they can all be traced back to a question of tact. It all started at a meeting of delegates of the Anthroposophical Society in Switzerland in the summer,[59] when the Swiss members felt themselves to be drowned out by members who happened to be in Switzerland at the time. They felt they were being pushed aside. Everything they felt thus comes down to a question of tact. The Swiss members felt that the others talked much too much, that they themselves had not been able to get a word in and that people from elsewhere had given them all kinds of advice which failed to take account of the situation in Switzerland. The whole matter obviously stems from that meeting. At the last meeting of delegates the matter was cogently discussed, but on the other hand a great deal was brought forward which people found impossible to understand. As I was in the chair at that meeting of delegates I know how certain things said met with absolutely no understanding, so it would be a good thing if the wishes expressed then could be brought forward again in a comprehensible form. This is what I hope from today's meeting. Who would like to speak?

Herr Geering-Christ explains his point of view.

DR STEINER: That is quite right. The matter is not at all complicated if you look at the facts, and Herr Geering has put it very clearly. If the matter is properly faced it will find a perfectly simple solution. I should also like to add that the whole matter has been put on a new footing by the foundation of the General Anthroposophical Society of which Herr Steffen, being the one who will represent the Swiss element within the General Anthroposophical Society, is the Vice-president. The whole matter has been placed on a new footing as a result of the institution of this Vorstand.

Looking at the structure as a whole it becomes obvious that part of the trouble at the meeting of delegates in the summer, which made for such bad feeling,[60] stemmed from the fact that at that time the German council saw itself as the 'Vorstand' for the worldwide Society and behaved accordingly. This was what hurt the feelings of the Swiss delegates, was it not? So there are several contributory factors, which Herr Geering suggested in one way or another at the end of his speech. There is an administrative matter for the Swiss Anthroposophical Society which will naturally be settled at a meeting of Swiss members. So on the one hand there are the affairs of the Swiss Society and on the other there is a question of tact. I do hope that these matters of tact will be settled in the near future.

The General Anthroposophical Society, within whose framework our present discussions lie, can of course only discuss the arrangement of the relationship between the branch at the Goetheanum and the Swiss Anthroposophical Society. This is what we ought to be discussing today. Everything else should be left to a meeting which the Anthroposophical Society in Switzerland will hold. This question of bringing order into the relationship between the branch at the Goetheanum and the Anthroposophical Society in Switzerland is something that can concern us very much. At the last meeting of delegates on 8 December 1923, when the wishes on this matter were expressed, I believed that a solution could be found. You will agree that for external and internal reasons the branch at the Goetheanum cannot be seen by the outside world as something separate from the Swiss Society. But I thought that the solution could lie in arranging matters internally in such a way that the branch would have neither a seat nor a vote, or at least not a vote, at meetings of delegates of the Anthroposophical Society in Switzerland.

Today, however, I believe that the view expressed by Herr Geering is very much justified, namely that a change in this direction is not necessary. The moment our Swiss friends can come to a general conviction that they could get on perfectly well with the branch at the Goetheanum when other things are not allowed to interfere, at the moment when our Swiss friends can come to that conviction, there will, I believe, be no need to change anything. I would like you to have a specific discussion on whether there are any wishes that lie in this direction. Once this question has been fully discussed it will then be a matter for the Anthroposophical Society in Switzerland, who will elect their General Secretary or whatever kind of officer they may want to have. Once this has been discussed we shall actually have completed our consideration of the Swiss affair. I think the difficulty is partly due to the Swiss council having not been particularly strongly consolidated so far. The chairmen of the various branches had simply been nominated as the council. Obviously a council like this is a rather elastic entity and nobody really knows what it is, since the council does not function properly. If a properly functioning council can come into being in the Swiss Society, the whole matter will sort itself out. I do not believe that it will be possible for those not living in Dornach to form a majority in Dornach. So I would ask you to seize on a formulation which will bring about a change in the relationship of the branch at the Goetheanum with the Anthroposophical Society in Switzerland.

Herr Schweigler has something to say.

DR STEINER: Does anyone else wish to speak to this point?

HERR GEERING-CHRIST: Could we now proceed to a vote among the Swiss delegates?

DR STEINER: I was just about to ask the Swiss friends whether they agree with the aims set out by Dr Hugentobler, Herr Geering and Herr Schweigler. Would those Swiss friends who do, please raise their hands. (They do.)

This is a clear expression of the wish of our Swiss friends to keep the branch at the Goetheanum within the bosom of the Swiss Anthroposophical Society. All the other questions are matters for the Swiss Anthroposophical Society and do not belong in this meeting. So we have dealt with the matter that needed attention within the framework of the General Anthroposophical Society.

Does anyone else wish to speak about these questions while they can be discussed at this smaller meeting?

Fräulein Dr Vreede, as the secretary of the branch at the Goetheanum, states that of the 150 members of the branch 70 are in fact Swiss members.

Dr Grosheintz wishes to speak.

DR STEINER: That is quite correct. In a Society such as ours it will never be possible to avoid the appearance of questions in every field which have to be settled by tact alone. You will remember that in *The Philosophy of Freedom* tact plays a special part among the moral principles. However much may be regulated by means of statutes, I am actually convinced that pedantic statutes can be the source of much that has to be settled by tact. So I do agree that if things are carried out in the manner suggested by Dr Grosheintz just now, we shall manage things alright by means of tact. Much will depend on this.

Frau Weiss asks a question.

DR STEINER: I do not think that Dr Grosheintz meant this in a statutory way. He was speaking of something that has to be applied in each case as it arises if it is felt to be necessary. And this is exactly what I mean by a 'question of tact'. You have to have at your fingertips a sense for what might be necessary. I am altogether of the opinion that in the management of a society not much can be achieved by a pedantic head. It may have its place elsewhere, certainly, but in the management of a society such as the one to be founded here a pedantic head is quite harmful. What we need are sensitive fingertips. The more we can manage the Society through our sensitive fingertips the better will things be.

Mr Monges asks whether the relationship of Honolulu to the General Anthroposophical Society is to be similar to that of the branch at the Goetheanum.

DR STEINER: Honolulu belongs to the General Anthroposophical Society. It has nothing to do with all these questions. Everything we have been discussing up to now has concerned the relationship between the branch at the Goetheanum and the Anthroposophical Society in Switzerland. The branch in Honolulu has nothing to do with the branch at the Goetheanum nor with the Anthroposophical Society in Switzerland.

Does anyone else wish to speak about anything, for instance matters which could do with a preliminary airing prior to the general discussion with all the members? Somebody might wish to bring up a point for preliminary discussion in this smaller circle.

HERR LEINHAS: There was the matter of the contribution to be paid to the General Anthroposophical Society.

DR STEINER: Perhaps I could ask Dr Guenther Wachsmuth to report on this.

Dr Wachsmuth reports.

DR STEINER: It will not help us much, my dear friends, if we discuss whether every country should participate in paying membership contributions. It will only help us if they do all pay. There is very little point in knowing now whether they will pay or not. The only fruitful thing to do is to take the general picture as the basis and to endeavour from this general picture to state a figure which promises to be sufficient for the General Anthroposophical Society to achieve what it has to achieve. I would therefore be in favour of stating a standard figure and then leaving open, of course, what the groups, the national groups, can agree to in practice. Of course the figure can be exceeded by an unlimited amount, approaching, though never achieving, the lavish scale on which Carnegie[61] acted. And less can also be contributed, for instance by the countries with very weak currencies, down to what in mathematics is termed the vanishing point. In practice we shall see what can be done. I do not know how closely it will be possible to approach the scale of Carnegie, but I am quite certain that the vanishing point, as they say in mathematics, will have a definite part to play. Therefore, having regard to all that we can know today, I do believe that a standard figure should be fixed and that deviations from this can be arranged in individual discussions. So I think it would be right to lay down that each group should pay 12 Schillings for each of its members, that is 1 Schilling per month. I can assure you that even if this Schilling is really contributed we shall have the greatest difficulty in carrying out the things we intend to do here. This must not be allowed to weigh on people. For those who cannot pay, the amount will have to be reduced, and we shall have to reduce our plans accordingly. But I do believe that we could agree on a standard contribution, from the groups, of 12 Schillings per member. Any other arrangement would lead to the Anthroposophical Society being able neither to live nor die, so that once again for financial reasons nothing worthwhile would be achieved. We shall be criticized and people will not understand that we cannot achieve anything if our hands are tied.

So this is not intended to be an absolute demand. It is a general standard. If it turns out to be impossible, it nevertheless expresses what we would need; and we shall then simply have to reduce it. This is perfectly possible. But I do think that it is necessary to make a statement of where one stands.

Mr Collison asks about a joining fee.

DR STEINER: The joining fee would not be included in this. It is something that goes into the general fund. But the calculation can be made on the basis of the subsequent contributions. I am simply reckoning with a monthly amount for every member of 1 Schilling, or annually 12 Schillings. This is what I am reckoning with. Perhaps I may be allowed to disclose that the Vorstand did consider this but only spoke in pictures regarding how these matters might be settled. My suggestion is what has come to me personally as a result of those pictures.

Mademoiselle Sauerwein explains her point of view.

BARONESS DE RENZIS: That would amount to 50 Lire. It would be utterly impossible for Italy!

Mademoiselle Sauerwein replies.

DR STEINER: Of course this may be so. It would simply mean that the standard contribution for individual groups would have to be set at a sufficiently low level. But I do not see that this means we cannot set the standard at the level that seems to us necessary after making some very exact calculations. What will happen in reality? Try to imagine it! I can say that under the conditions pertaining at present there will definitely be payments from not more than at most three to four thousand members, or rather payments will not be made for more than three to four thousand members. If you picture this to yourselves you will also have a picture of the amount we shall have at our disposal here each year. So you see the only sensible thing to do is to set the level of membership contributions like a budget. To set the level without regard to the future is pointless. If we want to make calculations we have to make them with figures. We have to be able to count on a certain income. If this income fails to appear we are then obliged to replace the shortfall from other sources in another way, perhaps from voluntary contributions and so on. Simply to fix an amount which bears no relationship to what we need here seems to me impossible. If we are to fix an amount — otherwise we might as well go straight to voluntary contributions — then it must be on the basis of what we need here. No other basis can be fruitful.

Fräulein Schwarz asks some questions.

DR STEINER: The *Verein des Goetheanum* can only receive contributions towards the rebuilding of the Goetheanum. And the rebuilding of the Goetheanum has nothing to do with the administration of the Anthroposophical Society. These are two quite separate things. I presume you are referring to the membership fee for the *Verein des Goetheanum*? The relationship of the

Anthroposophical Society to the *Verein des Goetheanum* is something that can still be discussed during this conference. With regard to the membership of the *Verein* I think some kind of method will have to be found if those gathered here in any way wish it. You have to consider that with regard to the rebuilding of the Goetheanum the membership fees for the *Verein* are so minimal as to be almost negligible. The membership contributions are almost negligible! And in future they will be negligible; in the past they were at least used for the most part for the payment of interest on loans. But for the building of the Goetheanum in future it will not be possible to get involved with loans. A sinking fund (*à fonds perdu*) will be the only option. So then the membership contributions to the *Verein des Goetheanum* will have to be put to a use other than that of paying interest. We shall be speaking about the building of the Goetheanum. In future perhaps it will be possible to bring about an agreement with the General Anthroposophical Society. This is a question that would go too far for the moment, since we have not yet got beyond the matter of the membership contribution.

Does anyone wish to speak to the question of the membership contribution?

Mr Kaufmann explains that a little while ago Dr Wachsmuth had mentioned an amount of 7 Schillings for the contribution and that the English delegates had come with the mandate to agree to 7 Schillings.

DR STEINER: If the method I have suggested is chosen, then it will encompass every other method. But I merely maintain that it is impossible to mention a sum from the start in the knowledge that it will be no good for anything. Whether or not something is obligatory is not so much the point. The point is that the amount can be counted on under all circumstances. In the picture that has emerged we have certainly counted — or I have certainly counted — on the countries with strong currencies treating the amount more or less as though it were obligatory. To go below the nominated sum would require individual negotiations. But if we want to go below it now, it would have been better if we had started by negotiating the amount in the first place. We could have started the discussion by considering the amount — I know this would have gone against our moral sense — and once the discussion had revealed that the General Anthroposophical Society could not be maintained we could have decided not to found it in the first place. There is no other way but to think realistically. We cannot found a Society which is incable of surviving. But now I have said that it will be possible to give less than the stated amount and then the centre here will have the task of raising the difference. This statement makes the payment of the membership contribution no hardship at all, for it is simply a statement of what is actually needed. I should be sorry if the matter of the membership contribution were to create a mood of dissatisfaction. But it is not necessary for this to happen, my dear friends. However, it is on the other hand necessary that the general enthusiasm for our cause which rightly exists, and which has been expressed over the last few days, should not come to grief over the bagatelle of the membership contribution. That would be 'ahrimanic'. My dear friends, people are so quick to say this in other settings!

Dr Büchenbacher recounts that the Free Anthroposophical Society in Stuttgart made it possible for a colleague to exist by paying him 2, 5 or 10 percent of the weekly payments. He says that though conditions in Germany are very difficult, nevertheless if everybody pulls his or her weight things can be managed.

DR STEINER: I should merely like to point out that discussion leading to such matters cannot really belong in our present agenda. I am convinced that if we were to listen to all the pros and cons of paying or not paying the contribution we should of course hear as many justified reasons as there are people in this room, and later, in the meeting with all the members, that would mean eight hundred justified reasons. Surely we cannot make this the content of our discussion. If we are to continue, we must discuss how else we are to manage. We must discuss from the point of view of the General Anthroposophical Society how else we are to manage. I can see no possibility of managing in any other way. It seems likely that we shall not get what we need, but I see no way of managing with less. However, I do see a possibility that the special wishes might be taken into account. Assume that not a single group can pay the required amount. So instead of 36,000 Schillings we should receive 5,000 Schillings, and then we shall have to see how to replace the 31,000 Schillings with something else. Above all it will be an uncomplicated and obvious situation. But it will be different from situations elsewhere; we cannot proceed by fixing budgets. Imagine a national budget being fixed if every citizen is allowed to pay whatever he likes! You cannot fix a national budget in this way! Or can you, Duke of Cesaro? Can you ask each citizen what he wants to pay per year or do you have to fix a sum and tell him what he must pay?

THE DUKE OF CESARO: You can, but you can't force him!

DR STEINER: This is just it; we shall not be able to enforce anything! And this can be the very reason why it might be much more easy to agree than if it were a matter of being forced. We have taken into account the matter of not being forced.

Mr Collison asks whether this might not be a bit of an obstacle as regards acquiring new members.

DR STEINER: Suppose a group was in a position in which it could only expect a yearly sum of 4 Schillings or 4 Francs from each member. If this were the case it would of course not be able to pay 12 Schillings or 12 Francs to us. Perhaps it could pay only 2 Schillings or even nothing. The question of how to deal with new members is a matter that is left entirely to the groups, who will then say to us: We cannot pay more than so much for each member. Under these circumstances it will always be possible to manage.

Herr Ingerö declares on behalf of Norway that about 3,000 Schillings per year could be paid.

Dr Zeylmans van Emmichoven declares that taking Holland as a whole, the sum will be met.

DR STEINER: This is how the matter was always handled during the time when we were still the German Section of the Theosophical Society. Individual members were not forced to pay, but the groups were able to pay the full sum to the German Section by making up any shortfall out of larger payments by some members. In those days, though, the contributions were far smaller. This is no longer possible today. I have often described to you the conditions under which it was possible to manage with the old, modest contributions. I have described to you how *Luzifer-Gnosis* was produced and sent out in the early days.[62] These are conditions which cannot be brought back today. So all in all, so far as I can see, there can be no other picture than that of needing 12 Schillings in the future for each member of the General Anthroposophical Society. Is there any member of the Vorstand who thinks differently?

FRAU DR STEINER: No indeed. While I was closing down the publishing company and our flat in Berlin recently I was so interested to find the endless envelopes again, all addressed by hand by Dr Steiner, while each entry in the post book had been checked by me. We saw to every little detail ourselves and then carried the whole mailing to the post office in a laundry basket. These memories came back to me in Berlin. Nobody likes doing things like this these days. But it was most interesting to look back and experience once again how every detail was attended to by Dr Steiner and myself in those days.

DR STEINER: These are things which simply come about and there is no point in arguing about them. You didn't argue about them; you didn't even talk about them. These things are simply there, to be done out of the necessity of the moment. But once something comes under discussion you simply have to state how much you need. It is only possible to discuss something if you have a proper basis. Does anyone else wish to speak about this?

FRAU PROFESSOR BÜRGI: I wish to commit myself to paying the contribution on behalf of the Bern branch.

HERR HAHL: I wish to agree to what has been said.

DR STEINER: My dear friends, we must adjourn the meeting now so that we can go to the lecture. I shall announce when and where we shall continue.

Continuation of the Foundation Meeting

29 DECEMBER, 10 O'CLOCK IN THE MORNING

DR STEINER:

My dear friends!

Today our agenda begins by giving us the pleasure of the lecture by Herr Werbeck.

Louis Werbeck gives his lecture on 'The Opposition to Anthroposophy'.

DR STEINER: Dear friends, let us have a fifteen-minute break before continuing with yesterday's meeting of members.

DR STEINER: My dear friends! Let us hear again today the words which are to resound in our soul both here and later, when we depart and carry out with us what is intended here:

Soul of Man!
Thou livest in the limbs
Which bear thee through the world of space
In the spirit's ocean-being.
Practise spirit-recalling
In depths of soul,
Where in the wielding will

Of world-creating
Thine own I
Comes to being
Within God's I.
And thou wilt truly live
In the World-Being of Man.

For the Father-Spirit of the heights holds sway
In depths of worlds begetting being.
Seraphim, Cherubim, Thrones!
Let there ring out from the heights
What in the depths is echoed
Speaking:
Ex Deo nascimur.

Soul of Man!
Thou livest in the beat of heart and lung
Which leads thee through the rhythm of time
Into the realm of thine own soul's feeling.
Practise spirit-awareness
In balance of the soul,
Where the surging deeds
Of the world's becoming
Thine own I
Unite
With the World-I.
And thou wilt truly feel
In the Soul-Weaving of Man.

For the Christ-Will in the encircling round holds sway
In the rhythms of the worlds, bestowing grace on the soul.
Kyriotetes, Dynamis, Exusiai!
Let there be fired from the East
What through the West is formed
Speaking:
In Christo morimur.

Soul of Man!
Thou livest in the resting head
Which from the grounds of eternity
Opens to thee the world-thoughts.
Practise spirit-beholding
In stillness of thought,
Where the eternal aims of Gods
World-Being's Light
On thine own I
Bestow
For thy free willing.
And thou wilt truly think
In the Spirit-Foundations of Man.

For the world-thoughts of the Spirit hold sway
In the being of worlds, craving for light,
Archai, Archangeloi, Angeloi!
Let there be prayed from the depths
What in the heights will be granted
Speaking:
Per Spiritum Sanctum reviviscimus.

Let us once again take hold of these words in meaningful sections. Here we have:

[Rudolf Steiner writes on the blackboard as he speaks. See Facsimile 4, Page XVI, bottom.]

Practise spirit-recalling

What takes place in the soul of man is related to all being in the cosmos of spirit, soul and body. Thus this 'Practise spirit-recalling' especially points to what is heard in the call to the Seraphim, Cherubim and Thrones when the manner in which they work in the universe is characterized:

Seraphim, Cherubim, Thrones!
Let there ring out from the heights
What in the depths is echoed.

We have the right cosmic concept when we picture in our soul how the voices of Seraphim, Cherubim and Thrones resound in the universal word and are heard because they find an echo in the depths of the grounds of world existence, and how what is inspired from above and what resounds from below, the universal word, emanates from Seraphim, Cherubim and Thrones.

In the second verse we have:

Practise spirit-awareness

This is related to the second hierarchy: Kyriotetes, Dynamis, Exusiai. To characterize them we imagine their voices in the universal word working as expressed in the words:

Kyriotetes, Dynamis, Exusiai!
Let there be fired from the East
What through the West is formed.

The third member of man's existence is:

Practise spirit-beholding

To this we add the indication of how the third hierarchy enters with its work into the universal word:

Archai, Archangeloi, Angeloi!
Let there be prayed from the depths
What in the heights will be granted.

[As shown on the blackboard]

Practise spirit-recalling
S. Ch. T.

Let there ring out from the heights
What in the depths is echoed.

Practise spirit-awareness

K. D. Ex.

Let there be fired from the East
What through the West is formed.

Practise spirit-beholding

A. AA. Ang.

Let there be prayed from the depths
What in the heights will be granted.

Here we have the opposite of the first hierarchy in whose case the voices resound downwards while their echo comes up from below. And we have here the voices heard coming from beings who pray for something from below and whose prayer is answered from the heights downwards into the depths. From above downwards: from the heights towards the depths; from the encircling round: East and West; from below upwards: from the depths into the heights.

My dear friends! Something left over from earlier is a letter to the Vorstand of the Anthroposophical Society in Dornach from the Polish Anthroposophical Society which has not been represented here: 'The working groups in Poland — Cracow, Lemberg,

Warsaw — have resolved to found the Polish Anthroposophical Society. The Society shall serve the ideas of Anthroposophy by revealing the treasures of its spiritual teachings to the widest circles and by working among the Polish people in a time of destiny, helping them to recognize their mission. For the celebration of the laying of the Foundation Stone, the newly-founded Anthroposophical Society in Poland sends to the leader and founder of the international Anthroposophical Movement, Dr Steiner, this expression of their highest respect. The Polish Anthroposophical Society urgently requests that he may concern himself with it and not deny it his protection and guidance. For its part, it commits itself . . . (the final words were obscured by noise).

For the Warsaw circle:
For the Lemberg circle:
For the remaining circles:
Luna Drechsler as their representative.'

Furthermore from Cologne on the Rhine: 'For the celebration of the laying of the Foundation Stone in 1923 I wish you and . . . (unclear) that the significance of this laying of the Foundation Stone may be revealed to all the world. With cordial greetings, Gottfried Husemann.'

My dear friends, I now consider that for the moment the Vorstand has put before you the main concerns that had to be brought to you. In the next few days there will still be the matter of a draft of some By-Laws or rules of practice to be attached to the Statutes. But now our main concern, before any other discussions, is that our dear friends should have a chance to express what they wanted to say. Here is a list of those who wish to speak or report, and I think it would be best, in order to save time, not to proceed along given lines — for if you do this you waste time — but to bring to completion what our respected, dear friends have to say. So I would like to ask whether you agree that those friends who have already asked to speak should now have their say.

They are Herr Leinhas, Dr Kolisko, Dr Stein, Dr Palmer, Herr Werbeck, Dr Lehrs, Miss Cross, Mademoiselle Rihouët, Mr Collison, Frau Hart-Nibbrig, Herr de Haan, Herr Stibbe, Herr Zagzwijn, Frau Ljungquist.

Dr Wachsmuth points out that these requests to speak were made at the beginning and referred to general matters, not specific themes.

DR STEINER: Then let me ask for the names of those friends who now wish to say something. It is naturally necessary, for the further progress of the meeting, that those friends or delegates who are concerned about something should express this. So now in a comprehensive, general discussion let me ask all those who wish to do so to speak about what concerns them with regard to the Anthroposophical Society which has been founded here.

MR COLLISON: Later on could we please speak about education.

DR STEINER: Would anyone like to speak about something entirely general? If this is not the case, dear friends, then let us proceed to the discussion of more specific aspects. According to the programme we have a discussion on the affairs of the Society and on educational questions. Perhaps someone first has something to say with reference to Herr Werbeck's lecture and so on?

Herr Hohlenberg wishes to speak.

DR STEINER: Herr Hohlenberg will speak on the subject of the antagonism we face.

Herr Hohlenberg does this.

DR STEINER: The best thing will be if I leave what I have to say on this subject till the conclusion of the discussion. A good deal will still be brought forward over the next few days.

The next person who wishes to speak about the affairs of the

Society, and also the Youth Movement, is Dr Lehrs. May I invite Dr Lehrs to speak.

Dr Lehrs speaks about the Free Anthroposophical Society.

DR STEINER: My dear friends! I do not want a misunderstanding to arise in respect of what I said here a few days ago. Dr Lehrs has understood me entirely correctly, and any other interpretation would not be correct. I did not mean that what was suggested then no longer applies today. I said that I had naturally felt it to be tragic that I had to make the suggestion of creating a division between the Anthroposophical Society in Germany and the Free Anthroposophical Society. But this suggestion was necessary; it was the consequence of the situation as it was then. And now it is equally necessary that this Free Anthroposophical Society should continue to exist and work in the manner described by our young friend from various angles. So please consider Dr Lehrs' interpretation of what I said a few days ago to be entirely correct.

I assume that Herr Hans Ludwig Pusch wishes to speak to what Dr Lehrs has said, so may I ask Herr Hans Ludwig Pusch to speak now.

Herr Hans Ludwig Pusch speaks about the aims and endeavours of German young people in Hamburg.

DR STEINER: Could I ask you to continue with your report at this point tomorrow. We have to keep to the times on the programme.

We shall continue this meeting tomorrow after Dr Schubert's lecture on 'Anthroposophy, a Leader towards Christ'. May I now ask those friends who wish to speak, or who feel they must speak for definite reasons, to let me know this evening after the lecture so that I can gain an impression of the number of speakers and make room in the agenda. Please bear in mind that we must make the most fruitful use of the days at our disposal. Apart from what has already been announced in connection with my three last lectures, it will also be necessary to have some smaller, specialist meetings with the doctors present here. Other smaller meetings will also have to be planned.

Now let me announce the next part of the agenda: This afternoon at 4.30 the Nativity Play; in the evening at 8.30 my lecture. Tomorrow morning at 10 o'clock the lecture by Dr Schubert on 'Anthroposophy, a Leader to Christ'. This will be followed by the continuation of today's meeting which we have had to interrupt in the middle of a speech. Unfortunately we shall probably have to do this again to enable us to carry out the proceedings in a rational manner. The meeting is now adjourned till tomorrow.

I still have a few announcements to make and would ask you to remain in your seats. First of all, please do all you can to avoid crowding at the entrance. I have been told that older people who are more frail than the young have been put in danger, so please avoid this and give consideration to others.

Secondly, Dr Im Obersteg, Centralbahn Platz 9, Basel, who has frequently arranged rail and sea travel for us, has offered to make the necessary arrangements for those who need them for their return journey. In our experience Dr Im Obersteg's service is exceptionally reliable. Chiefly it will be a matter of taking over ship and rail tickets for the western countries such as Norway, Sweden, England, Holland, France, Spain, Italy and so on. You can either go direct or arrange it through us. Will those who have wishes in this respect please approach Dr Wachsmuth.

Continuation of the Foundation Meeting

30 DECEMBER, 10 O'CLOCK IN THE MORNING

DR STEINER:

My dear friends!

The first point on the agenda today is the pleasure of a lecture by Dr Schubert on Christ and the spiritual world: 'Anthroposophy, a Leader to Christ.'

Dr Schubert gives his lecture. After an interval of fifteen minutes, Dr Steiner speaks:

My dear friends! Let us begin again today with the words of the self-knowledge of man coming from the spirit of our time:

Soul of Man!
Thou livest in the limbs
Which bear thee through the world of space
In the spirit's ocean-being.
Practise spirit-recalling
In depths of soul,
Where in the wielding will
Of world-creating
Thine own I
Comes to being

Within God's I.
And thou wilt truly live
In the World-Being of Man.

Soul of Man!
Thou livest in the beat of heart and lung
Which leads thee through the rhythm of time
Into the realm of thine own soul's feeling.
Practise spirit-awareness
In balance of the soul,
Where the surging deeds
Of the world's becoming
Thine own I
Unite
With the World-I.
And thou wilt truly feel
In the Soul-Weaving of Man.

Soul of Man!
Thou livest in the resting head
Which from the grounds of eternity
Opens to thee the world-thoughts.
Practise spirit-beholding
In stillness of thought,
Where the eternal aims of Gods
World-Being's Light
On thine own I
Bestow
For thy free willing.
And thou wilt truly think
In the Spirit-Foundations of Man.

Today, my dear friends, let us bring together what can speak in man in three ways:

[Rudolf Steiner writes on the blackboard as he speaks. See Facsimile 4, Page XVII top.]

[Practise]	*Practise*	*Practise*
spirit-recalling	*spirit-awareness*	*spirit-beholding*

This will properly be brought together in the heart of man only by that which actually made its appearance at the turning of the time and in whose spirit we now work here and intend to work on in the future.

At the turning of the time
The Spirit-Light of the world
Entered the stream of earthly being.
Darkness of night
Had held its sway,
Day-radiant light
Streamed into souls of men.
Light that gives warmth
To simple shepherds' hearts,
Light that enlightens
The wise heads of kings.

Light Divine
Christ-Sun
Warm thou our hearts,
Enlighten thou our heads,
That good may become
What we from our hearts would found
What we from our heads would direct
In conscious
Willing.

[Rudolf Steiner writes on the blackboard as he speaks]

That good may become
What we from our hearts would found,
What we from our heads would direct
In conscious
Willing.

[As shown on the blackboard]

[Practise]	*Practise*	*Practise*
spirit-recalling	*spirit-awareness*	*spirit-beholding*

That good may become
What we from our hearts would
found,
What we from our heads would
direct
In conscious
Willing.

DR STEINER: My dear friends! Yesterday's speaker, Herr Hans Ludwig Pusch, does not wish to continue. Instead, Dr Lehrs will say a few words on the theme. Please may I now ask him to speak.

Dr Lehrs completes what Herr Pusch had wanted to say the day before on the question of the Youth Movement.

DR STEINER: May I now ask Mrs Merry to speak.

Mrs Merry speaks about the work in England and brings the apologies of Mr Dunlop who has been unable to attend.

DR STEINER: My dear friends! I have spoken often and in different places about the extraordinarily satisfactory summer school in Penmaenmawr.[63] Perhaps I may be permitted to add to what I have said so often. I truly believe that an exceedingly significant step forward will have come about for the Anthroposophical Movement if everything Mrs Merry has just sketched can come into being over the next few years as fruits of the seeds of Penmaenmawr. We may believe that the very best forces are at work promoting the endeavours of the Anthroposophical Movement in this direction, for Mr Dunlop took this summer school at Penmaenmawr in hand in an extremely active manner, an inward, sensitive and indeed esoteric manner. In Penmaenmawr conditions were fulfilled from the start which we have never found to be fulfilled anywhere else, conditions that were necessary for the success of Penmaenmawr.

You see, my dear friends, we expected Mr Dunlop in Stratford, in Oxford, and even once in London, and now here in Dornach. So my picture of Mr Dunlop is that of the man about whom it is always said that he is coming and then he doesn't come. But he did come to Penmaenmawr! And it went so exceptionally well, so well that I only wish he were here today so that we might once more thank him most heartily. I really did believe that Mr Dunlop would be here. In London he said to me that he would do it differently next time; he would not say he was coming but instead he would simply come. So in London he did not say he was coming. And yet he still has not come! So after all I shall have to ask Mrs Merry most warmly to take our thanks back to him, the cordial thanks of this whole gathering for that extremely significant inauguration of a movement within the Anthroposophical Movement which has such good prospects because of the summer school at Penmaenmawr. Out of the spirit of the descriptions I have given of Penmaenmawr I am sure that you will agree to my asking Mrs Merry in your name to take to Mr Dunlop out hearty thanks for the inauguration of the summer school at Penmaenmawr, and also to my requesting him to continue to take such work firmly in hand, for in his hands it will succeed well.

May I now ask Herr van Bemmelen, the representative of the Dutch school, to speak.

Herr van Bemmelen reports on the work of the school in The Hague.

DR STEINER: Now may I ask Dr Unger to speak. He wishes to refer to the problems of the Society.

Dr Unger gives his lecture about the problems of the Society and concludes with the following:

Dear friends. The way in which responsibility devolves for instance on the individual Societies and the larger groups, as a result of the new Statutes, means that it will be necessary to pass this trust and this responsibility on further. Ways and means will have to come about which must not be allowed to remain fixed in the old structure that has come to be adopted. Instead situations must be livingly transformed so that people can be found who are capable through their very nature of carrying the central impulses further. Thus a matter that appears to be merely organizational immediately leads to a further question: How shall we be able to bring this impulse into the public eye? Once again we shall have to let experience play its part. The other day I ventured to make some suggestions about working in public. What Herr van Bemmelen has just said shows us that Holland is no exception to the way in which everywhere people are waiting to hear about Anthroposophy in a suitable form and in the right way. People are asking about the soul of man and about cultivating the soul in its true nature. Beyond this it will fall to us to find people among the general public who want to work further in this realm. Everywhere it must be made possible to open our doors and welcome people to the Society. Necessary for this above all is an understanding of the human being which can arise out of the warmth of love for our fellows combined with serious work in the anthroposophical sense. So the question of the next generation coming to the Society will be a far-reaching one. It has always been difficult to find people who want to continue with the work because for this it is necessary to create a situation within the Society which enables younger people to make a connection in the first place.

Today, especially, if I may say so, in Germany, many of the supports and conditions of the past, and of life as it has been for so long, are in general breaking down. In this situation younger people in particular — perhaps students who are finishing their university courses or maybe people who would like to work out of the artistic impulses of Anthroposophy — are forced instead to creep into some corner of ordinary economic life, collapsing as it is, in order merely to make a living. It ought to be a task of the Society, and especially the individual groups, to find ways of creating a foundation within Anthroposophy on which young people can live out what they have learnt in their studies. And out of this arises the most important question of all: How can that which is coming towards us by way of young, striving, life-filled strength be taken up into the School of Spiritual

Science? What form will make it possible, whether here in Dornach or elsewhere, to make studies possible that can lead to the future collaboration of these people? It is a problem which is already coming to the fore here and there but especially in Germany where there is a strong need for new colleagues but where those who ought to be working in the Society are often in such dire straits. We must find these people amongst the general public through our public work.

So the establishment of the School on the generous scale described to us so far can give us the hope that we need so badly. In the School as well as in the Society and in the groups there is a platform for tackling the problems which are arising.

The same applies to the scientific work in the institutions. Herr van Bemmelen has touched on the field of education, but similar questions could be asked with regard to scientific work. The influence of this Conference will lead to a flaring up of the will to work and to find ways. Other friends are sure to have questions about this too. Let us hope, when we return home and are asked about everything, that out of the experience of these discussions we shall be capable of giving genuinely concrete answers. So that we can come to this, problems that have arisen really must be brought forward, just as I have presumed to suggest certain things now. If other friends from the various countries bring forward these problems from different angles, let us hope that the new impulse in the General Society will be able to penetrate to every furthest corner, to all the groups and to all the individuals who are and who want to be members of this Society.

DR STEINER: May I now ask Herr van Leer to speak.

Herr van Leer speaks about the intention of sending in reports to Herr Steffen. He makes suggestions about how to divide up what is sent into different categories.

DR STEINER: I rather think that the purpose of this correspondence will best be served by taking the following into account. Without having discussed this with Herr Steffen I believe I can say more or less what he thinks, though perhaps he will have to correct me afterwards. The best reports will be those that come out of the individuality of the different correspondents. I think that all those friends I mentioned the other day, and also a number of others, are interested in what I meant by the life of the Society and cultural life in general. And I believe that most of these friends think about what comes to their attention with regard to either one or the other at least once a week, or even every day. Things go through one's mind; so one day they sit down and simply write down what has gone through their mind. As a result fifteen, or perhaps twenty, four-page letters will arrive here. It will be quite a task to read them all. Well, if twenty letters arrive, Herr Steffen will be kind enough to keep ten of them and give me the other ten. We shall manage. But we shall manage best of all if you spare us any categories. We need to hear how each individual feels in his heart of hearts, for we want to deal with human beings and not with schedules. Let everything remain a motley mixture; this will bring us the individuality of the writer in question and that is what interests us. We hope in this way to obtain the material we need, human material with which to fill our Supplements so that they in turn give a human impression with their all too human weaknesses.

Just write down on four pages, or sometimes even eight pages, what is in your heart of hearts. For us here the most interesting thing will always be the people themselves. We want to cultivate a human relationship with human beings and out of these human relationships we want to create something that will shine out even after it has gone through the process of being dipped in dreadful printer's ink. This is what I am talking about. It will be best of all if everyone can present himself in a human way to other human beings. Now, Herr Steffen, please correct me.

HERR STEFFEN: Certainly not. You have expressed exactly what is in my soul too. I only want to say that there is no question of this becoming too much work for me; it is part and parcel of my gifts as a writer that I enjoy reading reports of this kind. I always have to strive to see what is going on inside people's souls, so truly no letter can be too long. I don't believe it will be too much for me. I anyway enjoy reading several newspapers every day, but if interesting things come from our friends, then I greatly prefer to read them. As regards categories, an editor or a writer has only one, or rather two: the first is what he can use and the second is what he cannot use. That is all I wanted to say.

DR STEINER: Just imagine, after these discussions, what it would mean if these reports were to inspire Herr Steffen to write a novel or even a play! That would be the most wonderful thing I could think of.

MR COLLISON: I would like to know whether we might 'sometimes' receive a reply.

DR STEINER: I hope that the reply will be there every week in the Supplement. But if a special reply were to be necessary, then I would hope that one would be sent.

Now may I ask Herr Stibbe to speak.

Herr Stibbe reports on the opposition experienced in Holland,[64] referring particularly to Professor de Jong.

DR STEINER (referring to Herr Stibbe's report with regard to Professor de Jong): Yes indeed. He has tried to form a methodical concept of mystery wisdom by bringing it down to all kinds of spiritualist phenomena, as he describes in his book.

Now, dear friends. It will still be possible in the next day or two to speak further on the questions that have arisen out of this discussion. So far as I can see, the questions that have arisen are: reporting, and then the opposition. These are the tangible questions that have arisen so far. I cannot see any others taking shape yet.

Tomorrow we shall start our meeting at 10 o'clock and I shall begin by asking those friends to speak who have reports to give about the results of their research. Frau Dr Kolisko and Dr Maier, Stuttgart. Now may I ask Dr Schwebsch to speak. When he has finished I shall ask for a report on eurythmy in America to be read out.

30 DECEMBER, 10 O'CLOCK IN THE MORNING

Dr Schwebsch expresses the gratitude of the Waldorf School for the manifold assistance it has received.

DR STEINER: Following on from this, please allow me to touch on a few things. The first is that once the grave financial position of the Waldorf School had become known, interest in it was awakened really everywhere. We have seen particularly in Switzerland how the efforts of the members of the school associations led to the creation of numerous sponsorships. Mrs Mackenzie has endeavoured to form a committee in England to carry out collections in aid of the Waldorf School. The first donation has already been sent to me and I shall ask the leaders of the Waldorf School to accept this small beginning.

Now I have something else to say: So many thanks are owed to the world on behalf of the Waldorf School — Dr Schwebsch has already mentioned a number of things — that it is impossible to encompass everything in a moment. We ought to make a long list of all those to whom we owe thanks in one way or another on behalf of the Waldorf School. The interest in it is indeed great. Yet we shall ever and again have to continue to ask for an even greater interest. The support given so far has in the main been for the school itself. Less thought has hitherto been given to the pupils or those who might become pupils of the Waldorf School. There is one case, or rather two, which really touch us deeply. At a time when those living in Switzerland were in a position to purchase a great deal in Germany with very few Swiss Francs, two workers here at the Goetheanum felt they could put into practice a very praiseworthy idea, namely to send their sons to the Waldorf School. Considerable sacrifices were made by our friend, Pastor Geyer, when he undertook to care for these two schoolboys. We at the Goetheanum take the view that we should finance the actual school fees and whatever is needed for the school in the same way as other firms such as *Der Kommende Tag* and *Waldorf Astoria* pay for the children of their workers. But now that life for the children has suddenly become so expensive in Germany, more expensive than it would be here in Switzerland, it is no longer possible for the families of the boys to pay for their keep. Now both families and boys are faced with the sad prospect of their being unable to return to the Waldorf School after the Christmas holidays. So I should like to ask whether it would be possible to make a collection here in order, at least for the near future, to pay for the keep of the two boys in Stuttgart so that they can continue to go to the Waldorf School. What we need is 140 Francs a month for both boys together. We shall try to set up a money box for this. Perhaps Mr Pyle will be prepared to lend us one for donations specifically for this purpose. Maybe this is how we can do it.

Now would Dr Wachsmuth please read the resumé of the report on eurythmy in America.

Dr Wachsmuth reads a report from Frau Neuscheller on the progress made by eurythmy in North America.

DR STEINER: Dear friends, first I would like to ask those from further afield who wish to attend tomorrow's performance of the Three Kings Play to get their tickets today so that what remains can be available for Dornach friends tomorrow.

Secondly would you please note that my three last evening lectures will lead in various ways to a discussion of medical matters for the general audience. Then after the lectures there will be discussions about medical matters with the doctors who are here. Would therefore any practising doctors please come to the Glass House tomorrow morning at 8.30 for an initial meeting.[65] I am referring only to practising doctors. After 1 January there will be opportunity for others interested in medical questions to participate in other sessions.

Tomorrow morning at 10 o'clock we shall start with the continuation of today's meeting. I would ask you to let us begin with the two reports already mentioned. Then, both tomorrow and the next day, I shall take the liberty of speaking briefly on the idea of the future building in Dornach and I shall ask you to let me bring up for discussion some points on how this idea of the building in Dornach might be carried into reality. It would not be right to recommend that this meeting should be allowed to pass without any reference at all to the financial side of the idea of the building in Dornach. I shall leave it to you to say something after what I shall be obliged to bring forward very briefly tomorrow and the next day about the artistic aspect of the idea of the building in Dornach.

Then I would ask for time to be set aside in the afternoon at 2.30 for a meeting of Swiss members or their delegates. Herr Aeppli has asked for this meeting and has requested that I attend, or indeed take the chair. So I would ask the Swiss members to hold this meeting tomorrow afternoon at 2.30. This refers only to Swiss members since the matters to be discussed apply solely to the Swiss Anthroposophical Society.

This afternoon at 4.30 we shall see a performance of eurythmy, and my lecture will take place this evening at 8.30.

Meeting of practising doctors
31 December 1923 at 8.30 in the morning
in the Glass House

Continuation of the Foundation Meeting

31 DECEMBER, 10 O'CLOCK IN THE MORNING

DR STEINER:

My dear friends!

Once again as before we begin with the verses we have taken into ourselves:

Soul of Man!
Thou livest in the limbs
Which bear thee through the world of space
In the spirit's ocean-being.
Practise spirit-recalling
In depths of soul,
Where in the wielding will
Of world-creating
Thine own I
Comes to being
Within God's I.
And thou wilt truly live
In the World-Being of Man.

Soul of Man!
Thou livest in the beat of heart and lung
Which leads thee through the rhythm of time
Into the realm of thine own soul's feeling.

Practise spirit-awareness
In balance of the soul,
Where the surging deeds
Of the world's becoming
Thine own I
Unite
With the World-I,
And thou wilt truly feel
In the Soul-Weaving of Man.

Soul of Man!
Thou livest in the resting head
Which from the grounds of eternity
Opens to thee the world-thoughts.
Practise spirit-beholding
In stillness of thought,
Where the eternal aims of Gods
World-Being's Light
On thine own I
Bestow
For thy free willing.
And thou wilt truly think
In the Spirit-Foundations of Man.

And drawing all this together in the remembrance of the Event of Golgotha which gives meaning to the whole of earthly evolution:

At the turning of the time
The Spirit-Light of the world
Entered the stream of earthly being.
Darkness of night
Had held its sway,
Day-radiant light
Streamed into souls of men.
Light that gives warmth
To simple shepherds' hearts,
Light that enlightens
The wise heads of kings.

Light Divine
Christ-Sun
Warm thou our hearts,
Enlighten thou our heads,
That good may become
What we from our hearts would found
What we from our heads would direct
In light-filled
Willing.

And we imprint this into ourselves:
[Rudolf Steiner writes on the blackboard as he speaks. See Facsimile 4, Page XVII bottom.]

Light Divine,
Christ-Sun,

We imprint it in such a way that we especially relate to it the closing words, which will be spoken in their threefoldness once more tomorrow: how this Light Divine, this Sun of Christ shine forth so that like shining suns they can be heard from East, West, North, South. To this Light Divine and this Sun of Christ we relate especially the closing words which were spoken on the first day:

The spirits of the elements hear it
from
East, West, North, South:
May human beings hear it!

[As shown on the blackboard]

Light Divine
Chr.-Sun
The spirits of the elements hear it
from
E. W. N. S.
May human beings hear it!

31 DECEMBER, 10 O'CLOCK IN THE MORNING

DR STEINER: We come now, my dear friends, to the reports announced yesterday. Would Herr Maier please give his report first.

Dr Rudolf Maier, Stuttgart, speaks about 'The Connection of Magnetism with Light'.[66]

DR STEINER: It will be of the greatest importance that a truly anthroposophical method should be made customary in the different branches of scientific life by those individuals who are called to these branches within our anthroposophical circles. Indeed, seen from a certain point of view, this is of the utmost importance. If you seek the source of the great resistance of our time that has been appearing for decades against any kind of spiritual-scientific view, you will find that this resistance comes from the different branches of natural science. These different branches of natural science have developed in isolation, without any view of the world in general.

Round about the middle of the nineteenth century a general despair began to gain ground in connection with an overall view of the world. People said: All earlier overall views of the world contradict one another, and none of them has led anywhere; now it is time to develop the sciences purely on an exact foundation, without reference to any view of the world.

Half a century and more has passed since then, and now any inclination to unite a view of the world with science has disappeared from human minds. Even when scientific research itself urges an attempt to be made, it turns out to be quite impossible because there is insufficient depth in the spiritual-scientific realm.

If it should become possible for Anthroposophy to give to the different branches of science impulses of method which lead to certain research results, then one of the main obstacles to spiritual research existing in the world will have been removed. That is why it is so important for work of the right kind to be undertaken in the proper anthroposophical sense.

Today there is an abyss between art and science; but within science, too, there is an abyss between, for instance, physiology and physics. All these abysses will be bridged if scientific work is done in the right way in our circles. Therefore from a general anthroposophical point of view we must interest ourselves in these different things as much as our knowledge and capacities will allow. A scientific impulse will have to emanate from the Anthroposophical Society. This must be made evident at the moment when we want to take the Anthroposophical Society into entirely new channels.

Now, dear friends, since our stomach needs a very tiny interval between the courses of this feast of spirit and soul, we shall ask Frau Dr Kolisko to give her report in two or three minutes' time.

DR STEINER: May I now ask Frau Dr Kolisko to give her report on her special field.

Frau Dr Kolisko speaks about the biological work of the research institute in Stuttgart, 'The Effects of Microorganisms'.[67]

DR STEINER: Now, my dear friends, you have seen that quiet work is going on amongst us on scientific questions and that it is indeed possible to provide out of Anthroposophy a stimulus for science in a way that is truly needed today. But in the present situation of the Anthroposophical Movement such things are really only possible because there are people like Frau Dr Kolisko who take on the work in such a devoted and selfless way. If you think about it, you will come to realize what a tremendous amount of work is involved in ascertaining all these sequences of data which can then be amalgamated to form the curve in the graph which is the needed result.

These experiments are, from an anthroposophical point of view, details leading to a totality which is needed by science today more urgently than can be said. Yet if we continue to work as we have been doing at present in our research institute, then perhaps in fifty, or maybe seventy-five, years we shall come to the result that we need, which is that innumerable details go to make up a whole. This whole will then have a bearing not only on the life of knowledge but also on the whole of practical life as well.

People have no idea today how deeply all these things can affect practical daily life in such realms as the production of what human beings need in order to live or the development of methods of healing and so on.

Now you might say that the progress of mankind has always gone forward at a slow pace and that there is not likely to be any difference in this field. However, with civilization in its present brittle and easily destructible state, it could very well happen that in fifty or seventy-five years' time the chance will have been missed for achieving what so urgently needs to be achieved. In the face of the speed at which we are working and having to work, because we can only work if there are such devoted colleagues as Frau Dr Kolisko — a speed which might lead to results in fifty, or perhaps seventy-five years — in the face of this speed, let me therefore express not a wish, not even a possibility, but merely, perhaps, an illusion, which is that it would be possible to achieve the necessary results in five or ten years. And I am convinced that if it were possible for us to create the necessary equipment and the necessary institutes and to have the necessary colleagues, as many as possible to work out of this spirit, then we could succeed in achieving in five or ten years what will now take us fifty or seventy-five years. The only thing we would need for this work would be 50 to 75 million Francs. Then we would probably be able to do the work in a tenth of the time. As I said, I am not expressing this as a wish nor even as a possibility, but merely as an illusion, though a very realistic illusion. If we had 75 million Francs we could achieve what has to be achieved. This is something that we should at least think about.

In a few minutes I shall continue by starting to give a few indications about the idea of the future building in Dornach, indications which I shall continue tomorrow.

(A short interval follows, before Dr Steiner's lecture.)

The Idea of the Future Building in Dornach

Lecture by Rudolf Steiner

31 DECEMBER, IN THE MORNING

My dear friends!

As you may imagine, I have recently given much thought to the idea of the building in Dornach, and the situation will most certainly necessitate the earliest possible execution of this idea of this building in Dornach.

A great many of you were present in the summer when the financing of the future Goetheanum was discussed.[68] Everything that came to light then, when our friends revealed their willingness to make infinite sacrifices, and all the observations of the situation I have made since then, force me to the opinion that there is no other way but to proceed as rapidly as possible to the construction of a Goetheanum here, even if externally this Goetheanum cannot present the image we would dearly have liked to promise ourselves.

It seems to me that this Goetheanum must be erected in such a way as to make it usable as expediently as possible.

But if the idea about the building expressed at the meeting in the summer were to be realized, it would definitely not be possible to use it in a suitable way once it was finished. For is it not so that, in considering all the possibilities, we must look, might I say, through the walls, that is through the walls of the wallets of our dear friends. I know very well that what I am about to put to you will be met, out of the utmost good will, by many objections. And yet I still believe that the situation will prove me right when I say that the best way to proceed will be to plan for a Goetheanum of which the actual building costs do not exceed 3 to 3½ million Francs. Only then, even with the utmost willingness for sacrifice, shall we be in a position truly fruitfully to serve the intentions inaugurated in our new Statutes.

It would not be at all sensible if, as the Anthroposophical Society, we were to spend every last penny simply on the building itself. This would not be a good thing to do. So I do believe that the right idea would be to spend about 3 to 3½ million on the building to start with. If it is to be built in accordance with the situation as it actually is, then it must be as resistant as possible to damage such as that which unfortunately destroyed the old Goetheanum. And, as I have already pointed out in my articles in *Das Goetheanum*,[69] it must make available as much space as possible for anthroposophical activities. So we shall have to restrict ourselves somewhat. But I believe that just because of this we can be all the more certain of achieving what was pointed out yesterday, especially on the part of the young people: that above all a spiritual Goetheanum must exist here as soon as is in any way possible.

Today I want to start by explaining the ground-plan of the Goetheanum to you and then tomorrow I shall speak more about the elevation, the facade. I want to shape the ground-plan and the whole distribution of the space to be taken up by the Goetheanum in the following way.

The Goetheanum will not be as round a building as the old Goetheanum was. It is all very well to ask why I have not brought the model to show you, my dear friends. But you must not forget that this new Goetheanum is to be built in a relatively new material, concrete. And to give a concrete building a truly artistic character in keeping with the material is exceedingly difficult; the solution to this problem is very demanding.

You know Dr Grosheintz has had a house built near here which I have attempted to design in a style appropriate to concrete.[70]

But though I still believe that this style might be considered satisfactory for a dwelling to a certain degree — but only to a certain degree — it would nevertheless be impossible to build a second house to exactly the same plan. In any case it certainly did not yield an architectural style for a Goetheanum built of concrete. For the new Goetheanum it will be necessary to depart — essentially — from the idea of a circular building; we shall come back not to a circular building but to one that is more rectangular, a building with angles.

You can see the intention in the small building lower down the hill that was built to provide a hall for eurythmy practice.[71] It is built in a different material, but it shows that an angular building has considerable potential.

Now since there is the need to provide stages for eurythmy and the Mystery Dramas, it will be necessary to combine an angular building with a circular one. In addition, the new Goetheanum will have to provide space for the various activities. We shall need studios and we shall need lecture rooms. The single small white hall in which the fire first broke out a year ago had turned out to be quite inadequate for our purposes. So the next Goetheanum would have to be built in such a way that it would have a lower level — a ground floor — and an upper level. The upper level would, essentially, be the large auditorium for lectures and for those who come to hear and see the performances of eurythmy, the Mystery Dramas and other things. And on the lower level, beneath this auditorium, would be smaller rooms, divided off by walls, which would provide space for artistic and scientific purposes.

I also intend to create a space for the administration of the General Anthroposophical Society, so that this can be carried out direct from the Goetheanum.

In the idea of this building I also want to solve a certain problem in what seems to me a practical way. The plan will be such that there will be a stage at the rear with a rounded form. (Please don't take any notice of the proportions in this drawing.) The stage will essentially form a semi-circle. It will be enclosed by store-rooms. And then extending forwards there will be at the upper level the auditorium and at the lower level the various rooms, with a passage-way in between so that in future there will be more freedom of movement in this new Goetheanum than there was in the old. In the old Goetheanum you stepped straight inside from a vestibule at the entrance. Here, so that there can be freedom of movement, there will be a heated area in which it will be possible to meet and converse in all kinds of ways. And this passage-way will give access to the various rooms on the lower level. [See Facsimile 5, Page XIX bottom.]

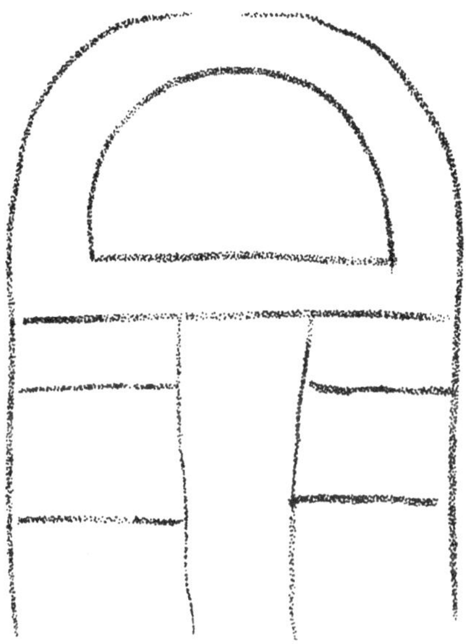

Then, going up a staircase, you will come to the large auditorium from which you look on to the stage or the space where lectures and other things will take place.

The practical problem I just mentioned is the following: In the old Goetheanum great inconvenience was caused by the fact that eurythmy rehearsals had to take place on the stage itself. When visitors came from elsewhere, and I hope they will continue to come in the future, they wanted to see everything; but the auditorium was needed for the work, so it was never possible to allocate time properly in a way that was needed for rehearsals and preparations for performances.

I now want to solve this problem by having on the ground floor, that is the lower level, a stage of exactly the same size as that on the upper level. The one on the upper level will serve for the actual performances while the one down below, having identical measurements, will be for rehearsals only. So there will be a room down below which can serve for all rehearsals up to the dress rehearsal, thus leaving the upper auditorium free at all times. The lower hall will have an ante-room just for those taking part in the rehearsals, where they may wait and sit down. On the upper level the stage will give straight on to the auditorium. The auditorium will be the same size as the plan of the rectangular part of the building.

In this way it will be possible to work in a practical manner in all the available space. It will not be necessary to make the new Goetheanum very much taller than the old Goetheanum, since I am not considering a new cupola. I am endeavouring to create a design for the roof which will consist of a series of planes arranged in relation to one another in a way which will, I believe, be no less aesthetically attractive than a cupola.

So we shall enter into the Goetheanum through a facade on the main front which I shall describe tomorrow. There we shall find the staircase leading to the main upper space; and we shall have a passage-way from which the different rooms are reached, and so on. There will also be entrances at the sides. By making the stage space smaller on plan than the store area, and by extending the walls forwards, we will gain space for the different rooms. At the top it will be possible to light the whole space with daylight, so that we can alternate between daylight, when it is there, and artificial light when we need it.

In this way it will be possible to have a really practical building in which every cubic foot of space can be used to the full. A great deal will be able to go on in this building all at once, whereas in the old building only one thing at a time could take place.

You must consider, my dear friends, that this is not simply intended to be an improvement — which perhaps some might consider a dis-improvement — but it is designed to take account of all the developments that have come about. I have often stressed amongst ourselves that if you want to live in reality and not in ideas, then the realities of the time must be given particular recognition. The time in which one lives is a reality. But it is difficult to generate an understanding for this time as being something real. There are still people today who represent the threefolding of the social organism with the very sentences I used to use with regard to the conditions prevailing at the time, in 1919. History is indeed advancing so rapidly just now that if someone describes things in the way they were described in 1919 this seems to be hundreds of years out of date. Thus, since things have after all been happening in the Anthroposophical Movement, you cannot build in 1924 as you did in 1913 and 1914. In 1913 and 1914 the idea of the Goetheanum arose simply out of the realization that an artistic space would have to be created for the Mystery Dramas. At that time we really only thought of the Mystery Dramas and the lectures. But much has happened since those days and I only wish that even more had happened, but I hope that quite soon a good deal more will happen even without the 75 million Francs I spoke about earlier. This must certainly be taken into consideration.

The thing that has happened since 1919 is that eurythmy has been developed.[72] In 1913 it did not yet exist, it has only developed since. Therefore it cannot be maintained that what was good enough then can be good enough now. Furthermore, although I was assured at the time that the building could be executed at a cost of much less than one million German Reichsmarks, nevertheless, as you know, the cost in the end was at least seven or eight times as much. So we do not want to do our sums in the abstract this time. We want to reckon with certain quite definite figures. The building must now be executed in such a way that we can start to carry out what is contained in our Statutes as soon as possible. This can only happen if we erect it in the manner described.

Even so, it will be possible to win, from the intractable material of concrete, forms that offer something new to the artistic eye. The old forms of the Goetheanum — I shall have more to say to you about these things this evening — will have to belong to history, which means your hearts, my dear friends. Forms moulded in concrete will have to be something entirely different.

Much will have to be done on the one hand to force the intractable material of concrete into forms which the eye of the human soul can follow artistically and on the other hand to mould seemingly decorative features, which are actually a consequence of the concrete itself, in an artistic and sculptural way, so that the material of concrete can for once be revealed in an artistic manner.

I ask you now to regard this idea as the seed out of which the Goetheanum shall actually emerge. I have stated that I alone am allowed to work on the artistic creation of the Goetheanum and it will not be possible to take on board to any great extent any of those offers or suggestions which have already been made —of course with the best intentions. There is no point in telling me of buildings in concrete that have been put up here or there, or of factories here or there that are working efficiently. If the Goetheanum building is to come about in concrete, it will have to emerge from an original idea, and nothing that has so far been achieved in concrete can serve as a basis for what is to come into being here.

This, my dear friends, is what I wanted to say to you today. It was not in any way intended to put a stop to the collections already set in train by our dear friend van Leer or by others representing the different countries. The sum originally envisaged will still be needed if we are to carry out what must, of necessity, be carried out. Perhaps I can spur on your zeal in this direction even more by saying that we shall try to use the money you collect in the most economical way by putting it towards anthroposophical work in the sense that it will be used for running the Goetheanum and that the Goetheanum will be built using the smallest amount possible. We shall endeavour here to bring a Goetheanum into being in the shortest possible time.

Tomorrow I shall speak about the image the Goetheanum will present to the outside, namely its facade.

I now want to return to something that is being brought to me from many sides like a kind of derivative of fear. On all sides I am being asked how the three Classes and the Sections of the School of Spiritual Science at the Goetheanum are to be handled. My dear friends, in the first place the Sections are no one's concern. The Sections are being set up for the work here. There is no need for us to discuss the Sections. They will exist in accordance with whatever is achieved. So really we can only speak about the General Anthroposophical Society as the foundation, and about the three Classes. And I believe that everything relevant is stated with absolute clarity in our Statutes. In Paragraph 5 it says: 'Members of the Society will be admitted to the School on their own application after a period of membership to be determined by the leadership at the Goetheanum. They enter in this way the First Class of the School of Spiritual Science. Admission to the Second or Third Classes takes place when the person requesting it is deemed eligible by the leadership at the Goetheanum.'

'Paragraph 7. The organizing of the School of Spiritual Science is, to begin with, the responsibility of Rudolf Steiner, who will appoint his collaborators and his possible successor.'

These sentences express, I believe, with absolute clarity that it is necessary to apply to me personally either in writing or in person; it would be better to start by saying in writing, since there will be too many personal applications to be dealt with on the spot. The matter will be taken from there. That is what it says here. The storm of queries is perhaps not so much the result of unclarity as of the necessity, my dear friends, to become accustomed to clarity. Perhaps unclarity is what is wanted in some quarters. Pedantry must be excluded, and bureaucracy will be banished across the border, but in everything that emanates from here — at least this is what we intend — absolute clarity shall reign. From what is written here it is clear that a little note is all that is needed. The little note should be addressed to me personally. And you will see how the answer will be given. You must have confidence.

That is what I wanted to say. Herr Hahl has asked to speak about the building of the Goetheanum. Please would you now speak.

Herr Hahl speaks on this subject.

Open Discussion of Swiss Delegates under the Chairmanship of Rudolf Steiner

31 DECEMBER, 2.30 IN THE AFTERNOON

AT 2.30 in the afternoon of 31 December a meeting of the Swiss Anthroposophical Society took place in the Architects' Office. Herr Aeppli had called this meeting and had asked Dr Steiner to be present and take the chair.

Members of the Vorstand of the General Anthroposophical Society present are: Dr Steiner, Albert Steffen, Fräulein Vreede, Dr Wachsmuth. Later also Frau Dr Steiner.

Herr Aeppli greets Dr Steiner and requests him to take the chair.

Dr Steiner opens the meeting called for the purpose of a free discussion at the request of the delegates of the Anthroposophical Society in Switzerland:

I thank Herr Aeppli most warmly for his kind words. Now let us begin the meeting. Who would like to make a contribution to this open discussion? Would anyone wishing to speak please do so.

Frau Professor Bürgi, Bern, requests Dr Steiner to become the Chairman of the Swiss Anthroposophical Society.

DR STEINER: I am somewhat surprised by Frau Professor Bürgi's suggestion. For — at least in the long run — we cannot very well depart from the stipulation of the incompatibility of the offices of the central Vorstand with other offices. Thus I too would not be able to take on any other position in some part of the Anthroposophical Society in the long run. But quite apart from that, if we are to enter into a provisional arrangement for the time being, would not Herr Steffen be a better choice as General Secretary for Switzerland? It seems to me that if we are going to enter into a provisional situation, then Herr Steffen would be the right person. Of course it is entirely up to you to have a discussion about it. But it seems rather a problem, or indeed senseless, for me to assume the position of Chairman of the Swiss Society when the only reason preventing Herr Steffen is the fact that he is a member of the central Vorstand. I am in the very same position. Perhaps you would speak further on this.

HERR STEFFEN: I would want to decline. It does not seem to be fitting.

DR STEINER: But my dear Herr Steffen, why not? Since it is to be provisional, I cannot see why not! But perhaps there is another way of getting out of this fix. Perhaps we can achieve both ends, dear friends: bringing about a Swiss leadership for the Swiss Anthroposophical Society and, arising out of the local situation, creating a close link with the central Anthroposophical Society. Or ought it not to be possible for there to be a close link between the central Anthroposophical Society, which has its seat here in Switzerland, and the Swiss Anthroposophical Society? Perhaps we can get out of this fix by seeing to it that *we* in principle maintain the incompatibility while *you* express it by choosing a kind of General Secretary apart from us yet at the same time confer on both of us the chairmanship as members of the Vorstand of the central Anthroposophical Society. It would then be that the Swiss Society comes to the resolution, arising out of this meeting of its delegates, that it is an obvious thing for the central Vorstand to be regarded also as the head of the Swiss Anthroposophical Society. And the Swiss Anthroposophical Society then appoints an acting General Secretary. If we were to do it like this, it would not have to be provisional, for it would be an expression of the very best of all situations: The Swiss members have no fear for their independence in that they simply take into their bosom the whole of the Anthroposophical Society. This is how I think we could solve this problem. Herr Steffen and I together will take on the chairmanship in our capacity as Presidents of the Anthroposophical Society.

DR HUGENTOBLER: Truly we could not have come up with a better solution!

DR STEINER: Would anyone else like to speak?

Herr Keller suggests that the choice of General Secretary be left to the Vorstand.

DR STEINER: It is of course rather difficult for the Vorstand to make this choice if the matter is not discussed first. I am sure I am not giving away esoteric secrets by saying that it is extremely difficult to discover which individual is so popular all over Switzerland as to be generally accepted as the administrator. Perhaps a little discussion on the matter might contribute to achieving a result. The office will then be exercised in close contact with Herr Steffen and myself. And then what Frau Professor Bürgi said would probably no longer apply in the way it would have done had an independent General Secretary been chosen. What she said was that the Swiss Society was in an exposed position through being so close to the Goetheanum and so on, and that therefore it would be important for the office to be exercised in a suitable manner. But now, since you have been so good as to chose us to take on this office, these arguments may not apply quite so sharply any longer. I rather think that now the person's popularity will be all that matters. But would anyone else like to say something?

Dr Grosheintz believes that it is perhaps not necessary to have a General Secretary in addition to the present Vorstand.

DR STEINER: Would not people prefer that a person be nominated by the meeting so that the various administrative tasks can be better carried out? Surely people would prefer this? I would like to hear what people think.

EDGAR DÜRLER: We of the 'New Generation' branch suggest Dr Oskar Grosheintz.

DR STEINER: Dr Oskar Grosheintz has been suggested. Are there any other suggestions?

Herr Thut would like further clarification of the duties incumbent on this person.

DR STEINER: Now that we are making a new beginning, should we not start afresh with new arrangements and disregard the old ones? Could we not give up the old ways and reorganize things starting from the roots? From an objective point of view I don't think there is anything against the Swiss Anthroposophical Society being constituted in such a way that its main representation lies with the General Anthroposophical Society in the way we have just decided. However, on the level of feelings I do want to avoid a sense possibly arising later on that the Swiss Anthroposophical Society is being patronized in any way or treated as a second-rate child. In actual fact this would not be possible, for by embracing it in the first place it is shown to be a first-rate child. This would indeed have to be the case. But nevertheless, a hint of a feeling could arise somewhere that the Swiss Society is only an appendage of the General Anthroposophical Society. Tact also has a part to play in this, and in practice I don't think it would happen. But if anyone here does have a hint of any such feeling in his heart, then please do express it now, so that we can really come to a conclusion on this matter. Otherwise it would probably be best with regard to Switzerland simply to make allowances for the old ways to which people are so attached and to carry out the general administration ourselves. In this case Herr Thut's suggestion would be the right one: simply to let the Swiss Anthroposophical Society be administered along with the General Anthroposophical Society. And for any constitutional matters having a substantial inner significance for the Society we would then call a meeting of whatever representatives the different branches wished to send. By doing this from time to time we would be expressing what people have become so attached to in Switzerland, namely the democratic element. I think that would then be the best way to get on. We would always call on the individual members. This would be possible in Switzerland because it is such a small country, but it would not be possible in any other national Society. It would also not be necessary for these meetings to take place always at the Goetheanum. They could be in different places since it is so easy to get everywhere. In fact it would be quite a good thing if these meetings of members were what are usually called wandering meetings. Having meetings from time to time in Bern, Zurich, Olten and so on, always combined, presumably, with one of my lectures, would be the best way of managing our affairs in Switzerland.

HERR THUT: It was not my intention to cling to this old organization at all costs. I merely wanted clarity about which aspects would remain and which would not, so as to be as clear as possible about how the things that are still in question would work.

DR STEINER: In that case I would consider that Herr Thut, and probably most of you here, would prefer it if the representation of the Swiss Society were carried out here by the General Anthroposophical Society? Routine matters can easily be attended to by the administration and no special secretary would be needed for this. And then, in order to keep in contact with the different parts of Switzerland, it would be best if we could nominate, as an advisory group for the Vorstand here, three, four or five men and women who would be trustees, to whom we could turn when necessary and with whom we could hold the wandering meetings. These would not have to be so very frequent, but the group of trustees would give us contact with the different parts of Switzerland. Perhaps this is what people would like?

HERR STORRER: If this were to be the case, then of course the 'New Generation' group would withdraw its suggestion.

DR STEINER: Would anyone else like to speak?

Dr Usteri asks a question.

DR STEINER: Your question refers to the Programme. But this is a matter of the agenda each day. You said that you arrived this morning and found the meeting in the hall was not what you expected? Was it not? Well you see we have had to depart from the Programme because it was not possible in the plenary gathering to speak in depth about all the questions that need discussing unless we had constantly adjourned the meetings and had had a running agenda for the members' meetings. That is why I myself departed in the daily agendas from the original Programme. But the agenda for the following day has always been announced in detail the day before. Thus the meeting of doctors in question took place this morning. What a pity that you did not have a chance to ask someone who was here yesterday. Any member would have been able to tell you that there was going to be a meeting of practising doctors in the Glass House at 8.30 this morning.

For you see: We wanted to make this particular Christmas Conference as fruitful as possible and do as much as we could to prevent everything from being watered down in general discussion. That is why medical matters were to be discussed among practising doctors only; so they were removed from the general meeting and are to be dealt with in three meetings of which the first took place this morning at 8.30, the second tomorrow and the third probably also — the time is yet to be announced. Thus the things announced in the Programme are in fact being dealt with in an even better way than had originally been made known. A general discussion amongst all the members would not have led to any better outcome. I have even made sure that all the meetings which do not concern all members but only particular groups have also been announced in the general meeting, so that those not concerned with a particular meeting nevertheless know that it is taking place. That you did not find this out was probably due to the fact that you did not arrive before 8.30, when you would have had an opportunity to ask someone. I don't think a

General Secretary would have been able to inform you any better than any of the members if you had got there this morning. In House Friedwart you could have obtained exact information.

But of course there could also be very good reasons for nominating a General Secretary. This is something we could discuss further. There was no vote about it, but I should like to take a vote on this. Would those friends who are in favour of Albert Steffen and myself continuing as chairmen of the Swiss Anthroposophical Society please raise their hands. (They do.) Would those who are against also please raise their hands. (Nobody does.) So, the suggestion has been adopted. Now it is a question of whether we decide to let the administrative office of the General Anthroposophical Society take over the routine administration of the Swiss Anthroposophical Society and whether we set up a group of elders, or for that matter younger people, to whom we can turn from time to time when necessary or when something has to be decided.

Dr Usteri supports this suggestion.

Herr Geering supports Dr Usteri.

Herr Thut asks whether representation by a General Secretary would not be more advantageous than that by the representatives of the groups.

DR STEINER: I think it would be best if the individual branches were to suggest their delegates to us. The group of delegates can be as large as the number of branches that exist. The disadvantage hitherto has been that the group of representatives of the branches has at the same time been seen as the council. A council like this is no good for anything. But here — perhaps I am boasting, but this is what we intend — if the administration is firmly taken in hand by the leadership of the Anthroposophical Society, then it will be up to this leadership to take the initiative and call the delegates of the branches together for a meeting. In such a case a rather large group of delegates would probably not pose any particular difficulty. So I think it will be quite manageable for every single branch to nominate a representative for this circle. This, it seems to me, will be the best way. But if any branches wanted to join together to send a delegate, that would also be possible. But it is not necessary for this to be done today. It would perhaps be better to have a thorough discussion in the branches themselves and let us know who has been chosen sometime during the next two or three weeks. Then our administration will be entirely democratic, which is much favoured in Switzerland.

Now I would like to ask whether there is anything else you wish to bring up. I cannot imagine that you do not also have other wishes, urges, longings on your mind.

Herr Aeppli would like to know whether the question of the administration has now been settled.

DR STEINER: The meetings would take place anyway, and as for the purely administrative matters, they would be reported to this group so that the administration would be relieved of the responsibility if the council would accept the responsibility. Would anyone else like to speak?

DR USTERI: Now that there has been such applause, I presume that a formal vote on the two points is not necessary.

DR STEINER: Actually, I would ask you to vote once there is no one else who wishes to speak. Now does anyone else wish to speak on the matter of this group or on what I have said about the group relieving the administration?

HERR STORRER: I should like to suggest that the small branches send one and the larger branches two delegates. But then we should have to define what we mean by 'large' and 'small'.

Herr Trinler says that what matters is not whether there are one or two but that they are the right people!

DR STEINER: Would anyone else like to say something about this?

So are you making this proposal? The proposal is that the small groups send one and the larger groups two delegates.

Herr Trinler says something (inaudible).

DR STEINER: The two proposals are in agreement with one another, they are not contradictory; but we shall have to define 'larger' and 'smaller'. So what is a large and what is a small group?

HERR STORRER: Looking at the Swiss branches, I would say that the large ones are those at the Goetheanum, in Bern, in Basel, in Zurich and in St Gallen.

DR STEINER: But you could imagine that a branch which is small today might grow large later on. We do need a figure to tell us when a group is starting to become a large one.

HERR STORRER: A small group has not more than ten members.

DR STEINER: So ten and less is a small branch; eleven and over a large branch.

HERR TRINLER: A branch with as many as a hundred members does not necessarily achieve any more than a small one.

HERR THUT: It is not a matter of what the branch achieves. Perhaps forty or fifty could be the number determining a large group.

Herr Schweigler asks how he should understand the matter of deciding about the delegates: Would this be by a vote or simply by acclaim? Which is best?

DR STEINER: The situation varies from one country to another. You will have heard that in England I suggested that the selection of representatives be made not according to branches but according to whatever figure is arrived at by dividing the total English membership by seven. I think this would be a very good method for England, but it would not be good to apply this way of thinking to Switzerland. Here I think we should aim in this group for two delegates from branches with over fifty members and one from those with fewer than fifty members. Apart from this, the difference is not particularly important. I think that would be best in this case. A branch with ten members can perhaps work better than a branch with two hundred members, certainly. But that applies to all forms of democratic representation, and I do not believe that you can base any particular rule on this. Otherwise you would have to say: Those branches which work well send two representatives and those which work badly send one. But this would be rather difficult to determine! And a branch which does not work well will certainly not believe such a thing of itself. (Laughter)

DR HUGENTOBLER: I don't think Herr Schweigler realizes that there are things about which you cannot vote.

Herr Schweigler denies this. Dr Hugentobler answers (inaudible).

DR STEINER: So if I have understood this correctly, then the proposal regarding the groups of delegates is as follows: Firstly the group of delegates is instituted, and secondly branches of over fifty members send two representatives and branches of under fifty members send one.

A MAN ASKS: Are the branch leaders not the people best suited?

DR STEINER: But the branch leaders are not decided by the meeting of delegates but by the branches themselves! It has nothing to do with whoever might be the branch leader at the moment.

A MAN: But (inaudible).

HERR GEERING-CHRIST: That is a misunderstanding on the part of this gentleman!

DR STEINER: The initiative has to lie with somebody. And now the initiative will lie with us here in Dornach and we shall be supported by the delegates. The meeting of delegates will be a kind of control body. It does not have to work as a council. A difficulty only arises if there is a council scattered all over the place that never does anything. That is where the difficulty lies.

DR USTERI: Have we accepted Dr Hugentobler's proposal that there should be a vote?

DR STEINER: It has been proposed that there should be a vote. Very well. Dr Hugentobler's suggestion was the most far-reaching, namely that the branches choose their own delegates and let us know in due course, whereby branches of over fifty members will send two and those with fewer than fifty will send one. Does anyone want me to divide this proposal into two parts? If that is not the case, then I now propose the vote for both the questions and ask those in favour to raise their hands. Who is against? The proposal seems to have been adopted.

So now the whole of the administration and leadership of the Society in Switzerland has been constituted.

Does anyone else wish to speak about a matter that concerns the Swiss Society?

HERR STOKAR: I should like to ask the present chairman, Dr Steiner, for his opinion on whether the Swiss Society should now come to grips with the Statutes. As stated in the Statutes, it is now up to us to discuss the Statutes and work out a suitable form for our national Society, perhaps by adding to the general Statutes.

DR STEINER: That will of course be the subject of the first meeting of delegates, and it will be our task, as the council of the Swiss Society, to work out a draft. On the basis of this draft the first meeting of delegates will be able to discuss with us how we adopt the draft statutes or else modify them or whatever. This will surely be in order on the basis of the decisions made today.

HERR STOKAR has another question: When there are official public announcements to be made, will they be made from here or will the representatives in the different towns be expected to make them?

DR STEINER: First of all there will be an official report in the first supplement to *Das Goetheanum*,[73] and apart from this official report a good number of friends have been present and experienced it all for themselves. They will pass on anything they consider important. That is how I see it. As I see it, people are actually obliged to speak within the circle of the Society about what they have experienced here, and they could also speak about it wherever else they like in a tactful way such as is appropriate when speaking in public.

Dr Hugentobler wants the links with Dornach to be better.

HERR GEERING-CHRIST: Will nothing be made public?

DR STEINER: Let me repeat what I have just said: Members should feel obliged to speak amongst the members about whatever they have experienced. About whatever they have experienced! But they should also feel in duty bound to bring these things out into the world in, shall I say, a tactful manner. And I include the press in this. It will be possible to do it in a suitable way and we shall make sure that it is done in a suitable way. Indeed, I should like to say anyway — and as far as I know the whole Vorstand, which I have been so very instrumental in bringing into being, supports this — that I count courtesy as something that ought to exist extensively within our Society. We need courtesy. Some of us regard it as the most terrible thing that could have happened that one of our most valued members in Switzerland[74] has been lost to us. He was a member of the Goetheanum committee and one of the reasons he was able to give was that he once entered the Goetheanum, as a member of the committee, and was then thrown out. There have been many such examples of 'discourtesies'. We shall very urgently have to make it our task that courtesy is not the least of the unwritten paragraphs of our Statutes. We shall have to make very, very strenuous efforts in this direction. I presume that what Dr Hugentobler meant encompassed a good deal of this.

It was no small task for the provisional Vorstand to find quarters for all the many people who have come here, and some are indeed lodged in the most primitive and dreadful quarters. Yet they managed. But that does not make the work any less! In addition to all this — please be patient for a few more moments — we shall have to succeed gradually in being truly courteous in every way both towards Switzerland and towards the outside in general!

One speaker says that people could be more observant and take more into account: Yesterday evening someone had arrived in Dornach who had lost his membership card two or three years ago. Every seat was occupied and it was impossible to find one anywhere, and so on.

DR STEINER: In that particular case it would not have helped if the Swiss Society had had a representative or a council since it was a meeting of the General Anthroposophical Society. We should have been delighted if only you had come up to our table at the front. This is the very reason why I made sure that the Vorstand should be visible right from the start. They will be visible at every future meeting and I hope, knowing the Vorstand as I do, that they will also be courteous in future. So please be so good as to turn to the Vorstand during this Conference and things should be alright. Are there any more questions?

GENERAL REPLY: No.

DR STEINER: It seems to me that we have more or less reached the end of our agenda, and as far as the question of courtesy is concerned, let us rather carry it out in practice! I think we can now close this meeting. Please permit me to close the meeting.

The Envy of the Gods — The Envy of Human Beings

Looking back to the burning of the Goetheanum on New Year's Eve 1922/23

•

Lecture by Rudolf Steiner

31 DECEMBER, 8.30 IN THE EVENING

My dear friends!

We stand today under the sign of a grievous memory and we shall by all means place what is to be the content of today's lecture within the sign of this grievous memory. Those of you who were present then will remember how the lecture I was permitted to give just a year ago in our former building[75] followed a path which led from the description of earthly, natural conditions upwards into the spiritual worlds and into the revelation of these spiritual worlds out of the starry script. You will remember how it was possible, then, to link the human heart, the soul of man, the human spirit, and all that belongs to it, with all that can be discovered on the path outwards into not only the wide realm of the stars but also into what depicts the world of the spirit through the wide realm of the stars, like a cosmic script. The last thing I was permitted to write down on the blackboard in that hall which was taken from us so soon afterwards, that last thing was intended to raise the human soul up into spiritual heights. On that very evening the link was made with that to which our Goetheanum building was to be dedicated in its whole being. So now, as though in a continuation of that lecture given here a year ago, let me begin by speaking about that to which the link was then made.

If in the times before the burning of Ephesus men spoke about the Mysteries, then those who in their heart and soul understood something of the nature of the Mysteries said, in essence: Human knowledge, human wisdom has an abode, a dwelling place in the Mysteries. And if in those olden times there was talk of the Mysteries among the spiritual leaders of the world, that is if there was talk in supersensible realms about the Mysteries — allow me to use these expressions even though they describe only figuratively how thoughts are sent down from the supersensible realms and how the supersensible works in the sense-perceptible realm — if in supersensible realms there was talk about the Mysteries, then what was said went, in essence, like this: In the Mysteries, human beings set up an abode where we gods can find those human beings who bring us offerings and who understand us in their act of offering. For indeed those who knew about such things in the ancient world were generally aware that in the Mystery centres gods and human beings encountered one another and that all that carries and maintains the world depends on what takes place in the Mysteries between gods and human beings.

But there are words which have even come down to us in external history. These words handed down through history can deeply move our human hearts, especially when they can be seen taking shape out of very special events, when the shape they take is formed as though in letters of bronze, visible in spirit only for a moment and written into the history of humankind. Such words are always seen when one looks in spirit towards the deed of Herostratos,[76] the burning of the temple at Ephesus. In the flames the ancient words stand out: The envy of the gods.

Among the manifold words that have come down to us from olden times, which can be seen in the life of those times in the manner I have described, I do believe that this is one of the most terrible to be found in the physical world: The envy of the gods. In those olden times the word 'god' was used to describe anything that lived as a supersensible being without ever needing to appear on earth in a physical body. And in those times people distinguished between many and varied races of gods.

But those divine spiritual beings who are so closely linked with mankind that the human being in his inmost nature has come into existence through them and has been sent by them on his journey through the ages, those beings we sense in the majesty and in the minutest appearances of outer nature, those divine spiritual beings cannot become envious. Yet in olden times the envy of the gods denoted something very real. Following the human race in its development up to about the time of Ephesus we find that indeed the more advanced human individuals had taken for themselves much of what the good gods had been glad to give them in the Mysteries. It is quite right to say that an intimate relationship exists between the good human hearts and the good gods, a relationship made ever more close in the Mysteries. Thus the realization came about in the souls of certain other luciferic and ahrimanic godly beings that human beings were being drawn ever closer to the good gods. And thus arose the envy of the gods towards man. Again and again we hear in history that a human being striving for the spirit, if he meets with a tragic destiny, is described as having been a victim of the envy of the gods.

The ancient Greeks knew of this envy of the gods and they traced much of what took place in external human evolution back to this envy of the gods. The burning of the temple at Ephesus made it obvious that a certain further spiritual development of mankind is only possible if human beings realize that there are gods, that is supersensible beings, who are envious of the further progress of humankind. This has coloured the whole of history since the burning of the temple at Ephesus, or I could say since the birth of Alexander.[77] And a proper conception of the Mystery of Golgotha, too, must take into account that we look into a world that is filled with the envy of certain races of gods. From soon after the Persian wars the atmosphere of soul in Greece had been filled with the consequences of this envy of the gods. And what was then accomplished at the time of Macedonia had to be carried out in full awareness of the envy of the gods reigning over the face of the earth in the spiritual atmosphere. Yet it was carried out courageously, boldly, in defiance of misunderstandings on the part of both gods and men.

And there came down into this atmosphere filled with the envy of the gods the deed of that God who was capable of the greatest love that can possibly exist in the world. We see the Mystery of Golgotha in its true light only if we can add to everything else also the image of the clouds in the ancient world, in Hellas, Macedonia, the Near East, North Africa, Southern Europe; the image of those clouds that are an expression of the envy of the gods. Wondrously warming, gently gleaming, there falls into this cloud-filled atmosphere the love that streams through the Mystery of Golgotha.

This interaction was, if I may describe it thus, a matter which at that time took place between gods and human beings. Now, in our time, in the age of human freedom, it is something that has to take place down below, here in physical human life. And the manner in which it takes place can indeed be described. In olden times, down on the earth, one thought of the Mysteries thus: Human knowledge, human wisdom finds an abode in the Mysteries. But among the gods it was said: When we descend into the Mysteries we find there the offerings of human beings, and in the human being who makes his offering we are comprehended.

The burning of the temple at Ephesus marked the beginning of the age in which the Mysteries in their old form gradually began to disappear. I have told you how they continued to endure here and there, sublimely, for example, in the Mysteries of Hibernia, where the Mystery of Golgotha was celebrated in the divine cultus simultaneously with the actual physical event over in Palestine. They knew of it solely through the spiritual communication that existed between Palestine and Hibernia. There was no physical communication. Nevertheless, in the physical world the Mysteries receded more and more. The external abodes, which were places of encounter between gods and human beings, increasingly lost their significance. By the thirteenth and fourteenth centuries they had lost it almost entirely. Those who wanted to find the way, for example to the Holy Grail, had to know how to follow spiritual paths. In olden times, before the burning of the temple at Ephesus, the paths to be trodden were physical paths. In the Middle Ages the paths were spiritual.

In particular a spiritual path had to be followed by one who sought instruction in the truly Rosicrucian way from the thirteenth or fourteenth century onwards, but even more so from the fifteenth century. The temples of the Rosicrucians were profoundly hidden from any external physical experience. Many true Rosicrucians frequented the temples, but these temples could not be found by any external, physical human eye. But it was possible for pupils to find these aged Rosicrucians who lived here or there like hermits of wisdom, hermits of the holy human deed. They could be found by those who could comprehend the language of the gods speaking out of gently shining eyes. I am not talking figuratively. I do not want to speak in pictures. I am telling you of an actual reality which was extremely significant at the time to which I am pointing. The pupils found their Rosicrucian teacher if they had first gained the capacity to understand the language of the heavens speaking out of gently shining physical eyes. In the fourteenth and fifteenth centuries in Central Europe these remarkable personalities were to be found living in the most modest surroundings, in the most unassuming human accommodation. They were filled with the divine spirit; in their inner being they were linked to the spiritual temples which existed but to which access was truly as difficult to find as was that to the Holy Grail described in the well-known legend.

Looking at what took place between one of these Rosicrucian teachers and his pupil, we can overhear many a conversation that describes in the form appropriate for more recent times the divine wisdom as it exists on the earth. The instruction was profoundly concrete. A Rosicrucian teacher was discovered in his solitude by a pupil who had enthusiastically endeavoured to seek and find him. A pupil gazed into the gently shining eyes out of which flows the speech of gods and, modestly, he received something like the following instruction.

Look, my son, at your own being. You bear with you that body which your external, physical eyes can see. The very centre of the earth sends to this body the forces which make it visible. This is your physical body. But look around you at your own environment on the earth. You see stones; they are permitted to exist on the earth; their dwelling place is on the earth. Once they have taken on a shape, they can maintain it through the forces of the earth. Look at the crystal. It bears a form and through the earth it retains this form of its own nature. Your physical body is incapable of this. If your soul departs from it, then the earth destroys it, it dissolves it into dust. The earth has no power over your physical body. It has the power to shape and to maintain the transparent, wonderfully formed shapes of the crystal; but it has no power to maintain the shape of your physical body; it has to dissolve it into dust. Your physical body is not of this earth. Your physical body is of supreme spirituality. To Seraphim, Cherubim and Thrones belong the form and shape of your physical body. Your physical body does not belong to the earth; it belongs to those spiritual forces which are the highest as yet accessible to you. The earth can destroy it but never build it up.

And within this your physical body lives your etheric body. The day will come when your physical body is taken in by the earth in order to be destroyed. Then your etheric body will dissolve into the widths of the cosmos. The widths of the cosmos can dissolve this etheric body but they cannot build it up. Only those divine, spiritual beings belonging to the hierarchy of the Dynamis, Exusiai and Kyriotetes can build it up. You unite with your physical body the physical substances of the earth. But that which is in you transforms the physical substances of the earth in such a way that within them there is no longer anything resembling whatever is physical in the environment of your physical body. Your etheric body moves everything in you that is liquid or watery. The juices that stream and circulate are under the influence of your etheric body. See your blood: Exusiai,

Dynamis, Kyriotetes cause this blood as a liquid to circulate through your arteries. You are human only in your physical body. In your etheric body you are still animal, but an animal enspirited by the second hierarchy.

What I have been saying to you compressed into a few words was the subject of long instruction by that teacher in whose gently shining eyes the pupil heard the speech of heaven. Then the attention of the pupil was drawn to the third member of the human being, which we call the astral body. The pupil was shown how this astral body contains the impulse to breathe and to be involved with everything that is aeriform in the human organism, with everything that pulses as air through the human organism. The earthly realm may endeavour, for ages after the human being has stepped through the portal of death, to rumble about in the aeriform realm. For years the clairvoyant eye can discern the astral bodies of those who have died rumbling about in the atmospheric phenomena of the earth. Yet the earthly realm with all its environment is incapable of doing anything to the impulses of the astral body except dissolve them. The beings of the third hierarchy, Archai, Archangeloi, Angeloi, alone can form it.

Thus, deeply moving the heart of his pupil, the teacher said: In your physical body, by taking in and transforming the mineral kingdom, by taking in the human realm and working on it, you belong to Seraphim, Cherubim, Thrones. In so far as you are an etheric body, you are animal-like in the etheric realm, but you belong to the spirits called the spirits of the second hierarchy, Kyriotetes, Dynamis, Exusiai; in so far as you weave in the fluid element you do not belong to the earth but to this hierarchy. And by weaving in the aeriform element you do not belong to the earth but to the hierarchy of Angeloi, Archangeloi, Archai.

Having undergone sufficient instruction in this way, the pupil no.longer felt related to the earth. Going out, he sensed, from his physical, etheric and astral bodies were the forces that joined him through the mineral world with the first hierarchy, through the watery earth with the second hierarchy and through the encircling air with the third hierarchy. It was clear to him that he lives on the earth solely through the element of warmth which he bears within him. Thus the Rosicrucian pupil felt the warmth he bears within him, the physical warmth, to be what is actually the earthly, human element in him. And he learnt increasingly to feel that this physical warmth is related to warmth of soul and warmth of spirit. Human beings living in later times have increasingly forgotten how their physical content, their etheric content and their astral content is related to the divine world through the solid element, the fluid element and the aeriform element. But the Rosicrucian pupil knew this full well. He knew that the warmth element is that which is truly earthly and human. At the moment when the pupil of the Rosicrucian master realized this mystery of the connection between the element of warmth and the human, earthly element, he knew how to link his human element with the spiritual world.

Before entering those often quite unassuming dwellings inhabited by such Rosicrucian teachers, the pupils were shown, usually without their seeking it and in a seemingly miraculous manner — the one in this way and the other in another way, often coincidentally, so outwardly it seemed — they were shown that they must seek to link their own spirit with the spirit of the cosmos. And when the pupil had received from his teacher the instruction about which I have just been speaking, then, yes then he could say to his teacher: I now depart from you having received the greatest consolation possible on earth; by showing me that warmth is truly the element of earthly man you have enabled me to link my physical aspect with the realm of soul and spirit; I take the soul element not into my solid bones, not into my liquid blood, not into my airy breath, but into my element of warmth.

In utmost peace those who had received such instruction departed, in those days, from their teachers. And out of the peace in their countenance which expressed the outcome of that great consolation, out of the peace in their countenance there developed gradually that gentle glance through which the speech of heaven can resound. Thus profound instruction in the realm of the soul was available right into the first third of the fifteenth century, hidden away from those events of which external history tells us. An instruction took place which encompassed the total human being, an instruction that permitted the human soul to link its own being with the sphere of the cosmos and of the spirit.

This spiritual mood has entirely drained away during the course of the last few centuries. It no longer belongs to our civilization. A superficial civilization, estranged from the gods, has spread itself over what were once the dwelling places that saw what I have just described to you. Here one stands today with the memory, which can only be called up in the light of the astral world, of many a scene resembling the one I have described. Hence our basic mood when we first look back to those ages that are often described as being so dark, and then look out into our present time. But when we look back in this way our heart is stirred — through the spiritual revelations that can once more be received by mankind since the final third of the nineteenth century — by a deep longing to speak in a spiritual way once more to human beings. And this spiritual way of speaking is not dependent on abstract words alone; it calls for all manner of signs in order to be all-embracing. And a language needed for those spiritual beings who are to speak to modern mankind, such a way of speaking existed indeed in the forms of our Goetheanum, burnt down a year ago. Truly these forms were to have spoken out into the world the ideas told to the audience from the platform. Thus in a certain way the Goetheanum was something that could, in an entirely new form, remind us of something ancient.

When the one approaching initiation entered into the temple at Ephesus, his glance was drawn to that statue about which I have spoken during these days, that statue which called to him in words of the heart: Unite with the world ether and you shall see the earthly realm from etheric heights. Thus did many a pupil at Ephesus view the earthly realm from etheric heights. And a certain race of gods grew envious. But centuries before the Mystery of Golgotha courageous human beings nevertheless found ways, despite the envy of the gods, to carry forward —weakly, perhaps, but not so weakly that it remained without effect — that which had worked since the days of ancient and holy human evolution right up to the time of the burning of the temple. And if our Goetheanum could have been finally completed, then once again, as we entered from the West, our glance would have fallen on that statue which would have challenged the human being to know himself as a cosmic being placed between the forces of Lucifer and the forces of Ahriman with the inward, divinely sustained equilibrium of his being. And when our glance fell on the forms of the pillars, the architraves, they spoke a language that was a continuation of what was expressed from the platform in the ideas which worked as though interpreting the spirit. The words continued to resound along the sculpted forms. And up above, in the dome, were scenes to be seen, scenes which brought human evolution closer to spiritual sight. In this Goetheanum there was indeed, for those who had a feeling for it, a memory of the temple at Ephesus.

But that memory grew terribly painful when the burning torch was applied to this very Goetheanum in a manner that was not at all dissimilar to ancient times, not at all dissimilar especially as regards the moment of evolution in which the Goetheanum was, of itself, to have become the bearer of a renewal of spiritual life.

My dear friends, our pain was profound. Our pain was inexpressible. But we formed the resolve to continue our work for the spiritual world unhindered by the most sorrowful and most tragic event that could possibly have come upon us. For in our heart of hearts we could say that in the flames rising up from Ephesus was written the envy of the gods, at a time when human beings still had to follow rather more without freedom the will of good or evil gods.

In our day human beings are organized more towards freedom. And a year ago, in the night of New Year's Eve, we saw before us the devouring flames. The red blaze shot skywards. Dark blueish, reddish-yellow lines of flame curled through the seething sea of fire, generated by the metal instruments contained in the Goetheanum, a gigantic sea of flame containing the most varied shades and colours. And gazing into this sea of flame with the coloured lines darting hither and thither one could not but read words which spoke to the pain in one's soul: the envy of human beings.

Thus what speaks from epoch to epoch in human evolution comes together, link by link, even in the greatest of misfortunes. An unbroken thread runs from the words that give expression to the greatest misfortune at a time when human beings still looked up to the gods without freedom, a time when they ought to have been making themselves free of this unfreedom. An unbroken thread of spiritual evolution runs from that misfortune which bore, inscribed in the flames, the words about the envy of the gods. This unbroken thread runs right through to our own misfortune in a time when human beings ought to be finding the strength for freedom, a misfortune in which the flames bore the incription: the envy of human beings. In Ephesus the statue of the goddess; here in the Goetheanum the statue of the human being, the statue of the representative of man, Christ Jesus, into whom, identifying ourselves with him, in all humility, we thought to merge in knowledge, just as in olden times, in their own way, no longer quite comprehensible to mankind today, the pupils of Ephesus merged into Diana of Ephesus.

We do not lessen our pain by viewing in the light of history what took place on New Year's Eve last year. When I was permitted to stand for the last time on that platform that had been set up in harmony with the whole of the building, the intention had been to guide the eyes of the listeners, to guide the eyes of their souls towards the ascent from earthly realms into starry realms that express the will and the wisdom, the light of the spiritual cosmos. Many of the spirits who taught their pupils in the Middle Ages in the manner described just now stood, I know, as godparents at that moment. And an hour after the last word had been spoken I was called to the burning Goetheanum. We spent the night of New Year's Eve last year watching the Goetheanum burning.

The mere utterance of these words, dear friends, conjures up an inexpressible response in all our hearts, in all our souls. When something like this has swept across a hallowed place in human evolution, there have always been a few who have vowed to work on in the spirit devoted to what had once been physical even though whatever it had been was no longer present. And gathered now as we are on the anniversary of that misfortune of the Goetheanum, let us be aware that our souls will be living in the proper mood for this our gathering if we all vow to carry on in spirit through this wave of progress in human evolution that which was present in physical form, as a physical image and a physical shape in the Goetheanum, visible to our physical eyes, before being snatched away from our physical perception by a Herostratos-deed. Our pain attaches itself to the old Goetheanum. We shall only become worthy of having been permitted to build that Goetheanum if today in remembering it we vow, before whatever is best and most divine in each one of our souls, to keep faith with the spiritual impulses that had been given an outer form in that Goetheanum. It was possible for this Goetheanum to be taken from us. The Spirit of this Goetheanum, if our will is truly upright and honest, cannot be taken from us. And least of all will it be taken from us if at this solemn and festive hour, separated by so short a time from the moment a year ago when the flames leapt up from our beloved Goetheanum, if at this moment we not only feel the pain anew but also vow out of this pain to keep faith with that Spirit for whom, over ten long years, we were permitted to build this abode.

Then, my dear friends, when this inner vow flows from our heart in all honesty and uprightness, when we can transform the pain and suffering into the impulse for doing deeds, then shall we transform the sorrowful event into a blessing. The pain cannot diminish because of this, but it behoves us to find out of this very pain the incentive to act, the incentive to do deeds in the spirit.

And so, my dear friends, let us look back to the terrible flames of fire which filled us with such inexpressible sorrow. But let us also, in making that vow before whatever forces are the best and most divine in each of us, feel the holy flame in our hearts, the flame which is to enlighten and warm that which was willed in the Goetheanum, by bearing this will onwards through the waves of progress in human evolution. So now, more profoundly, we repeat those words which I was permitted to speak over there, a year ago almost at this very moment. I said, in essence: We are living on the eve of a new year, let us live towards a new cosmic year. If only the Goetheanum still stood amongst us, we could renew this exhortation at this moment! It no longer stands amongst us. Yet I believe that just because it no longer stands amongst us we are permitted, on this eve of another new year, to renew this exhortation with a force increased many times over. Let us bear the Soul of the Goetheanum over into the new cosmic year, and let us endeavour to build in the new Goetheanum a worthy monument to the body of the old Goetheanum, a worthy memorial!

My dear friends, may this link our hearts to the old Goetheanum which we had to consign to the elements. May it link our hearts also to the Spirit, to the Soul of this Goetheanum. With this vow before whatever is best within our being we want to live on not only into the new year. In strength of deed, bearing the spirit, leading the soul we want to live on into the new cosmic year.

My dear friends, you greeted me this evening by standing in memory of the old Goetheanum. You are living in the memory of this old Goetheanum. Let us stand once more as a sign that we vow to work on in the Spirit of the Goetheanum with whatever best forces we can find in the image of our inner human being. Indeed, so be it. Amen.

Thus let us continue, my dear friends, as long as we are able, in accordance with the will that unites our human souls with the souls of the gods with whom we wish to keep faith in the spirit, in the spirit out of which we sought this faith with them at a certain moment in our lives, at that moment when we sought the spiritual wisdom of the Goetheanum. Let us understand how to keep this faith.

Continuation of the Foundation Meeting

1 JANUARY 1924, 10 O'CLOCK IN THE MORNING

DR STEINER:

ONCE MORE, my dear friends, we shall welcome to our souls what is to inspire us and bring us strength during this Conference:

Soul of Man!
Thou livest in the limbs
Which bear thee through the world of space
In the spirit's ocean-being.
Practise spirit-recalling
In depths of soul,
Where in the wielding will
Of world-creating
Thine own I
Comes to being
Within God's I.
And thou wilt truly live
In the World-Being of Man.

For the Father-Spirit of the heights holds sway
In depths of worlds begetting being:
Seraphim, Cherubim, Thrones!
Let there ring out from the heights
What in the depths is echoed
Speaking:
Ex Deo nascimur.

1 JANUARY, 10 O'CLOCK IN THE MORNING

Soul of Man!
Thou livest in the beat of heart and lung
Which leads thee through the rhythm of time
Into the realm of thine own soul's feeling.
Practise spirit-awareness
In balance of the soul,
Where the surging deeds
Of the world's becoming
Thine own I
Unite
With the World-I.
And thou wilt truly feel
In the Soul-Weaving of Man.

For the Christ-Will in the encircling round holds sway
In the rhythms of the worlds, bestowing grace on the soul.
Kyriotetes, Dynamis, Exusiai!
Let there be fired from the East
What through the West is formed
Speaking:
In Christo morimur.

Soul of Man!
Thou livest in the resting head
Which from the grounds of eternity
Opens to thee the world-thoughts.
Practise spirit-beholding
In stillness of thought,
Where the eternal aims of Gods
World-Being's Light
On thine own I
Bestow
For thy free willing.
And thou wilt truly think
In the Spirit-Foundations of Man.

For the world-thoughts of the Spirit hold sway
In the being of worlds, craving for light:
Archai, Archangeloi, Angeloi!
Let there be prayed from the depths
What in the heights will be granted
Speaking:
Per Spiritum Sanctum reviviscimus.

Today we shall inscribe a simple rhythm into our souls:

[Rudolf Steiner writes on the blackboard as he speaks. See Facsimile 5, Page XVIII top.]

Thou livest in the limbs

For the Father-Spirit of the heights holds sway
In depths of worlds begetting being.

Thou livest in the beat of heart and lung

For the Christ-Will in the encircling round holds sway
In the rhythms of the worlds, bestowing grace on the soul.

Thou livest in the resting head

For the world-thoughts of the Spirit hold sway
In the being of worlds, craving for light.

[As shown on the blackboard]

Thou livest in the limbs
For the Father-Spirit of the heights holds sway
In depths of worlds begetting being.

Thou livest in the beat of heart and lung
For the Christ-Will in the encircling round holds sway
In the rhythms of the worlds, bestowing grace on the soul.

Thou livest in the resting head
For the world-thoughts of the Spirit hold sway
In the being of worlds, craving for light.

I thus write down for you the rhythms as they resound together because they do indeed encompass an image of the starry constellations. We say: Saturn is in the sign of Leo, or Saturn is in the sign of Scorpio. Rhythms depend on this, rhythms that go through the world. An image of primeval spirit lives in such rhythms in the way I have written them down for you over the course of these last days, having taken them from our verses which are inwardly organized through and through in accordance with the realm of spirit and soul.

Now to continue with our meeting, Herr Krebs would like to speak.

Herr Krebs speaks.

DR STEINER: On the question of the opposition, Herr Wolfgang Wachsmuth and then Herr Hardt wish to speak.

Herr Wolfgang Wachsmuth speaks about books and the question of the opposition.

DR STEINER: Obviously, if such a group is formed, then if it needs advice in one matter or another it will find this advice here. That is what I would like to say as a direct reply to the question. Does anyone else wish to speak with regard to the question of the opposition?

Herr Werbeck speaks on the question of the opposition.

DR STEINER: I would now ask Herr Hardt to speak. (He does not respond.) Now Herr Leinhas would like to speak.

Herr Leinhas speaks about the question of the opposition and about the press.

DR STEINER: Dr Stein will speak next.

Dr Walther Johannes Stein speaks on the question of the opposition.

DR STEINER: I would now like your permission to proceed to the matter of the rebuilding of the Goetheanum.

The Rebuilding of the Goetheanum

Lecture by Rudolf Steiner

1 JANUARY, IN THE MORNING

I SHALL TAKE the liberty of adding a few remarks to what I said yesterday, after which I shall invite contributions from those who have asked to speak.

You will remember that I endeavoured to solve the problem of the outside of the Goetheanum as well as was possible at the time by treating it as a building problem. A number of aspects were, though, made more difficult than they need have been by the speed at which the building was expected to be constructed. Nevertheless I believe that the shaping of the facade, of the portals, of the windows and window surrounds did portray outwardly the inner content of the Goetheanum, which was essentially a circular building.

Now, as I attempted to describe it to you yesterday, the impression is to be of a building that is partly circular and partly rectangular, having no longer a ground-plan that is circular. And it will be necessary to find for the forms a modern style that is appropriate for concrete as a building material.

Such things are always exceedingly difficult. It is of course easier to work in an abstract way out of the forms, and then choose the material, than it is to accept the material as the necessary given factor and then search for the forms out of this material, forms which are also partly determined by the circumstances which I described to you yesterday. Now, since we do not have time to go into more detail, I want to show you one essential feature, the underlying theme of the portals and of the windows, so that you can see how I want to let the inner formative force that was latent in the old forms assert itself once more also in the new forms of the intractable material, concrete.

I want the walls, coming down from the roof which is shaped in flat surfaces, to give the eye a definite impression of load. I want to bring it about that this downward pressure is caught and held, also for the eye, by the portal as well as the window surrounds. I also want to bring it about that inwardly the spiritual impression is of a portal that draws you in, or a window that takes in the light in order to usher it into the space within. But at the same time I want to bring it about that in a certain way this form reveals how the Goetheanum is to be a kind of shelter for the one who seeks the spirit within it. This will also have to be expressed by the portal. So let me describe what is to be revealed. [See Facsimile 5, Page XX.]

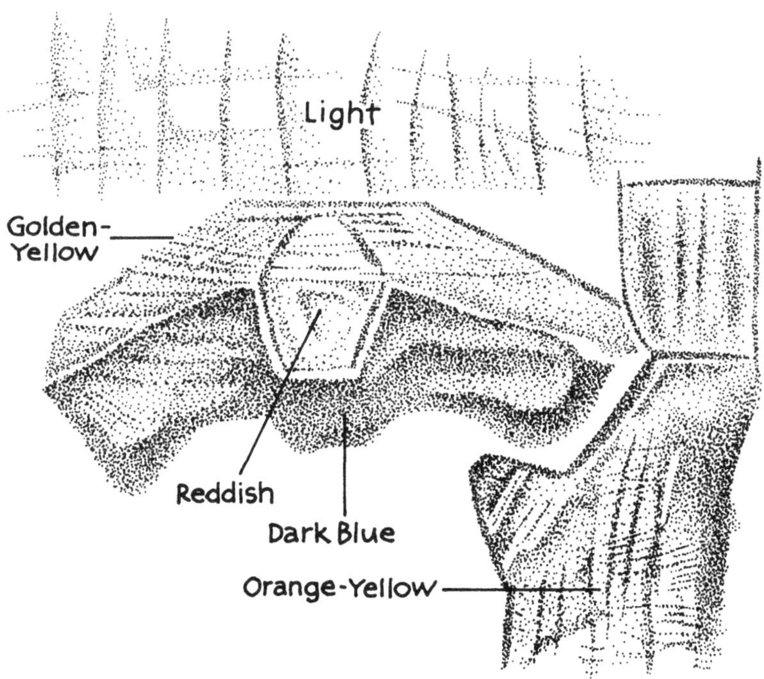

For instance, on the west front the roof will rise up like this. So I want the next thing appearing after the roof to be a kind of small form growing out of this roofing. Let me make it easier for you to see by using different colours to draw what will, of course, be all the same colour.

So this will jut out (lemon-yellow); it will be immediately above the head of someone who is standing before the portal, about to enter. Below that will be a portion, something that could be seen as a portion of a pentagon, but only a portion (reddish). The remainder of the pentagon would be above. And the whole of this is carried by a form which recedes (blue). So what you remember as rounded forms in the earlier Goetheanum[78] will here appear as something angular. You must imagine that *this* comes forward like a kind of roof (lemon-yellow), *this* goes back inwards (blue), and *this* becomes visible in the background (whitish). And the whole of this is to be supported by a pillar shape to the left and to the right in such a way that this pillar or column receives this protective form which appears above the head of the one who enters; it receives this protective form in another form (orange-yellow) like this, but at the same time it carries the roof part with an appropriate form which grows out of it.

This form will be used for both the side and main portals and for the windows. And in the use of this form we shall be able to achieve a really integrated external impression. It will show on the one hand how the load pressing down from above is carried and on the other hand how the pillars rise up in order to support that which comes out from the inside, revealing itself and needing to be received.

The essential thing about an angular building is the harmony between the forces of support and load. If we are to carry this out in an organic building, every part must reveal the indwelling character of the totality. The pillars in the old building reached from bottom to top. Now they will be metamorphosed so that on the lower level, the ground floor, they will develop like roots — architecturally conceived, of course. Out of these the actual pillars will grow on the upper level, becoming bearers of the whole. They will then bring the forms of the roof to completion from within outwards. The roof will not be terminated horizontally but rather in the way the cupola was terminated. The pillars and columns will be metamorphosed into supporting elements while at the same time expressing what in the old Goetheanum was to have been expressed in the roundness of the building.

We shall have to endeavour to calculate how basic the forms will have to be, merely hinted at perhaps, in order to keep the whole building, given this shape, within 3 to 3½ million Francs. Once we have made this decision — and I do not believe that any other is possible — then we shall I hope, and if the willingness of our friends to make sacrifices does not let us down, soon be in a position to begin construction and the building will then appear as a new Goetheanum in the place where the old one stood and in a much more basic and simple form.

I would now like to call on Herr van Leer, who has asked to speak on this matter.

Herr van Leer wants to found a World Goetheanum Association, resembling a World School Association, for the running of the Goetheanum.

DR STEINER: Yes, my dear friends, I cannot see any objection to the creation of a body of people who are members of a Goetheanum Association or something similar even if they are not members of the Anthroposophical Society. The question will be, though, as to what the members of such an organization can be called upon to do. It will be very difficult to win members merely by saying that they should pay money for the Goetheanum or for any other of our ventures. But perhaps in future Anthroposophy as such, as represented now here in Dornach, will become more and more known in the world. Perhaps people who are not in the first instance courageous enough to become anthroposophists will see that fruitful work can be done out of Anthroposophy and with Anthroposophy. Then it might be possible to say to people: Look, this is a spiritual movement; maybe you are not interested now; but help it to mature, do something so that the people involved can get going and show what they can do. It is quite likely, if we carry out into the world what has been discussed here during this Conference, that an Association such as that envisaged by our dear friend van Leer might indeed become a possibility.

Do not forget that a good deal of what is now included in the Statutes is of necessity bound up with the complete openness of the Society. You will see that much will change in practice. And once there is an understanding everywhere of what is connected with this openness of the Society, then it could very well be that a form such as that suggested just now by van Leer will be found. This openness will have to be taken very, very seriously by us. And on the other hand we here at the Goetheanum, this Vorstand, will have to take very seriously the fact that in future there can be no more working under cover. It will no longer be possible to say: If we approach people about a threefold social order or about Anthroposophy, they don't want to know about this, but they are interested in the things themselves. This is something that has done us the most damage of all over the last few years, or indeed over a longer period too, because it has brought us inwardly into a sphere of untruthfulness. The work going out from Dornach in future in all realms of life will be uprightly and honestly declared in full openness as being for Anthroposophy. Then people will know for what they are giving their money. And if we work from this angle then I do believe that a form such as you have suggested will become possible. It will never be possible if people have to ask what they are supposed to give money for.

This is what I believed I ought to say. If this is done, then the prospects are quite good. Would anybody else like to speak on the question of the rebuilding?

Miss X believes that eurythmy can show the public a great deal of what Anthroposophy is about. She asks for pictures, pictures of eurythmy and the picture of Frau Dr Steiner for publication in South America.

Mr Monges hopes to arouse interest in America. 'Americans have to see before they will give.'

DR STEINER: Does anyone else wish to speak?

Herr Donner speaks about the financial situation.

DR STEINER: Does anyone else wish to speak?

Mademoiselle Sauerwein asks whether the 12 Schillings are for the Society or the Goetheanum.

DR STEINER: In order to clarify the question Mademoiselle Sauerwein has brought to our agenda, I should report to you on the meeting in committee the other day of the General Secretaries of many different countries with the Vorstand and with representatives of the Swiss groups. I must tell you what conclusions were reached. It was a matter of completing the only point of the Statutes which could not be finalized before they were printed. We have adopted the Statutes, but one small point remained open because I said that it would be better to discuss it in a smaller circle first; and that was the matter of the annual contribution to be made by the groups for each member.

I brought the following points of view to that smaller circle. You see, an anthroposophist — let me say this, though of course it will be easily questioned — an anthroposophist does not entertain illusions but must think realistically, for the future too. To think realistically is to say that one will need this much money for a particular project, that is, to make a preliminary annual budget which is likely to be sufficient. For the founding of the Anthroposophical Society there is no sense financially in talking a great deal about what each individual thinks should be paid annually for each member. The only sensible thing to do is to say how much we need and then to calculate how much this is likely to come to when it is divided by the number of paying members. I have concerned myself very fundamentally with this question ever since I decided — with the agreement of the members of the Vorstand whom I considered to be the right ones — to take the Presidency of the Anthroposophical Society into my own hands. All I can do is to tell you the conclusion given to me as a result of my considerations: If we really want to run the Society which you yourselves have decided shall exist, the only thing we can do is ourselves lay down the amount which we need from every group for each member. All we can do is enter at this point in the Statutes the membership contribution to be made by every group for each of its members: 12 Schillings annually. That is only 1 Schilling monthly. You can work out what a minute amount that is per day! But we cannot manage without these 12 Schillings annually for each member. We could, of course, have started off the other way round, though I don't know whether this would have been more dignified. We could first have said: We need 12 Schillings from every member and then we shall found the Anthroposophical Society. Perhaps that would have been more practical. However that may be, the Society will only be realistically founded when we have these 12 Schillings annually.

Now, my dear friends, there are sure to be many groups who will say that they cannot raise this amount. There are groups whose membership fees would not even cover this, and they all want to keep at least half of the membership fee for themselves! So in the cases where this is so it will be a matter of negotiating with them how much they can reduce their contribution. And the missing amount will have to be raised in another way. We still need this missing amount. But this minimum sum which we need will have to be the standard, and then groups can go below it, which is bound to happen, as we well know from experience, down even to the vanishing point. The vanishing point is often reached. But I hope that there will also be instances of the opposite, right up to the level of Carnegie, though of course never quite reaching the infinite! Anyway, this is the suggestion that I wanted to make in a smaller circle. And this smaller circle did not by any means agree immediately. But I do believe that most have meanwhile come to see that there is no other way. Countries also do it like this. You cannot set up a budget and then ask every single citizen: How much can you pay? This is not how it is done. We admittedly have no means of enforcing collection, and of course we want no such thing, for there must be freedom amongst us, including that of saying how much we need. So if you like, please do say what you think, or at least vote on whether you agree in general, in principle, to the payment of 12 Schillings per member, always remembering that everyone can negotiate how much below this it is necessary to go. I had to say this if this matter was to be discussed. (Applause)

Mademoiselle Sauerwein says that these 12 Schillings will be contributed by France because they are needed and she would like to know the date by which payment is required.

DR STEINER: The date will be a matter of administration. In the very near future — since time is too short to do so at the Conference — we shall issue By-Laws to the various groups and in these we shall say when the contributions can be paid. They do not all have to come in at the same time. The method will gradually emerge, and agreements can be made with the different groups as to when it suits them to pay. Certainly we shall not shirk. Does anyone want to speak to this question of the membership contribution?

Mr Pyle suggests that agreement be expressed immediately on the point that the 12 Schillings per year would be raised somehow, since they were absolutely necessary.

DR STEINER: It has been suggested that we vote straight away on this question of the membership contribution. Does anyone want to speak about this suggestion, which is actually a matter for the By-Laws? Only on the suggestion, not on the question. If that is not the case, then I now call for a vote on this suggestion. Will those friends who are in favour of the standard membership contribution being set at 12 Schillings with the given proviso please raise their hands. (They do.) Will those member-friends not in favour now also please raise their hands. There seems to be cordial agreement on this point.

I intended to bring up this point at the end of today's agenda, but it has now been settled. So after this interruption we can continue with the agenda if anyone still wants to speak about the rebuilding of the Goetheanum or about Herr van Leer's suggestion.

Mrs Merry wishes to speak.

DR STEINER: Would anyone else like to speak on this?

Herr Koschützki touches on the question of finance. He considers that work at research institutes is the most suitable for obtaining money for the Goetheanum from non-anthroposophists.

DR STEINER: So long as these things are in future always shown to be intimately bound up with Anthroposophy. It would be wrong to give the impression of merely wanting to do some research through ordinary science. In future we want to put things before the world simply as they emerge from the central core of Anthroposophy. Of course there is a good deal which does have to be presented in public in a way that is not possible through pictures, since pictures at best bring something supersensible into the realm of the sense-perceptible. But we are supposed to present the supersensible to the world. This is of course difficult, more difficult than presenting something sense-perceptible, but we must succeed. And we shall succeed. But please have the courage to present the supersensible and not something that appears as though through a mask. This has brought us enough harm.

Does anyone else wish to speak?

Herr Leinhas speaks about the building of the Goetheanum and about the organization. He believes that friends can be won on the basis of pointing out what is said in the Statutes.

DR STEINER: Does anyone else wish to speak?

Dr Kruger speaks of personal impressions and of his feelings for what has been experienced here as a primeval founding.

DR STEINER: Now, dear friends, let me throw the discussion open for any subject people might still want to mention.

Herr Geuter says that the journal *Anthroposophie* and the

articles of Herr Steffen and Dr Steiner are particularly valuable for disseminating Anthroposophy.

DR STEINER: Does anyone else wish to speak about anything?

Dr Zeylmans speaks from the medical point of view. There is surely no realm more in need of renewal than that of medicine. About thirty-five doctors were present at the founding of the small clinic in The Hague and by the end they were very enthusiastic about the lectures. It can certainly be said that we do not want anything different but we do want more. The lectures heard up to now have been marvellous, but what is needed is not only a bridge such as this but also an entirely new kingdom in one's heart in order as a doctor to become a healer in the sense of earlier times. He therefore especially welcomes the founding of the Medical Section.

DR STEINER: You will allow me, my dear friends, to add a few words after my lecture this evening about such questions as, for instance, the shaping of the medical work and how we think about it. I shall do so then because I want to ask any friends who would still like to say something in brief about one thing or another to do so now. The farewell words I myself want to say and also what I want to say about questions such as that brought up so kindly by Dr Zeylmans just now I shall say in connection with my lecture this evening. So would anyone who still has a short contribution to make please do so.

Herr Wullschleger, a teacher, speaks about the question of a school in Switzerland, considers a school in Basel to be absolutely necessary and requests support of every kind.

DR STEINER: Now we have come to the end of our agenda. Or rather we should say that time has brought us to the end of our agenda. It will be satisfying this afternoon, on the very day on which we saw for the first time from the grounds just outside here the ruins still in flames, on this very anniversary of that terrible day we shall meet here at 4.30 for a social gathering. The thought of meeting for such a gathering on this very day can be particularly dear to us when for one or another it may be possible to speak together in the most intense and best and intimate way such as will seem suitable for this very day of mourning and remembrance and such as our heart must long for. So at 4.30 we shall assemble here for our social gathering. At 8.30 my final lecture will take place. The practising doctors are requested to meet me again tomorrow morning at 8.30 down in the Glass House. I shall make any further announcements this evening.

Anything which one or another of you might still have wished to say will now remain unsaid. But just as last time it was possible for one or two things intended for more than a personal conversation to be said to everyone during the Social Gathering, so this time, too, it will be possible to speak to the members during the Social Gathering if anyone wishes to do so.

Now will those friends from Germany who wish to travel tomorrow at 10.45 please raise their hands so that Dr Wachsmuth can see how many there are wishing to travel tomorrow morning. Now will those wishing to take the evening train please raise their hands. It will not be easy to arrange for anyone to stay any longer. Only those who have had their passes extended properly can remain. It is not possible to endanger future meetings here by allowing the authorities to notice that fifty or more people are leaving later than intended. If only a few depart, it will not be possible to arrange for extra lodgings. Also would you please hand in any unused meal tickets at House Friedwart. In addition would you please hand in the blankets you have used at House Friedwart because we shall need them for future meetings. Then would those friends who have not yet collected their passes from House Friedwart please do so, because we have no use for them. We would of course gladly travel away on behalf of every one of you if we only could. Finally, for those friends still here, there will be a eurythmy performance at 7 o'clock tomorrow evening. The programme will include a repeat of 'Olaf Asteson'.

On the Right Entry into the Spiritual World: The Responsibility Incumbent on Us

Lecture and words of farewell by Rudolf Steiner

1 JANUARY, 8.30 IN THE EVENING

My dear friends!

We are gathered together for the last time in this Conference from which much that is strong and important is to go forth for the Anthroposophical Movement. So now let me shape this final lecture in a way that connects it inwardly, in its impulse, with the various prospects thrown open to us by this series of lectures as a whole,[79] but also in a way that will allow us to gain a sense for the future, especially the future of anthroposophical endeavour.

When we look out into the world today we see something that has already been there for many years: a tremendous amount of destructiveness. There are forces at work that give us an inkling of the abysses into which western civilization is still to plunge. Looking at those individuals who externally are the cultural leaders in the various fields of life, we notice how they are enmeshed in a terrible cosmic sleep. They think, and until recently most people thought, that until the nineteenth century mankind was childlike and primitive in its insights and views, and that now that modern science has entered into all the various fields truth has at last arrived, truth that must be upheld forever.

People who think like this are, without knowing it, living in a state of tremendous arrogance. On the other hand, here and there amongst mankind today there are some inklings that things are perhaps not as the majority would like to imagine.

Some time ago I was able to give a number of lectures in Germany organized by the Wolff agency.[80] The audiences were exceptionally large, so that people here and there began to notice that Anthroposophy was something for which people were looking. All kinds of foolish voices were raised in antagonism, among them one which was not much more intelligent than any of the others but which nevertheless expressed a kind of presentiment. It consisted of a note in a newspaper referring to one of the lectures in Berlin. This notice in the newspaper said: Listening to stuff like this you get the impression — I am quoting the article approximately — that something is happening not only on the earth but also in the whole of the cosmos that is calling mankind to a form of spirituality that is different from what has existed so far; even the forces of the cosmos, not merely earthly impulses, are demanding something of mankind; a kind of revolution in the cosmos which must lead man to strive for a new spirituality.

So there was this voice, which was in its way quite remarkable. For it is true: The proper impulse for what must now go forth from Dornach must, as I have emphasized from various angles over the last few days, be an impulse arising not on the earth but in the spiritual world. Here we want to develop the strength to follow the impulses coming from the spiritual world. In the evening lectures during this Christmas Conference I have spoken about manifold impulses present in historical development so that your hearts might be opened to take in spiritual impulses which still have to stream into the earthly world and are not taken from the earthly world itself. Everything that has hitherto borne the earthly world in the right way has had its source in the spiritual world. And if we are to achieve something fruitful for the earthly world, we must turn to the spiritual world for the appropriate impulses.

My dear friends, this encourages me to point out that the impulses we are to bear away with us from this Conference must be linked to a great sense of responsibility.

Let us spend a few minutes on the great responsibility that is now incumbent on us as a result of this Conference. In recent decades it has been possible for someone with a sense for the spiritual world to wander, in spiritual observation, past many personalities, gaining bitter sensations with regard to the future destiny of mankind on earth. It has been possible to wander past one's fellow human beings in the manner available to spiritual insight, observing how they lay aside their physical and etheric bodies in sleep and live in the spiritual world with their ego and astral body. Wandering among the destinies of those egos and astral bodies while human beings slept has, in recent decades, given rise to experiences which can point to a heavy responsibility incumbent on the one who can know such things. These souls, having left behind their physical and etheric bodies between going to sleep and waking up, were often to be seen approaching the Guardian of the Threshold.

The Guardian of the Threshold has entered the awareness of human beings in many and various ways during the course of human evolution. Many a legend and many a saga — for this is the form in which the most important things are preserved, rather than that of historical records — many a legend and many a saga tells of the approach by one personality or another to the Guardian of the Threshold in order to receive instruction on how to enter the spiritual world and then return once more to the physical world. Entering rightly into the spiritual world must bring with it the possibility of returning to the physical world at any moment with the full ability to stand on both feet as a practical and thoughtful human being, not as a dreamer, not as a dreamy mystic.

Throughout all the thousands of years during which human beings have striven to enter the spiritual world, this has been the fundamental stipulation of the Guardian of the Threshold. But especially in the final third of the nineteenth century hardly any human beings were to be seen approaching the Guardian of the

Threshold in a state of wakefulness. And even more so in our own time, when mankind as a whole has the historical task of passing by the Guardian of the Threshold in one way or another, do you find, when wandering in the spiritual world, that souls are asleep when they approach the Guardian of the Threshold as egos and astral bodies. This most significant picture meets us today: There stands the Guardian of the Threshold surrounded by groups of sleeping human souls who do not have the strength to approach him in a waking state but who approach him instead while they are asleep.

Witnessing this scene, you become aware of a thought which is bound up particularly with what I would like to call the germination of a necessary great responsibility. The souls who thus approach the Guardian of the Threshold in a state of sleep demand entry into the spiritual world. They demand to be allowed to wander across the threshold in a state of sleep; their consciousness is that of a sleeping human being — which so far as the waking state is concerned remains unconscious or subconscious. And countless times the voice of the grave Guardian of the Threshold is heard: For your own good, you may not cross the threshold; you may not gain entrance to the spiritual world. Go back! For if the Guardian of the Threshold were to allow them to enter without more ado, they could come over into the spiritual world with all the concepts passed on to them by today's schools, today's education, today's civilization; with all those concepts and ideas with which human beings have to grow up nowadays from their sixth year onwards right, you could say, until the end of their earthly lives.

These concepts and ideas have a particular characteristic: If you enter into the spritual world with them, with the way you have become with them through present-day civilization and schooling, you become paralysed in your soul. And on returning to the physical world you would be void of thoughts and ideas. If the Guardian of the Threshold did not gravely reject these souls, if he were not to reject many, many of today's human souls but were to let them step over into the spiritual world, then, waking up on their return, waking up at the decisive moment on their return, they would have the feeling: I cannot think; my thoughts do not grasp my brain; I have to live in the world without thoughts. For the world of abstract ideas which human beings today attach to everything is such that one can indeed go into the spiritual world with them but one cannot bring them out again. And when you watch this scene, which is experienced today by more souls than you would ordinarily imagine, you say to yourself: If only these souls could be successfully protected from experiencing also in death what they are now experiencing in sleep. For if the inner condition experienced before the Guardian of the Threshold were to endure for a sufficiently long period of time, if human civilization were to remain for a long time under the influence of what can be taken in in schools by way of what is traditionally passed down by civilization, then sleep would become ordinary life. Human souls would pass through the portal of death into the spiritual world and then be incapable of bringing any strength of ideas with them into their new life on earth. For though you can enter the spiritual world with today's thoughts, you then cannot leave it with them. You can only leave it in a state of soul paralysis.

You see, present-day civilization can be founded on the kind of cultural life that has been nurtured for so long. But life cannot be founded on it. It would be possible for this civilization to endure for a while. During their waking hours, the souls would have no inkling of the Guardian of the Threshold; then while they slept they would be turned away by him so that they should not become paralysed; and the final consequence would be that a human race would be born in the future without any understanding, without any possibility of applying ideas to life when they were born in this future time, so that the faculty of thinking and living in ideas would have disappeared from the earth. A sick human race, living only in instincts, would have to populate the earth. Terrible feelings and emotions alone, without orientation through the force of ideas, would come to dominate human evolution.

Indeed, the soul failing to gain entry into the spiritual world, and being turned away by the Guardian of the Threshold in the way I have just described, is not the only sad sight to meet the one who has spiritual vision. If such a one were to take with him a human being from eastern civilization on his journeyings to where the sleeping souls can be observed approaching the Guardian of the Threshold, then such an eastern human being would be heard to utter spirit words of terrible reproach towards the whole of western civilization: See, if this goes on, then the earth will have fallen into barbarism by the time those living today return for a new incarnation; people will live by instincts alone, without ideas; this is what you have brought about by falling away from the ancient spirituality of the orient.

Thus a glimpse like this into the spiritual world bears witness to a strong sense of responsibility for the task of man. And here in Dornach there must be a place where it is possible to speak, to those who wish to listen, about every important direct experience of the spiritual world. Here there must be a place where the strength is found to point to those little traces of the spirit not only in the cleverly put together dialectical and empirical scientific manner of the present time. If Dornach is to fulfil its task, then it must be a place where human beings can hear openly about what is going on historically in the spiritual world and about the spiritual impulses which then enter into the world of nature and govern it. Human beings must be able to hear in Dornach about genuine experiences, genuine forces and genuine beings of the spiritual world. This is where the School of true Spiritual Science must be. And we must henceforth not shy away from the demands of modern scientific thought which causes human beings to approach the earnest Guardian of the Threshold in a state of sleep in the way I have described. In Dornach it must be possible to win the strength, spiritually, to look the spiritual world in the eye, to learn about the spiritual world.

Therefore we shall not let loose a tirade of dialectics on the inadequacy of present-day scientific theory. Instead I had to draw your attention to the position in which this scientific theory, and its consequences in ordinary schools, places the human being with regard to the Guardian of the Threshold. If we can face up to this in our soul in all earnestness during this Conference, then this Christmas Conference will send a strong impulse into our souls which can carry them away to do strong work of the kind needed by mankind today, so that in their next incarnation human beings will be able to encounter the Guardian of the Threshold properly, or rather so that civilization as a whole will measure up to the Guardian of the Threshold.

Compare today's civilization with that of former times. In all former civilizations there were ideas, concepts, which were turned first of all towards the supersensible world, towards the gods, towards the world which engendered, which created, which brought forth. Then with those concepts, which belonged above all to the gods, it was possible to look down onto the earthly world in order to understand it with concepts and ideas which were worthy of the gods. And if souls then approached the Guardian of the Threshold with these ideas which had been formed in a manner that was worthy of the gods and that had a value for the gods, then the Guardian said: You may pass, for you are bringing with you into the supersensible world something that is directed towards this supersensible world even during the time of your life on earth in a physical body; therefore when you return to the physical, sense-perceptible world sufficient strength will remain to prevent you from becoming paralysed through having seen the supersensible world. Nowadays human beings elaborate concepts and ideas which, in accordance with the genius of the times, they want to apply solely to the physical, sense-perceptible world. These concepts and ideas deal above all with anything that can be weighed and measured, but they are not at all concerned with the gods. They are not worthy of the gods and they are of no value to the gods. That is why the souls who have fallen entirely under the spell of the materialism of these ideas which are unworthy of the gods and valueless for the gods are met, when they cross the threshold in sleep, by the thundering voice of the Guardian of the Threshold: Do not step across the threshold! You have misused your ideas for the sense-perceptible world; therefore you must remain with them in the sense-perceptible world; if you do not want to become paralysed in your soul, you cannot enter with them into the world of the gods.

Such things have to be said, not because it is necessary to brood upon them but so that heart and mind and soul may become filled to the brim with them. Then we may come into the mood that will be the right mood to bear away from this solemn Christmas Conference of the Anthroposophical Society. The most important thing of all is the mood of soul we bear away with us, a mood of soul for the spiritual world that gives us the certainty: In Dornach a central point for spiritual knowledge will be created.

That is why it was so good to hear Dr Zeylmans speak this morning about a field which is to be cultivated here in Dornach, the field of medicine, and to hear him say that it is no longer possible to build bridges from ordinary science to what is to be founded here in Dornach. If we have the ambition to make what grows in the soil of our own medical research into something that can stand the scrutiny of present-day clinical requirements, then we shall never achieve any definite goal in the things that really make up our task, for then other people will simply say: Well, yes, here is a new method; we too have initiated new methods once in a while.

The important thing is that a branch of practical life, such as medicine, should be taken up into anthroposophical life. I think I understood rightly this morning that this is what Dr Zeylmans longs for. Did he not say in connection with this goal that someone who today becomes a doctor longs for impulses from a new corner of the universe. Let me tell you that in the field of medicine the work here in Dornach is to be carried on just as has that in a number of other fields of anthroposophical work which have remained within the bosom of Anthroposophy. With Dr Wegman as my helper, work is already in train on a system of medicine based entirely on Anthroposophy, a system which is needed by mankind and which will be presented to mankind quite soon. Equally it is my purpose to bring about the closest ties between the Goetheanum and the Clinic in Arlesheim which is working so beneficially. In the very near future such ties are to be brought about so that all that is flourishing there may be truly oriented towards Anthroposophy, which is indeed the intention of Dr Wegman.

In what he said, Dr Zeylmans was indicating with reference to one particular field what the Vorstand in Dornach will make its task in all the fields of anthroposophical work. Thus in future the situation will be clear. No one will say: Let us first show people eurythmy; if they hear nothing about Anthroposophy, then they will like eurythmy; and then, having taken a liking to eurythmy, if they hear that Anthroposophy stands as the foundation for eurythmy, they will take a liking to Anthroposophy as well. No one will say: First we must show people how the medicines work in practice so that they see that they are proper medicines, and will buy them; then, if they later hear that Anthroposophy is behind the medicines, they will also approach Anthroposophy.

We must have the courage to regard such a method as dishonest. Not until we have the courage to regard such a method as dishonest, not until we inwardly detest such a method will Anthroposophy find its way through the world. So in future here in Dornach we shall fight for the truth, not fanatically but simply in an honest, straightforward love of the truth. Perhaps this will enable us to make good some of what has so sinfully been made bad in recent years.

With thoughts which are not easy but which are grave we must depart from this Conference that has led to the founding of the General Anthroposophical Society. But I do not think that it will be necessary for anybody to go away with pessimism from what has taken place here this Christmas. Every day we have had to walk past the sad ruins of the Goetheanum. But as we have walked up this hill, past these ruins, I think that in every soul there has also been the content of what has been discussed here and what has quite evidently been understood by our friends in their hearts. From all this the thought has emerged: It will be possible for spiritual flames of fire to arise, as a true spiritual life for the blessing of mankind in the future, from the Goetheanum which is being built anew. They shall arise out of our hard work and out of our devotion. The more we go from here with the courage to carry on the affairs of Anthroposophy, the better have we heard the breath of the spirit wafting filled with hope through our gathering. For the scene which I have described to you and which can be seen so frequently, that scene of present-day human beings, the products of a decadent civilization and education, approaching the Guardian of the Threshold in a state of sleep, is actually not one which is found amongst the circle of sensitive anthroposophists. Here on the whole the circumstance is such that only a warning, one particular exhortation, resounds: In hearing the voice from the land of the spirit you must develop the strong courage to bear witness to this voice, for you have begun to awaken; courage will keep you awake; lack of courage alone could lead you to fall asleep.

The exhortation to be awake through courage is the other variation, the variation for anthroposophists in the life of present-day civilization. Those who are not anthroposophists hear: You must remain outside the land of the spirit, you have misused ideas for merely earthly objects, you have not gathered ideas which have value for the gods and which are worthy of the gods; you would be paralysed on your return to the physical, sense-perceptible world. But those souls who are the souls of anthroposophists hear: Your remaining test is to be that of your courage to bear witness to that voice which you are capable of hearing because of the inclination of your soul, because of the inclination of your heart.

My dear friends, yesterday was the anniversary of the day on which we saw the tongues of flame devouring our old Goetheanum. Today we may hope — since a year ago we did not allow even the flames to distract us from continuing with our work — today we may hope that when the physical Goetheanum stands here once more we shall have worked in such a way that the physical Goetheanum is only the external symbol for our spiritual Goetheanum which we want to take with us as an idea as we now go out into the world.

We have here laid the Foundation Stone. On this Foundation Stone shall be erected the building whose individual stones will be the work achieved in all our groups by the individuals outside in the wide world. Let us now look in spirit at this work and become conscious of the responsibility about which I have spoken today, of our responsibility towards the human being who stands before the Guardian of the Threshold and has to be refused entry into the spiritual world.

Certainly it should never occur to us to feel anything but the deepest pain and the deepest sorrow about what happened to us a year ago. But let us not forget that everything in the world that has any stature has been born out of pain. So let us transform our pain so that out of it may arise a strong and shining Anthroposophical Society by dint, my dear friends, of your work.

For this purpose we have immersed ourselves in those words with which I began, in those words with which I wish to close this Christmas Conference, this Christmas Conference which is to be for us a festival of consecration not merely for the beginning of a new year but for the beginning of a new turning point of time to which we want to devote ourselves in enthusiastic cultivation of the life of spirit:

Soul of Man!
Thou livest in the limbs
Which bear thee through the world of space
In the spirit's ocean-being.
Practise spirit-recalling
In depths of soul,
Where in the wielding will
Of world-creating
Thine own I
Comes to being
Within God's I.
And thou wilt truly live
In the World-Being of Man.

For the Father-Spirit of the heights holds sway
In depths of worlds begetting being.
Seraphim, Cherubim, Thrones!
Let there ring out from the heights
What in the depths is echoed
Speaking:
Ex Deo nascimur.
The spirits of the elements hear it
In East, West, North, South,
May human beings hear it.

Soul of Man!
Thou livest in the beat of heart and lung
Which leads thee through the rhythm of time
Into the realm of thine own soul's feeling.
Practise spirit-awareness
In balance of the soul,
Where the surging deeds
Of the world's becoming
Thine own I
Unite
With the World-I.
And thou wilt truly feel
In the Soul-Weaving of Man.

For the Christ-Will in the encircling round holds sway
In the rhythms of the worlds, bestowing grace on the soul.
Kyriotetes, Dynamis, Exusiai!
Let there be fired from the East
What through the West is formed
Speaking:
In Christo morimur.
The spirits of the elements hear it
In East, West, North, South,
May human beings hear it.

Soul of Man!
Thou livest in the resting head
Which from the grounds of eternity
Opens to thee the world-thoughts.
Practise spirit-beholding
In stillness of thought,
Where the eternal aims of Gods
World-Being's Light
On thine own I
Bestow
For thy free willing.
And thou wilt truly think
In the Spirit-Foundations of Man.

For the world-thoughts of the Spirit hold sway
In the being of worlds, craving for light.
Archai, Archangeloi, Angeloi!
Let there be prayed from the depths
What in the heights will be granted
Speaking:
Per Spiritum Sanctum reviviscimus.*

At the turning of the time
The Spirit-Light of the world
Entered the stream of earthly being.
Darkness of night
Had held its sway,
Day-radiant light
Streamed into souls of men:
Light that gives warmth
To simple shepherds' hearts,
Light that enlightens
The wise heads of kings.

Light Divine
Christ-Sun
Warm thou our hearts,
Enlighten thou our heads,
That good may become
What we from our hearts would found
What we from our heads would direct
In conscious
Willing.

And so, my dear friends,** bear out with you into the world your warm hearts in whose soil you have laid the Foundation

*According to the shorthand report, the final words of the verse were not spoken on this occasion.

**In the following sentences, as in the gathering on 25 December 1923 at which the Foundation Stone was laid in members' hearts, Rudolf Steiner once again changed from the formal mode of address to the more intimate 'Du'. (Tr.)

Stone for the Anthroposophical Society, bear out with you your warm hearts in order to do work in the world that is strong in healing. Help will come to you because your heads will be enlightened by what you all now want to be able to direct in conscious willing. Let us today make this resolve with all our strength. And we shall see that if we show ourselves to be worthy, then a good star will shine over that which is willed from here. My dear friends, follow this good star. We shall see whither the gods shall lead us through the light of this star.

Light Divine
Christ-Sun,
Warm thou
Our hearts,
Enlighten thou
Our heads!

On Behalf of the Members

HERR WERBECK: Dear and greatly respected Dr Steiner! Dear friends! There is no other way for this Conference, so immensely meaningful for our Society and our Movement, to end except in an outpouring of deeply moved gratitude to the one whose work of love on the earth has brought us all together here. But my dear friends, what can words express! Was not perhaps all that a word can do shown at the beginning of this Conference by our respected friend Albert Steffen when, indicating that gratitude cannot be expressed in words, he said: Our gratitude is inexpressible. And yet on the wings of these words he did express everything our human hearts can give. Dear friends! Words, addresses, resolutions and all the rest are, measured against our Conference, nothing but outdated, cheap requisites of the cultural life that is collapsing all around us. And no one knows the background to these cheap requisites better than the one who has spoken to us this evening, moving us in the depths of our being. What is or rather can become honest gratitude, this virtue of great profundity, we shall still have to practise with the help of the one who spoke to us today. He alone has shown us through his spiritual work what gratitude really is. If we understand him aright, then we know that for us anthroposophists the hour has come when we must set the deed of gratitude in the place of the word of gratitude. We must requite his great, his immeasurably great deed of love with whatever deed of gratitude our puny strength can muster. For to him who spoke to us this evening we owe nothing less than our own spiritual felicity. And we know that the worth it bears will be eternal. It pertains not only to the few years we may still have to breathe on this physical earth; the felicity he has bestowed on us will stretch ahead to our future incarnations too. We know that this has been a turning point for our further destiny. What we are permitted to experience through his deed of love is incalculably significant. But we know that the felicity brought by this love cannot be measured with the yardstick known to us from times preceding Anthroposophy, for it will be paired with severe pain, with fateful destinies. But we also know that it is nevertheless a felicity that will lead us to salvation. And when our knowledge is truly tempered with feeling, then we know that words of gratitude are meaningless in face of this fact and that our only answer to what we have received from here can be in deeds of gratitude. And we know, however weak our forces, that our deeds of gratitude can flow into his great deeds. And therefore we also know that they can flow into the plan for salvation that is given to mankind today. For just as the great deeds are devoted to human beings, so may also the small deeds be devoted to human beings. Over this mighty life's work stands the heading: Let everything be for the good of human beings. O my dear friends, we know that something superhuman, something divine is working in him! But when we answer with deeds directed towards human beings we know that our deeds of gratitude will be felt at a human level. Yesterday he expressed it with the mighty fire of his great heart: Faithfulness and yet more faithfulness. This is something human directed towards something human. And so my dear friends, please stand once more and let us say in our heart as we depart from this holy place: You great and pure brother of mankind, out of our forces that are so very weak we want to thank you; we want to thank you through our deeds, through overcoming what has to be overcome in the service of your holy mission for mankind. We beg you: Be with us with the heavenly strength of your fatherly blessing!

DR STEINER: My dear friends! I could not have said many of the things I have had to say during this Conference in the form in which I said them, and similarly I could not accept the kind words of our dear friend Werbeck, if I were to relate all this to a single weak individual. For actually in our circles these things should not be related to a mere individual. Yet, my dear friends, I know that I have been permitted to say what has here been said, for it was said in full responsibility looking up to the Spirit who is there and who should be and will be the Spirit of the Goetheanum. In that Spirit's name I have permitted myself over the last few days to say a great many things which ought not to have been put so forcefully had they not been expressed while looking up to the Spirit of the Goetheanum, to the good Spirit of the Goetheanum. So allow me, please, to accept these thanks in the name of the Spirit of the Goetheanum for whom we want to work and strive and labour in the world.

All that remains is to ask that the practising doctors come to the Glass House tomorrow morning not at half past eight but at ten o'clock.

I also have a message to read to you: 'Out of our strong sharing in the experience of the Christmas Foundation Conference in Dornach we greet the President of the Anthroposophical Society. We thank him and his colleagues in the Vorstand for taking on the leadership and we also thank him for the Statutes. From the members of the Anthroposophical Society in Cologne who are meeting together at the close of the year.'

This is all I have to say. Tomorrow evening at 7 o'clock there will be a eurythmy performance for those friends who are still here.

PART THREE

CONCLUSION & APPENDICES

Conclusion

by Marie Steiner to the First German Edition of 1944

THE WORK that now began, without the interruption of even a single day, was at first devoted to medical knowledge; its scientific aspect had to be filled full of genuine spiritual forces; the esoteric work for which the younger doctors were so intensely striving had to be deepened, so that the loving will and the healing will that requires so much selflessness in the practice of caring for the sick could be unfolded.

On 2 January 1924 the third of the lectures to doctors was given.[81] And also on 2 January the course of eight lectures[82] to younger doctors and medical students began; it continued till 9 January.

The evening lectures brought contemplations of the destinies of inner spiritual life between the ninth and the end of the twelfth century. *Rosicrucianism and Modern Initiation* is the title of the cycle running from 4 to 13 January.[83] In the final lecture we are led from the principle of Rosicrucian initiation up to the mystery of modern initiation and the beginning of the Age of Michael. A lecture given to members on 18 January[84] is of particular importance. It gives a concise account of the coming into being of the Anthroposophical Society, from its beginnings, through the war years and right up to the completion of the building in Dornach. In opposition to the institutions being founded chiefly in Stuttgart, and to the work of scientists who join the Society in considerable numbers, there arises the will to destroy it held by a well-organized coalition of opponents. The gauntlet is thrown down when the Goetheanum is burnt to the ground, and finally we come, in view of the newly created world situation to the new founding of the Society as the General Anthroposophical Society.

The question now demanding an answer of us is: How can Anthroposophy be represented before the world? That lecture of 18 January culminates in this question. It also gives us a greater understanding of the coming inauguration of the Classes. And in order to provide a firm basis for the spiritual schooling to be striven for, nine lectures give new aspects of a deeper penetration into the nature of Anthroposophy, made possible only by the work of many years, under the modest title of *Anthroposophy — an Introduction.*[85]

At the same time in *Das Goetheanum* began the series of what came to be called Dr Steiner's *Letters to Members.* In these he endeavoured to awaken and strengthen people's sense of responsibility for the forming of the life of the Society and of what went on in the different branches. They have recently been republished in the little book *Life, Nature and Cultivation of Anthroposophy.*[86] From this foundation Dr Steiner goes on to what he describes as the special fields of the different Sections at the Goetheanum. In the first few essays, under the title 'The School of Spiritual Science', he turns first to the promotion of the medical work with which he was at that time particularly concerned. Then he goes on to the tasks of the young people who search with such yearning for a spiritual view of the world. The perennial conflict between the generations, particularly strong at the time, is thoroughly examined. Youthful impetuosity, now emerging to the full rather exuberantly and immaturely amid the strife within the Society, is given an orderly field of work in the newly to be founded Section 'for the Spiritual Striving of Youth'. There follow other brief discussions.

Since a new edition of these essays has been long awaited, this seemed the appropriate moment to bring it out as a continuation of the proceedings of the Christmas Foundation Conference. So the next private publication under the title of *The Constitution of the School of Spiritual Science*[87] will contain in the main those essays as well as Dr Steiner's lectures of 18 and 30 January and an address given on 3 February. They treat of questions of dividing up the School into Sections and of the special significance of belonging to the Class.

Rudolf Steiner's Words of Welcome to the Social Gathering

1 JANUARY, 4.30 IN THE AFTERNOON

These words of welcome were taken down in shorthand by Helene Finckh. The gaps at the beginning arose because, as the greeting had not been announced, it took her by surprise.

. . . on the occasion of this painful anniversary . . . at such a crowded gathering I imagine that out of this grave mood the minds and souls of our anthroposophical friends must find one another in personal conversation. We need it, my dear friends. There will always be a need in our Society for human being truly to find human being, for heart to find heart, and for soul to find soul. But we need it particularly here where we have to gather in this makeshift room while directly next door stand the remains which so painfully remind us of what we endeavoured to have as an external sign for our sacred cause. It seems to me that each one of us must feel the urge this afternoon to find an opportunity in many directions to speak his or her mind about the pain and the sorrow, but also, in contrast, to fire the development and unfolding of the hope, courage and strength that we shall need for the future. Though spoken out of heartfelt sorrow, may these words, my dear friends, serve as a starting point for many and varied fruitful exchanges amongst us as anthroposophical friends this afternoon. May it be so!

Notes on the Verses

NOTES ON THE VERSES IN THE 1985 GERMAN EDITION

In this [German] Edition the verses are given as Rudolf Steiner spoke them during the Christmas Conference of 1923, as shown by the complete and reliable record in shorthand made by Helene Finckh. Previous editions [in German] contained variations in some of the verses, especially in the rendering of 25 December. This is explained as follows:

Rudolf Steiner gave the verses in two versions, both of which are recorded in his own handwriting (see Facsimiles 1 and 4 in the Supplement). The first version was used during the Conference. The second version was made for the printed record in the report 'Die Bildung der Allgemeinen Anthroposophischen Gesellschaft durch die Weihnachtstagung 1923' (The Formation of the General Anthroposophical Society through the Christmas Conference of 1923) in the first number of *Was in der Anthroposophischen Gesellschaft vorgeht. Nachrichten für deren Mitglieder* (What is Happening in the Anthroposophical Society. News for Members) of 13 January 1924. In this second version there are certain divergences from the text as spoken during the Conference. The most important of these are that the hierarchies are not named but approached under a general designation, and that the Rosicrucian motto is given in German and not in Latin.

The reason which moved Rudolf Steiner to make this alteration was given on a number of occasions by Marie Steiner, and recorded by one of her colleagues, Günther Schubert, as follows: 'She spoke repeatedly about her memory of the great difficulty Rudolf Steiner experienced in reaching the decision to publish the verses of the 1923 laying of the Foundation Stone. In the end he toned down the direct approach to the hierarchies by making the salutation more abstract. He wanted this toned-down version to be the one used exclusively within members' circles too, for he said that there was a law attached to esoteric mantrams of such a cultic nature: The force with which they return equal to that with which they are sent forth, and it is therefore necessary to ask oneself whether one will be strong enough to endure this.'

Marie Steiner originally wanted to take this into account when she published this record of the Christmas Foundation Meeting. However, it was only possible in respect of the words spoken on 25 December, for on 29 December the call to the hierarchies by name was included in Rudolf Steiner's subsequent discussion of the 'rhythms'. The relevant lines were not spoken on the other days.

In the present [German] edition the verses, including that of 25 December, are given as they were spoken and recorded in the shorthand report.

NOTE ON ELEMENTAL AND ELEMENTARY BEINGS

by Richard Seddon

From the 1985 Edition of the German text (GA 260) we can see that the manuscript used by Rudolf Steiner at the Foundation address on 25 December 1923 contained the words 'Das hören die Element*en*geister' (elemental spirits). During the address he spoke this in the first two verses, but in speaking the third verse he said 'Das hören die Element*ar*geister' (elementary spirits). The latter formulation was both spoken and written (on the blackboard) on 31 December, and spoken again (twice only) in the concluding address on 1 January. In the less intimate manuscript for printing we find simply 'Das hören die Geister'. What is at issue here?

In the second lecture on 12 April 1909 in *Spiritual Hierarchies*,[88] Rudolf Steiner describes four groups of elementary beings (Elementarwesen): the gnomes, undines, sylphs and salamanders, the 'beings of the elements', whose redemption depends on man's mode of perception; the beings responsible for the rotation of the earth (i.e. from east to west), dependent on man's willing; the beings responsible for the waxing and waning of the moon, dependent on man's feeling; and the beings responsible for summer and winter (the sun's apparent movement between north and south), dependent for their redemption on man's mode of thinking. The last three groups were referred to on 4 April 1912[89] as the Spirits of Rotation of Time, offspring of the First Hierarchy, who form the astral body of the earth; whereas the first group form the earth's etheric body. He had previously remarked on 16 May 1908[90] that spirit is just what the 'very useful' beings of this group do not possess.

One can only surmise that during his preparation Rudolf Steiner had chiefly but not only in mind the world of the elements (in which the etheric Christ first manifests); but that during the course of the Foundation address itself he felt the need to widen the formulation towards those elementary spirits who govern the relationships between sun and earth in east and west, north and south, and are related to man's willing, feeling and thinking rather than his percepts. It is in this interplay between sun and earth that live those 'offsprings of powers of sun' who form the garment of Michael and prepare the way for Christ, having thus such a direct connection with the Christmas Foundation.

The Printed Version of the Verses in German

(Note: Facsimiles of both Rudolf Steiner's handwritten versions, this one, which he prepared for the printer, and the earlier one which he had with him when he spoke each day during the Conference, will be found in the Plates.)

Menschenseele!
Du lebest in den Gliedern,
Die dich durch die Raumeswelt
In das Geistesmeereswesen tragen:
Übe *Geist-Erinnern*
In Seelentiefen,
Wo in waltendem
Weltenschöpfer-Sein
Das eigne Ich
Im Gottes-Ich
Erweset;
Und du wirst wahrhaft *leben*
Im Menschen-Welten-Wesen.

Denn es waltet der Vater-Geist der Höhen
In den Weltentiefen Sein-erzeugend:
Ihr Kräfte-Geister
Lasset aus den Höhen erklingen,
Was in den Tiefen das Echo findet;
Dieses spricht:
Aus dem Göttlichen weset die Menschheit.
Das hören die Geister in Ost, West, Nord, Süd:
Menschen mögen es hören.

Menschenseele!
Du lebest in dem Herzens-Lungen-Schlage,
Der dich durch den Zeitenrhythmus
In's eigne Seelenwesensfühlen leitet:
Übe *Geist-Besinnen*
Im Seelengleichgewichte,
Wo die wogenden
Welten-Werde-Taten
Das eigne Ich
Dem Welten-Ich
Vereinen;
Und du wirst wahrhaft *fühlen*
Im Menschen-Seelen-Wirken.

Denn es waltet der Christus-Wille im Umkreis
In den Weltenrhythmen Seelen-begnadend;
Ihr Lichtes-Geister
Lasset vom Osten befeuern,
Was durch den Westen sich formet;
Dieses spricht:
In dem Christus wird Leben der Tod.
Das hören die Geister in Ost, West, Nord, Süd:
Menschen mögen es hören.

Menschenseele!
Du lebest im ruhenden Haupte,
Das dir aus Ewigkeitsgründen
Die Weltgedanken erschliesset:
Übe *Geist-Erschauen*
In Gedanken-Ruhe,
Wo die ew'gen Götterziele
Welten-Wesens-Licht
Dem eignen Ich
Zu freiem Wollen
Schenken;
Und du wirst wahrhaft *denken*
In Menschen-Geistes-Gründen.

Denn es walten des Geistes-Weltgedanken
Im Weltenwesen Licht-erflehend:
Ihr Seelen-Geister
Lasset aus den Tiefen erbitten,
Was in den Höhen erhöret wird:
Dieses spricht:
In des Geistes Weltgedanken erwachet die Seele.
Das hören die Geister in Ost, West, Nord, Süd:
Menschen mögen es hören.

In der Zeiten Wende
Trat das Welten-Geistes-Licht
In den irdischen Wesensstrom;
Nacht-Dunkel
Hatte ausgewaltet;
Taghelles Licht
Erstrahlte in Menschenseelen;
Licht,
Das erwärmet
Die armen Hirtenherzen;
Licht,
Das erleuchtet
Die weisen Königshäupter.

Göttliches Licht,
Christus-Sonne
Erwärme
Unsere Herzen;
Erleuchte
Unsere Häupter;
Dass gut werde,
Was wir
Aus Herzen gründen,
Was wir
Aus Häuptern führen
Wollen.

Three English Versions of the Verses

Alternative Translation of the Printed Version by George Adams (1927)

Soul of Man!
Thou livest in the limbs
Which bear thee through the world of Space
Into the ocean-being of the Spirit.
Practise *Spirit-recollection*
In depths of soul,
Where in the strength sublime
Of world-creative life
Thine own I grows to full being
In the I of God.
Then in the being of the World of Man
Thy *Life* will be true.

For the Father-Spirit of the Heights
Reigns in the depths of the World, begetting life.
Spirits of Strength!
May there ring forth from the Heights
The call that is re-echoed in the Depths,
Saying:
From the Divine springeth Mankind.
Spirit-beings hear it in East and West and North and South:
May human beings hear it!

Soul of Man!
Thou livest in the beat of heart and lung
Which guides thee through the rhythm of the Ages
Into the feeling of thine own Soul-being.
Practise *Spirit-meditation*
In the balance of the soul,
Where the surging deeds
Of cosmic evolution
Unite thine own I
With the I of the World.
Then in the working of the Soul of Man
Thy *Feeling* will be true.

For the Christ-Will in this horizon's Round
Reigns in the rhythms of the World, blessing the soul.
Spirits of Light!
May there be kindled from the East
The flame that is moulded by the West,
Saying:
In Christ Death becomes Life.
Spirit-beings hear it in East and West and North and South:
May human beings hear it!

Soul of Man!
Thou livest in the resting head
Which from the well-springs of Eternity
Unlocks for thee the Thoughts of the World.
Practise *Spirit-penetration*
In restfulness of thought,
Where the eternal aims of God
Grant light of cosmic being
To thine own I-
For free and active Will.
Then in the spiritual founts of Man
Thy *Thought* will be true.

For the Cosmic Thoughts of the Spirit
Reign in the being of the World, praying for light.
Spirits of Soul!
May there ascend from the Depths
The prayer that is heard in the Heights,
Saying:
In the cosmic Spirit-Thoughts the Soul awakes.
Spirit-beings hear it in East and West and North and South:
May human beings hear it!

At the turning-point of time,
The Spirit-Light of the World
Entered the stream of Earthly Evolution.
Darkness of Night
Had held its sway;
Day-radiant Light
Poured into the souls of men:
Light that gave warmth
To simple shepherds' hearts,
Light that enlightened
The wise heads of kings.

O Light Divine!
O Sun of Christ!
Warm Thou our hearts,
Enlighten Thou our heads,
That good may become
What from our hearts we would found
And from our heads direct
With single purpose.

Alternative Translation of the Printed Version
by Arvia MacKaye Ege

Soul of Man!
Thou livest in the limbs,
Which bear thee through the world of space
Into the ocean of spirit being:
Practise *spirit-recalling*
In depths of soul,
Where in empowering
World-Creator-Being
Thine inmost I
In God's own I
Takes being,
And thou shalt truly *live*
In human world-all being.

For the Father-Spirit of the heights reigns
In the depths of the world, begetting being;
Ye Spirits of Strength,
Let out of the heights ring forth
What in the depths finds its echo,
Speaking thus:
Out of the Godhead is created mankind.

This is heard by the Spirits in East, West, North, South;
May human beings hear it!

Soul of Man!
Thou livest in the pulse of heart and lung,
Which leadeth thee through the rhythm of time
Into the feeling of thine own soul being:
Practise *spirit-communing*
In the soul's fine balance
Where the on-surging,
World-Evolving Deeds
Thine inmost I
With the World's own I
Unite,
And thou shalt truly *feel*
In human soul inner-working.

For the Christ-Will reigns in the spheres encircling us
In the rhythms of the world, shedding grace upon souls;
Ye Spirits of Light,
Let from the East be enkindled
What through the West takes on form.
Speaking thus:
In Christ death becomes life.

This is heard by the Spirits in East, West, North, South;
May human beings hear it!

Soul of Man!
Thou livest in the quiet of the head
Which from out eternal foundations
Lays open before thee the world-all thoughts:
Practise *spirit-beholding*
In thought, stilled through,
Where the eternal aims of the gods
Cosmic-Being's-Light
On thine inmost I
For thy free willing,
Are shedding,
And thou shalt truly *think*
In human spirit foundations.

For the Spirit's World-All Thoughts reign
In the being of the world, light-beseeching.
Ye Spirits of Soul,
Let out of the deeps be entreated
What in the heights may be heard,
Speaking thus:
In the Spirit's World-All Thoughts the soul awakens.

This is heard by the Spirits in East, West, North, South;
May human beings hear it!

At the turn of time
Cosmic-Spirit-Light descended
Into earthly stream of being;
Darkling night
Had run its course;
Day-clear light
Streamed within human souls;
Light
That enwarms
The humble shepherds' hearts;
Light
That enlightens
The wise heads of kings.

God-given light,
Christus-Sun,
Enwarm
For us our hearts,
Enlighten
For us our heads,
That good may be
What we
From our hearts do found,
What we
From our heads
Direct with single will.

Alternative Translation of the Printed Version
By Richard Seddon

Soul of Man!
You live within the limbs,
Which bear you through the world of Space
Into the ocean-being of the spirit:
Practise *spirit-remembering*
In depths of soul,
Where in the sovereign
World-Creator presence
One's own I
Within God's I
Gains Being;
And you shall truly *live*
In cosmic Being of Man.

For the Father-Spirit of the heights holds sway
In the depths of worlds begetting existence:
Ye Spirits of Power
Let from the heights ring out
What in the depths is echoed;
This resounds:
From the Divine mankind has Being.
This the spirits hear in east, west, north, south.
May men hear it.

Soul of Man!
You live within the beat of heart and lung,
Which leads you through the rhythms of Time
Into your own soul-nature's weaving feeling:
Practise *spirit-awareness*
In balance of the soul,
Where the on-surging
Deeds of world-becoming
One's own I
And I of world
Unite;
And you shall truly *feel*
In the soul-working of Man.

For the Will of Christ in all around holds sway
In the world rhythms bestowing grace on souls:
Ye Spirits of Light
Let from the east flame up
What through the west takes form;
This resounds:
In Christ death becomes life.
This the spirits hear in east, west, north, south.
May men hear it.

Soul of Man!
You live within the resting head,
Which from the grounds of eternity
Reveals the universal thoughts:
Practise *spirit-beholding*
In the calm of thought,
Where the eternal aims of Gods
World-Being's light
On one's own I
Bestow
For will in freedom;
And you shall truly *think*
In spirit-foundations of Man.

For the Spirit's cosmic thoughts hold sway
In world Being beseeching light:
Ye Spirits of Soul
Let from the depths be entreated
What in the heights finds hearing;
This resounds:
In the Spirit's cosmic thoughts the soul awakes.
This the spirits hear in east, west, north south;
May men hear it.

At the turning of the times
Cosmic Spirit Light descended
Into the earthly stream of Being;
Darkness of night
Had run its course;
Day-bright light
Shone forth in human souls;
Light
That warms through
The humble shepherds' hearts;
Light
That illumines
The wise heads of kings.

Godly Light,
Christ-Sun,
Warm through
Our hearts,
Illuminate
Our heads,
That may be good
What we
From hearts would found,
What we
Would from our heads
Guide in true-aimed willing.

Notes

The text in German of the lectures, addresses and contributions to discussions made by Rudolf Steiner is recorded in the shorthand report made by the trained stenographist Helene Finckh (1883-1960) and in some cases in her own transcriptions into longhand. The contributions of other participants in the discussions of the Foundation Meeting sessions were not taken down by Helene Finckh but by others. Helene Finckh then included them in her transcriptions into longhand. Contributions in the other discussions were taken down by her.

1 Facsimile of the Programme. The lectures given by Rudolf Steiner during the Christmas Foundation Conference are published in *World History in the Light of Anthroposophy*, Rudolf Steiner Press, London 1977, GA 233.

There is no record of the lectures given by other speakers during the Conference with the exception of Albert Steffen's own record of his lecture *Aus der Schicksalsgeschichte des Goetheanums* (History and Destiny of the Goetheanum) published in *Was in der Anthroposophischen Gesellschaft vorgeht. Nachrichten für deren Mitglieder*, Vol.1, 1924, Nos. 2 and 3.

On the Christmas plays performed during the Conference, see Rudolf Steiner *Weihnachtspiele aus altem Volkstum. Die Oberuferer Spiele* (Ancient Folk Plays for Christmas from Oberufer), Dornach 1981 and *Ansprachen zu den Weihnachtspielen aus altem Volkstum* (Talks on the Ancient Folk Plays), GA 274.

The talks introducing the three eurythmy performances which took place during the Conference are included together with the programmes in Rudolf Steiner *Eurythmie. Die Offenbarung der sprechenden Seele. Eine Fortbildung der Goetheschen Metamorphosenanschauung im Bereich der menschlichen Bewegung* (Eurythmy. Revelation of the Speaking Soul), GA 277.

2 See Marie Steiner von Sivers: *Rudolf Steiner und die Zivilisations-*

aufgaben der Anthroposophie. Ein Rückblick auf das Jahr 1923 (Rudolf Steiner and the Tasks of Anthroposophy for Civilization. A Review of the Year 1923), Dornach 1943. Planned as GA 259 within the Complete Works.

3 In 1921 and 1922, the largest German concert agency of the day, Hermann Wolff and Jules Sachs in Berlin, had organized a number of lecture tours for Rudolf Steiner.

4 In 1894 the 'Allgemeiner Deutscher Verband' (General German League), founded in 1891, was renamed 'Alldeutscher Verband' (Pan-German League). During World War I this organization advocated exaggeratedly nationalistic aims, and after the war it campaigned for the restitution of the monarchy.

5 Matthias Erzberger, 1875-1921. German parliamentarian and statesman, leader of the left wing of the Centre party and signatory of the Armistice of World War I. From 1919 to 1920 he was Vice-Chancellor and Finance Minister. Assassinated in 1921 by members of a nationalist organization.

6 Walther Rathenau, 1867-1922. German industrialist and politician. In 1921 appointed Minister of Reconstruction. In 1922 Minister of Foreign Affairs. Assassinated by nationalist fanatics in 1922.

7 Rudolf Steiner spoke in Munich on 15 May and in Elberfeld on 17 May 1922 on the theme of 'Anthroposophy and Spiritual Knowledge'. The Munich lecture has been published in *Blätter für Anthroposophie*, 1966, Nos 11 and 12. The Elberfeld lecture has not been published. On both occasions he had to leave the building by the back stairs and down side streets because of threats to his personal safety.

8 Major General Gerold von Gleich. In 1921 he published a denunciation of Rudolf Steiner *Rudolf Steiner als Prophet, Ein Mahnwort an das deutsche Volk* (Rudolf Steiner the Prophet. A Warning to the German Nation). Thereupon his son, Sigismund von Gleich, published a refutation *Wahrheit gegen Unwahrheit über Rudolf Steiner. Widerlegung der Hetzschrift des Generalmajors Gerold von Gleich* (Truth against Untruth. A Refutation of the Denunciation of Rudolf Steiner by Major General Gerold von Gleich). Published by *Der Kommende Tag*, Stuttgart, no date.

9 See Rudolf Steiner *Awakening to Community*, Anthroposophic Press, New York 1974. GA 257.

10 Johanna Mücke. See List of Names.

11 See *Correspondence and Documents 1901-1925. Rudolf Steiner and Marie Steiner von Sivers*, Rudolf Steiner Press, London 1988. GA 262.

12 See Rudolf Steiner *The Last Address*, Rudolf Steiner Press, London 1967. GA 238.

13 See Rudolf Steiner *Rosicrucianism and Modern Initiation*, Rudolf Steiner Press, London 1965. GA 233a.

14 See Rudolf Steiner *Anthroposophy — An Introduction*, Rudolf Steiner Press, London 1961. GA 234.

15 See Rudolf Steiner *Speech and Drama*, Anthroposophical Publishing Company, London 1960, GA 282; *Pastoral Medicine*, Anthroposophic Press, New York 1987, GA 318; *Kursus für die Priester der Christengemeinschaft über die Apokalypse des Johannes* (Lectures for the Priests of the Christian Community on the Apocalypse of John), Dornach GA 346 (not available); *Karmic Relationships, Volume 4*, Rudolf Steiner Press, London 1957, GA 238.

16 See Rudolf Steiner *Anthroposophical Leading Thoughts. Anthroposophy as a Path of Knowledge. The Michael Mystery*, Rudolf Steiner Press, London 1973. GA 26.

17 See Rudolf Steiner *The Course of my Life*, Anthroposophic Press, New York 1970. GA 28.

18 Since the destruction of the Goetheanum by fire, it had been necessary to fall back on the old carpentry workshop which had served as a hall for lectures and artistic performances from 1914 onwards.

19 See Rudolf Steiner *Mystery Knowledge and Mystery Centres*, Rudolf Steiner Press, London 1973. GA 232.

20 Reports of these meetings will be included in GA 259. See Note 2.

21 See Rudolf Steiner *Aufbaugedanken und Gesinnungsbildung*, Dornach 1942. To be included in the Complete Works in the series 'Zur Geschichte der anthroposophischen Bewegung und Gesellschaft' (The History of the Anthroposophical Movement and Society).

22 Report to be included in GA 259. See Note 2.

23 See Rudolf Steiner *Awakening to Community*, op cit.

24 See Marie Steiner's Foreword. In *Was in der Anthroposophischen Gesellschaft vorgeht* 1926, No.39, she remarked in a footnote: 'To avoid misunderstandings it should be said that the impression of a heap of rubble was gained entirely from the impossible tax burdens in Germany, the delays in customers' payments and the daily increase in the rate of monetary devaluation. Added to this was the sight of everything packed into a pile of crates. The company's intrinsic worth was such that under normal conditions it soon began to flourish once more.'

25 See Erich Zimmer *Rudolf Steiner als Architekt von Wohn- und Zweckbauten* (Rudolf Steiner. An Architect of Dwellings and other Buildings with Specific Purposes), Stuttgart 1971.

26 It had been necessary to enlarge the carpentry workshop in order to accommodate the influx of participants.

27 See Rudolf Steiner *Zur Geschichte und aus den Inhalten der ersten Abteilung der Esoterischen Schule 1904-1914* (On the History and from the Content of the Esoteric School 1904-1914). GA 264.

28 See the lecture given in Berlin on 3 February 1913 'Das Wesen der Anthroposophie' in *Schickalszeichen auf dem Entwicklungswege der Anthroposophischen Gesellschaft* to be included in the Complete Works in the series 'Zur Geschichte der anthroposophischen Bewegung und Gesellschaft'.

29 Rudolf Steiner's four Mystery Dramas were first performed during the years 1910 to 1913. See Rudolf Steiner *Four Mystery Plays*, Steiner Book Centre, Toronto, 1973.

30 Meeting of Delegates at the end of February 1923. See Note 23.

31 The three objects of the Theosophical Society are:

1. To form a nucleus of the universal brotherhood of humanity without distinction of race, creed, sex, caste or colour.

2. To encourage the comparative study of religion, philosophy and science.

3. To investigate unexplained laws of nature and the powers latent in man.

32 See Note 2.

33 See Rudolf Steiner's essay 'Lebensfragen der theosophischen Gesellschaft' (Existential Questions for the Theosophical Society) in *Luzifer-Gnosis. Gesammelte Aufsätze 1903-1908.* (Luzifer-Gnosis. Collected Essays 1903-1908). GA 34.

34 Rudolf Steiner had had the suggested Statutes printed and distributed to every participant. See Facsimile 2, Page VI – IX.

35 See Note 27.

36 This refers to criticism of Anthroposophy expressed by Hans Leisegang (1890-1951), lecturer at Leipzig University, in his book *Die Geheimwissenschaften* (The Occult Sciences), Stuttgart 1924.

37 See Rudolf Steiner/Ita Wegman *Fundamentals of Therapy. An Extension of the Art of Healing through Spiritual Knowledge,* Rudolf Steiner Press, London 1983. GA 27.

38 For the first time in the public lecture in Berlin on 15 March 1917 in Rudolf Steiner *Geist und Stoff, Leben und Tod* (Spirit and Matter, Life and Death). GA 66, and in the chapter 'Die physischen und die geistigen Abhängigkeiten der Menschenwesenheit' (Physical and Spiritual Dependencies of the Being of Man' in Rudolf Steiner *Von Seelenrätseln* (Of the Riddles of the Soul) GA 21.

39 Annie Besant, 1847-1933. From 1907, following the death of the Founder-President H. S. Olcott, President of the Theosophical Society.

40 Charles Webster Leadbeater, 1847-1934. Influential colleague of Annie Besant. Inspired the founding of the order 'Star of the East'.

41 Wilhelm Windelband, 1848-1915. Philosopher, 1882-1903 professor in Strasbourg.

42 See lectures in London on 2 and 3 September, Vienna on 2 October and The Hague on 15 and 16 November 1923 in Rudolf Steiner *Spiritual Science and the Art of Healing*, Anthroposophical Publishing Company, London 1950. GA 319.

43 See Rudolf Steiner *The Tension between East and West*, Hodder & Stoughton, London 1963. GA 83.

44 This designation for the extension built on to the carpentry workshop for the occasion of the Christmas Conference referred to 'the chilly draught which blew there permanently' (Ernst Lehrs *Gelebte Erwartung*, Stuttgart, 1979).

45 On the basis of a pencil drawing by Rudolf Steiner.

46 See Rudolf Steiner *Die Konstitution der Allgemeinen Anthroposophischen Gesellschaft und der Freien Hochschule für Geisteswissenschaft — Der Wiederaufbau des Goetheanum*. GA 260a. Different parts of this collection are available in English under the following titles: *Anthroposophical Leading Thoughts*, Rudolf Steiner Press, London 1973; *The Life, Nature and Cultivation of Anthroposophy*, Anthroposophical Society in Great Britain, London 1975; *The Constitution of the School of Spiritual Science*, Anthroposophical Society in Great Britain, London 1964.

47 On 8 December 1923. See Note 22.

48 See Note 46.

49 Rudolf Steiner *The Philosophy of Freedom*, Rudolf Steiner Press, London 1979. This fundamental work was first published in 1894.

50 Rudolf Steiner never gave a cycle of lectures in Bremen. The shorthand report definitely states 'Bremen', but this might have been a mishearing of 'Berlin'. In 1904 Rudolf Steiner did give a cycle of lectures in Berlin on German mysticism and its precursors. Three of these, on 'Platonische Mystik und Docta ignorantia' (Platonic Mysti-

cism and docta ignorantia) are included in Rudolf Steiner *Über Philosophie, Geschichte und Literatur. Darstellungen an der Arbeiterbildungsschule und der Freien Hochschule in Berlin 1901 to 1905.* (On Philosophy, History and Literature). GA 51. The references made at this point in the Meeting could be taken to refer to these lectures.

51 See Paragraph 1 of the Statutes.

52 In *Das Goetheanum* No.21 of 30 December 1923 on Rudolf Steiner's relationship to geometry. Now Chapter One of Rudolf Steiner *The Course of my Life*, op.cit.

53 Eduard von Hartmann, 1842-1906. *Philosophie des Unbewussten. Versuch einer Weltanschauung*, (Philosophy of the Unconscious), Berlin 1896. See also Rudolf Steiner *The Course of my Life*, op.cit. especially Chapter Nine.

54 See Rudolf Steiner *The Theory of Knowledge Implicit in Goethe's World Conception. Fundamental Outlines with Special Reference to Schiller*, Anthroposophic Press, New York 1940. GA 2.

55 See Rudolf Steiner's letters to Marie Steiner-von Sivers of 18 and 20 February 1911 in *Correspondence and Documents. Rudolf Steiner and Marie Steiner von Sivers*, op cit.

56 'Schulverein für freies Erziehungs- und Unterrichtswesen in der Schweiz', later 'Goetheanum-Schulverein', Dornach. Founded 1922. From 1924, after the Christmas Foundation Conference, under the directorship of Rudolf Steiner.

57 See Rudolf Steiner *Swiss Teachers' Course*, Report by Albert Steffen. English text available in typescript only. GA 306.

58 Meeting of delegates of the Swiss Anthroposophical Society on 8 December 1923. See Note 22.

59 See Note 60.

60 The international meeting of delegates in July 1923. See Note 22.

61 Andrew Carnegie, 1835-1919. American industrialist. Amassed

an enormous fortune the greater part of which he donated for scientific and social work.

62 See Rudolf Steiner *The Anthroposophic Movement. Its History and Life-Conditions in Relation to the Anthroposophical Society*, London 1933. GA 258.

63 Such reports are included in *Rudolf Steiner und die Zivilisationsaufgaben der Anthroposophie*. See Note 1. For the thirteen lectures given in Penmaenmawr see *The Evolution of Consciousness as Revealed through Initiation Knowledge*, Rudolf Steiner Press, London 1966. GA 227.

64 No further information is available.

65 See Rudolf Steiner *Physiologisch-Therapeutisches auf Grundlage der Geisteswissenschaft. Zur Therapie und Hygiene* (Physiology and Therapy based on Spiritual Science). GA 314.

66 See Rudolf Maier's article 'Über einen durch Anthroposophie gefundenen Zusammenhang zwischen Licht und Magnetismus' (On a Connection, Discovered through Anthroposophy, between Light and Magnetism) in *Gäa Sophia. Jahrbuch der naturwissenschaftlichen Sektion der Freien Hochschule für Geisteswissenschaft am Goetheanum*, Dornach 1926.

67 See Lilly Kolisko *Physikalischer Nachweis der Wirksamkeit kleinster Entitäten* (Physical Proof of the Working of Microorganisms), Stuttgart 1923.

68 During the international meeting of delegates in July 1923.

69 This refers to the articles *Das Goetheanum in seinen zehn Jahren* (The Goetheanum in the Ten Years of its Life) and *Goethe und Goetheanum* (Goethe and Goetheanum) written after the burning of the Goetheanum. They review the artistic intentions connected with the first Goetheanum, and look back on the establishment of anthroposophical work. See Rudolf Steiner *Der Goetheanumgedanke inmitten der Kulturkrisis der Gegenwart* (The Goetheanum Idea amid the Present Cultural Crisis). GA 36.

70 'House Duldeck' is situated to the south-west of the Goetheanum.

71 'Rudolf Steiner Halde', north-west wing.

72 See Rudolf Steiner *Die Entstehung und Entwickelung der Eurythmie* (The Appearance and Development of Eurythmy). GA 277a.

73 See Note 46.

74 Prof. Dr. med. h. c. Alfred Gysi. See List of Names.

75 Lecture of 31 December 1922 in Rudolf Steiner *Man and the World of Stars and the Spiritual Communion of Mankind*, Anthroposophic Press, New York 1963. GA 219.

76 In order to make his name known to posterity, the Ephesian Herostratos set fire to the Temple of Artemis in Ephesus in 356 BC.

77 Alexander the Great, 356-326 BC. From 336 King of Macedonia. Died in Babylon.

78 See Rudolf Steiner *Ways to a New Style in Architecture*, Anthroposophic Press, New York 1927. GA 286.

79 See Rudolf Steiner *World History in the Light of Anthroposophy*, op.cit.

80 See Note 3.

81 See Note 65.

82 Rudolf Steiner *Eight Lectures to Doctors*. English text available in typescript only.

83 See Note 13.

84 See Note 46.

85 See Note 14.

86 See Note 46.

87 See Note 46.

88 The second lecture on 12 April 1909 in Rudolf Steiner *The Spiritual Hierarchies. Their Reflection in the Physical World. Zodiac, Planets, Cosmos*, Anthroposophic Press, New York 1983. (GA 110)

89 The lecture of 4 April 1912 in Rudolf Steiner *Spiritual Beings in the Heavenly Bodies and in the Kingdoms of Nature*, Steiner Book Centre, Toronto 1981.

90 Lecture of 16 May 1908 in Rudolf Steiner, *The Influence of Spiritual Beings upon Man*, Anthroposophic Press, New York 1961. (GA 102)

Notes on the Facsimiles

FACSIMILES 1, 3, 5
Size of the sheets: 21 x 27.5 cm

FACSIMILE 2
Size of the sheet: 28 x 21.7 cm, folded 14 x 21.7 cm

FACSIMILE 4
Size of the sheets: approx. 100 x 150 cm
The originals have been preserved because black sheets of paper were attached to the blackboards. The dates were added later.

LOCATION OF THE ORIGINALS:
Facsimile 1 and Facsimile 4, Blackboard XI: in the Goethaneum, Dornach. All the others are held in the archives of the Rudolf Steiner Nachlassverwaltung *in Dornach.*

List of Names

WITH BIOGRAPHICAL NOTES

ABELS, JOAN (b. India – d. 1962 Heidenheim a. d. Brenz)
Eurythmist. Took part in the very first performance of eurythmy in 1913 in Munich, subsequently continuing the work in Dornach. After retiring from eurythmy, he took on the office work at the Canteen.

AEPPLI, WILLI (Accra 1894 – 1972 Basel)
Swiss teacher. Member of the Society from 1921. At the Christmas Foundation Conference he was the representative of the Swiss Anthroposophical Society. From 1927 to 1954 he taught at the Rudolf Steiner School in Basel, and in 1954 became an adviser to the Association of Waldorf Schools in Germany. Wrote books on education.

ALEXANDER THE GREAT
See Note 77.

BEMMELEN, DANIEL J. VAN (Indonesia 1899 – 1983)
Dutch member from 1921. In 1923 co-founder and teacher at the first Dutch Waldorf school, 'De Vrije School' at The Hague.

BESANT, ANNIE
See Note 39.

BRANDTNER, W.
Secretary to the Anthroposophical Society in Porto Alegre, Brazil, founded in 1920.

BÜCHENBACHER, DR HANS (Fürth 1887 – 1977 Arlesheim)
Lectured on the threefold social order. At the Christmas Foundation Conference he was the representative of the Free Anthroposophical Society in Germany. 1931-1935 President of the Anthroposophical

Society in Germany. Later leader of the Working Group for Philosophy and Psychology at the Goetheanum in Dornach.

BÜRGI-BANDI, LUCIE (Bern 1875 – 1949 Bern)
Member from 1907. On the Council of the Johannes branch in Bern. 1913-1925 on the Council of the *Bauverein*. In March 1925 appointed by Rudolf Steiner to join the administration group for the building of the Goetheanum. Founder member of the *Rudolf Steiner Nachlassverwaltung*.

CARNEGIE, ANDREW
See Note 61.

CESARO, DUKE GIOVANNI ANTONIO OF (Rome 1878 – 1940 Rome)
Son of Baroness de Renzis (see below). Member of various town councils in Sicily (Radical Party, later Social Democratic Party). Member of Parliament. 1922-24 Minister for Post and Telegraphy. Co-publisher of *Lo Spettatore*. Political writings. In 1926 he joined the anti-fascist National Alliance. At the Christmas Foundation Conference he was the representative of the Novalis group in Rome.

COLLISON, HARRY (London 1868 – 1945 London)
Lawyer, painter and writer. Member from 1910. Leader of the Myrdhin group in London. Authorized by Rudolf Steiner to translate his works into English. Founder of the Anthroposophical Publishing Company. From 1923 General Secretary of the English Anthroposophical Society.

CROSS, MARGARET FRANCES (Preston 1866 – 1962 Hemel Hempstead)
Owner and head of a private school, interested in Rudolf Steiner's work. The school subsequently became The New School, Kings Langley, Hertfordshire.

DONNER, UNO (Helsingfors 1872 – 1958 Arlesheim)
Engineer. Founded and ran textile factories, among others. Met Anthroposophy in London in 1913. 1923-1932, at Rudolf Steiner's suggestion, General Secretary of the Finnish Anthroposophical Society. Participated in the agricultural course given by Rudolf Steiner at Koberwitz, Breslau in 1924. From 1928 he endeavoured to run a large farm on bio-dynamic lines. A bequest in his will led to the founding of the Donner Institute for Religious History and Cultural Research at the University of Abo in Finland.

DRECHSLER, LUNA (b. Lemberg/Lvov – d. 1933 Poland, in her fifties)
Painter and sculptress. Active in political life (town council). Worked on the first Goetheanum. Initiated the founding of the Polish Anthroposophical Society and became its General Secretary.

DUNLOP, DANIEL NICOL (Kilmarnock 1868 – 1935 London)
Initially a member of the Theosophical Society. From 1918 a member of the Anthroposophical Society in England and leader of the Human Freedom group. Organiser of the summer schools in Penmaenmawr (1923) and Torquay (1924). Founder of the British Weleda Company. 1930-1935 General Secretary of the Anthroposophical Society in England.

DÜRLER, EDGAR (St Gallen 1895 – 1970 Arlesheim)
Businessman. Member of the Society from 1921. Worked for Futurum AG, Dornach, part of the time on the board of directors. Later member of the board of directors of Ilag AG, then Weleda AG, Arlesheim. Then for many years chairman of the board of directors.

EISELT, DR HANS (b. Prague – d. 1936 Prague)
Having met Anthroposophy early in life, he worked for it until his death. He was leader of the branch in Prague and also lectured and ran the administration of the national Anthroposophical Society. He took the shorthand notes when Rudolf Steiner lectured in Prague. At the Christmas Foundation Conference he was the representative of the council of the Society in Czechoslovakia.

ERZBERGER, MATTHIAS
See Note 4.

FERRERI, CHARLOTTE (d. 1924 in Milan)
Born in Honolulu as the daughter of an American missionary. Leader of the Leonardo da Vinci group in Milan. This group had resigned as a body from the Theosophical Society in 1913 and then joined the Anthroposophical Society. Later she was co-founder of a group in Honolulu. At the Christmas Foundation Conference she represented Honolulu.

FREUND, IDA (d. 1931 in Prague)
An active member from 1909/10 in Prague. Her public charitable work was honoured after her death by the establishment of an Ida Freund Foundation.

GEERING-CHRIST, RUDOLF (Basel 1871 – 1958)
Bookseller and publisher. Founder member of the German Section in 1902 and of the Paracelsus branch in Basel in 1906, of which he became the chairman in 1921. 1922/23 he was a member of the inner working group at the Goetheanum. From 1913-1925 he was a member of the council of the *Bauverein* and in March 1925 he was appointed by Rudolf Steiner to join the administration group for the building of the Goetheanum.

GEUTER, FRIEDRICH (Darmstadt 1894 – 1960 Ravenswood)
Met Anthroposophy through Herbert Hahn when both were working as interpreters at a prisoner of war camp for British and French prisoners. After a spell at *Der Kommende Tag*, he began his lifetime's curative work at the Sonnenhof under Ita Wegman. From 1929 onwards he lived and worked in England, founding two homes for mentally handicapped children.

GEYER, REVEREND JOHANNES (Hamburg 1882 – 1964 Stuttgart)
Heard Rudolf Steiner lecture for the first time when he was a student. Member from 1910. From 1912 pastor of the Protestant church. From 1919, at Rudolf Steiner's suggestion, a teacher at the Waldorf School in Stuttgart.

GLEICH, GENERAL GEROLD VON
See Note 7.

GNÄDIGER, FRANZ (d.1971)
Priest of the Christian Community. For a time secretary to Friedrich Rittelmeyer. At the time of the Christmas Foundation Meeting he lived in Zurich, from 1934 in Bern.

GOYERT, WILHELM RUDOLF (Witten a. d. Ruhr 1887 – 1954 Arlesheim)
Art dealer. Co-founder of the first Waldorf school in Cologne, named 'Neuwacht School' by Rudolf Steiner.

GROSHEINTZ, DR. MED. DENT. EMIL (Paris 1867 – 1946 Dornach)
Member from 1906 and co-founder of the Paracelsus branch in Basel. From 1908 to 1913 he was a member of the council of the German Section. In 1912 he placed a parcel of land he owned in Dornach at the disposal of Rudolf Steiner for the Goetheanum. From 1913 to 1915 he was deputy chairman of the *Bauverein*, from 1915 to 1924 chairman, and 1924/25 deputy chairman when Rudolf Steiner was chairman. In

March 1925 Rudolf Steiner appointed him chairman of the administration group for the building of the Goetheanum. In 1920 he was founder-member and president of the branch at the Goetheanum, which he remained until 1946. 1922/23 he was a member of the inner working group at the Goetheanum.

GROSHEINTZ, DR OSKAR (d. 1944 in Basel)
Member from 1907 and chairman of the Johannes branch founded in Bern on his initiative. Took part in the performance of the Mystery Dramas in Munich.

GYSI, PROFESSOR DR MED H. C. ALFRED (Aarau 1864 – 1957 Zurich)
Eminent researcher in the field of dentistry who did pioneering work on dental prosthetics. Lecturer and professor at the dental institute of the University of Zurich, of which he was a co-founder. In 1902 he was one of the three Swiss founder members of the German Section and chairman of the Zschokke branch in Zurich which he founded in 1908 and to which he gave house room until 1920. 'To his manner of working we owe the fact that Dr Steiner's most important Zurich lectures were scientific in character.' (Marie Steiner, *Erinnerungen I* (Memoires, I). In 1913, together with Dr Emil Grosheintz, Frau Marie Schief and Frau Marie Hirter-Weber, he was one of the four Swiss members to make the land on the Dornach hill available for the building of the Goetheanum. He was a member of the council of the *Bauverein* till 1920. At the beginning of the twenties Professor Gysi withdrew from the Anthroposophical Society.

HAAN, PIETER DE (Utrecht 1891 – 1968 Holland)
Member from 1912. Having been the intended General Secretary for Holland, he withdrew in favour of Zeylmans van Emmichoven when the latter was suggested by Rudolf Steiner. From 1964-66 manager of the *Philosophisch-Anthroposophischer Verlag* in Dornach.

HAHL, ERWIN (d.1958)
A native of Württemberg. Heard Rudolf Steiner lecture for the first time in 1919 in Stuttgart. From 1922 he worked in Yugoslavia, where he endeavoured to found a branch in Zagreb. At the Christmas Foundation Conference he was the representative of the work in Yugoslavia.

HARDT, DR MED HEINRICH (Stargard 1896 – 1981)
Met Anthroposophy in Rostock, where he was a student. Co-initiator

of the lectures Rudolf Steiner gave for young doctors in January and at Easter 1924 in Dornach. Later he was for many years the doctor at the Lauenstein home for the handicapped.

HART-NIBBRIG, FRAU J (b. Holland – 1957 Dornach in her late eighties)
Was a member of the Theosophical Society before 1913. From about 1924 she lived in Dornach. She was close to Marie Steiner.

HARTMANN, EDUARD VON
See Note 53.

HENSTRÖM, SIGRID
Member from 1911. From 1924 chairman of the branch in Stockholm. At the Christmas Foundation Meeting she was the representative of the Swedish Society.

HEROSTRATOS
See Note 76.

HOHLENBERG, JOHANNES (1881 – 1960 Kopenhagen)
Painter and writer. From 1923 General Secretary of the Danish Anthroposophical Society. From 1926 he was the joint publisher and from 1929 the publisher of the Scandinavian anthroposophical journal *Vidar* till it was closed down in 1940. From 1947 to 1954 he published the cultural and political journal *Øjeblikket* in Denmark.

HUGENTOBLER, DR JAKOB (d.1961)
Teacher. A member of the council of the Zschokke (later Paracelsus) group in Zurich and then of the Johannes branch in Bern.

HUSEMANN, GOTTFRIED (b.1900 – 1972 Arlesheim)
Co-founder and priest of the Christian Community.

IM OBERSTEG, DR ARMIN (b.1881 – 1969 Basel)
Eminent lawyer. Member from 1919. A helpful supporter of the Goetheanum. For many years president of the cafe and restaurant co-operative at the Goetheanum and legal adviser to Weleda AG.

INGERÖ, KARL (d.1972 in Oslo)
At the Christmas Foundation Conference he was the representative of

the Norwegian Anthroposophical Society. Rudolf Steiner and Marie Steiner were guests in his house on several occasions.

JONG, PROFESSOR DE
See Note 64.

KAISER, DR WILHELM (Péry 1895 – 1983 Dornach)
Astronomer. Met Rudolf Steiner in 1918. Worked with Dr Elisabeth Vreede in the Goetheanum archives for a while. Lectured extensively in Germany and Switzerland. Wrote many books.

KAUFMANN (LATER ADAMS), DR GEORGE (Maryampol 1894 – 1963 Birmingham)
Mathematician and physicist. Member from 1916. Acted as consecutive interpreter for English-speaking audiences for 110 lectures, conferences and conversations by and with Rudolf Steiner in England and Dornach. Translated several of Rudolf Steiner's works and wrote numerous books.

KELLER, KARL (Basel 1896 – 1979 Arlesheim)
Journalist and editor in Basel. Heard Rudolf Steiner lecturing for the first time in 1917. As a member of the staff of the Swiss news agency he was able to publicise an essay written by Rudolf Steiner in the autumn of 1924 on the rebuilding of the Goetheanum.

KELLERMÜLLER, JAKOB (Räterschen 1872 – 1947 Dornach)
Engaged by Rudolf Steiner as doorkeeper for the first Goetheanum, he performed this task until 1946.

KOLISKO, DR MED EUGEN (Vienna 1893 – 1939 London)
Member from 1914. From 1920 teacher and school doctor at the Waldorf School in Stuttgart. From 1923 to 1935 on the council of the German Anthroposophical Society. Then lived in England.

KOLISKO, LILLY (Vienna 1889 – 1976 Gloucester)
Collaborated with Rudolf Steiner at the biological research institute in Stuttgart, publishing works on the spleen and on microorganisms in 1922 and 1923.

KOSCHÜTZKY, RUDOLF VON (Upper Silesia 1866 – 1954 Stuttgart)
Member from about 1917. He was originally a farmer but worked as a war correspondent in the First World War. From 1922 priest of the

Christian Community. He participated in bringing about the agricultural course and then became a member of the management of the resulting research group of anthropsophical farmers.

KREBS, CHRISTIAN (d.1945)
A member in Sweden. Participated in the agricultural course given by Rudolf Steiner at Koberwitz, Breslau, in 1924.

KRKAVEC, DR OTOKAR
Member in Prague. At the Christmas Foundation Conference he was the representative of the council of the Society in Czechoslovakia.

KRÜGER, DR BRUNO (b.1887 – 1979 Stuttgart)
Public prosecutor in Berlin. From 1921 he worked with the federation for the threefold social order in Stuttgart, lecturing on this subject. After the failure of the threefold project he worked as a lawyer in Stuttgart.

LEADBEATER, CHARLES WEBSTER
See Note 40.

LEER, EMANUEL JOSEF VON (b. in Amersfoort – 1934 Baku)
Dutch wholesale merchant. Member from 1909. Giver of strong financial backing to the various institutions. 1922/23 president of the management committee of the International Laboratories and the Clinical and Therapeutic Institute AG in Arlesheim. In 1924 the first president of the first management committee of the Weleda AG, Arlesheim.

LEHRS, DR ERNST (Berlin 1894 – 1979 Eckwälden)
Scientist. Member of the Society from 1921. Teacher at the Waldorf School in Stuttgart. From 1923 a member of the committee of the Free Anthroposophical Society confirmed by Rudolf Steiner after the Christmas Foundation Conference, and thus an officer of the General Anthroposophical Society. Published scientific writings. From 1952 he taught at the seminar for curative education at Eckwälden.

LEINHAS, EMIL (Mannheim 1878 – 1967 Ascona)
Merchant. Member from 1909. In March 1920 co-founder, later managing director and finally liquidator of *Der Kommende Tag AG* in Stuttgart. From 1921 to 1923 in the central Vorstand of the Anthroposophical Society, from February 1923 a member of the council of the German Society in Stuttgart. Member of the *Rudolf Steiner Nachlassverwaltung*

from 1949. *Aus der Arbeit mit Rudolf Steiner. Sachliches und Persönliches* (Working with Rudolf Steiner), Basel 1950.

LEISEGANG, HANS
See Note 36.

LJUNGQUIST, ANNA (d.1935 in Dornach)
One of the early pioneers of anthroposophical work in Sweden. At the Christmas Foundation Conference she was the representative of the Swedish Anthroposophical Society.

MACKENZIE, PROFESSOR MILLICENT
Professor of education at University College, Cardiff, Wales from 1910. At her instigation, Rudolf Steiner gave a course of lectures for English teachers at the Goetheanum at Christmas 1920 and he was also invited to lecture at educational conferences in Stratford-on-Avon (Spring 1922) and in Oxford (August 1922). These public lectures in England led to the founding of the Educational Union under the chairmanship of Professor Mackenzie, the purpose of which was to gain an entry for Rudolf Steiner's educational ideas particularly in English and American organizations.

MAIER, DR RUDOLF (Schorndorf 1886 – 1943 Hüningen)
Member from about 1908/09. From 1920 to 1924 leader of the scientific research institute of *Der Kommende Tag AG* in Stuttgart.

MARYON, LOUISE EDITH (London 1872 – 1924 Dornach)
Sculptress working in Dornach from 1914. Collaborated with Rudolf Steiner in the field of the sculptural arts, especially on the wooden sculpture 'The Representative of Man between Lucifer and Ahriman'. On her initiative the coloured eurythmy figures came into being and also the three 'eurythmy houses' to provide living accommodation for those working at the Goetheanum. At the Christmas Foundation Conference she was chosen to be the Leader of the Section for the Sculptural Arts.

MAURER, PROFESSOR DR THEODOR (Dorlisheim 1873 – 1959 Strasbourg)
Writer and anthroposophical lecturer. At the Christmas Foundation Conference he was the representative for the Alsace.

MAYEN, DR MED WALTHER
He came from Breslau. Worked in connection with Anthroposophy in South America, including Porto Alegre in Brazil.

MERRY, ELEANOR (Durham 1873 – 1956 Frinton-on-Sea)
English writer and painter. Member from 1921. Together with D. N. Dunlop she organized the summer schools at Penmaenmawr (1923) and Torquay (1924).

MONGES, HENRY B. (1870 – 1954 New York)
Professor of architecture. Member from 1916. Participated actively in founding, shaping and maintaining the Anthroposophical Society in America. He was its first chairman, and from 1923 its General Secretary. He secured the publication rights for Rudolf Steiner in the USA, translated his works and founded a publishing company.

MORGENSTIERNE, ETHEL

MÜCKE, JOHANNA (Berlin 1864 – 1949 Dornach)
Belonged to the socialist trade union movement and was a member of the management of the workers' educational establishment where she met Rudolf Steiner during his time as a teacher there (1899-1904). Member from 1903. From 1908 until her retirement (1935) she was the business manager, first in Berlin and from 1924 in Dornach, of the *Philosophisch-Anthroposophischer Verlag* founded in 1908 by Marie Steiner for the publication of Rudolf Steiner's work. From the end of 1911 until 1913 she was on the council of the German Section and from 1921 to 1923 on the council of the German Anthroposophical Society. Her book *Erinnerungen an Rudolf Steiner und seine Wirksamkeit an der Arbeiter-Bildungsschule in Berlin 1899-1904* (Memories of Rudolf Steiner and his work at the Workers' Educational Establishment in Berlin 1899-1904) was published in Basel in 1955.

MUNTZ-TAXEIRA DEL MATTOS, FRAU (b.Holland – d. 1931 in Brussels)
At the Christmas Foundation Conference she was the representative of the Belgian Anthroposophical Society as its General Secretary. Translated works by Rudolf Steiner into French.

NEUSCHELLER-VAN DER PALS, LUCY (St Petersburg 1886 – 1962 Dornach)
Together with her husband she first heard Rudolf Steiner speak in 1908

in Berlin. Both thereupon became members. Later she took up eurythmy. With her husband she went to America in 1913 and there built up the eurythmy work and participated in the founding of the Rudolf Steiner School in New York. She moved to Dornach in 1959.

PALMER, DR MED OTTO (Feinsheim 1867 – 1945 Wiesneck)
Member from 1908 at which time he was a practising doctor in Hamburg. In 1921 at the request of Rudolf Steiner he took on the management of the *Klinisch-Therapeutisches Institut* in Stuttgart. From 1923 onwards a member of the council of the German Anthroposophical Society.

PEIPERS, DR MED FELIX (Bonn 1873 – 1944 Arlesheim)
Member from 1904. In 1906/7 established a private clinic in Munich. Played the role of Benedictus when the Mystery Dramas were performed in Munich (1910-1913). Co-founder of the *Bauverein* and member of its council from 1911 until 1925. From 1911 to 1913 a member of the council of the German Section. From 1915/16 leader of the anthroposophical work in Munich. From 1921 to 1924 worked as a doctor at the *Klinisch-Therapeutisches Institut* in Stuttgart.

POLLAK, RICHARD (Karlin, Prague 1867 – 1940 Dachau)
He and his wife were both artists and took part in the painting of the large dome of the first Goetheanum (1914-1919). In the concentration camp at Dachau he gave over a hundred anthroposophical lectures to those doomed to accompany him through death.

POLZER-HODITZ, LUDWIG COUNT OF (Prague 1869 – 1945 Vienna)
Member from 1911. In 1917 he used his influence to interest the Austrian government in Rudolf Steiner's movement for the threefold social order. From 1919 to 1921 he worked in Austria for the threefold movement. He became chairman of the Austrian Anthroposophical Society at its foundation in October 1923. At the Christmas Foundation Conference, he was the representative of the council of the Austrian Society.

PUSCH, HANS LUDWIG (1902 – 1976)
Actor. Participated in Rudolf Steiner's dramatic course given in 1924 and subsequently worked as a member of the Goetheanum stage ensemble under Marie Steiner. Moved to the USA in 1939 where he lectured, gave courses in speech formation and staged the Mystery Dramas.

PYLE, WILLIAM SCOTT (b.America – d.1938 The Hague)
Painter. From 1921/22 in Dornach. In 1929/30, together with his wife Mieta Pyle-Waller, he designed the scenery for the third and fourth Mystery Dramas. At the suggestion of Rudolf Steiner he worked at the production of new plant-based paints ('Anthea Paints').

RATHENAU, WALTHER
See Note 5.

REICHEL, DR FRANZ (d.1960 in Prague)
One of the representatives of the council of the Anthroposophical Society in Czechoslovakia.

RENZIS, BARONESS EMMELINA DE (d.1945 in Rome)
Member from 1909. Was one of the pioneers of the Anthroposophical Society in Italy. After Rudolf Steiner lectured there in 1909 she became the leader of a branch in Rome and concerned herself with the translation of his works into Italian.

RIHOUËT-COROZE, SIMONE (Paris 1892 – 1982 Paris)
Member from 1913. In 1921 she founded the Paris eurythmy school and the journal *Science spirituelle*. From 1931 to 1976 she was General Secretary of the Anthroposophical Society in France. Translated the works of Rudolf Steiner and published the journal *Triades*. Wrote *Rudolf Steiner, une Épopée de l'Esprit au XXe Siècle*, Paris 1951.

SAUERWEIN, ALICE (b.Marseille – d.1931 in Switzerland)
Sister of the prominent French journalist and anthroposophist Jules Sauerwein. Founded the Paris group 'Saint-Michel' for whom Rudolf Steiner gave lectures in 1913 and 1914. From its founding in 1923, she was the General Secretary of the French Anthroposophical Society till 1930.

SIMON, FRÄULEIN

SCHMIDT, HERR

SCHMIEDEL, DR OSKAR (Vienna 1887 – 1959 Schwäbisch Gmünd)
Chemist. Member from 1907. Participated in establishing the Weleda company and was a member of its management from the beginning and later in Schwäbisch Gmünd.

SCHUBERT, DR KARL (Vienna 1889 – 1949 Stuttgart)
Member from about 1910. In February 1920 Rudolf Steiner requested him to take on the remedial class at the Waldorf School in Switzerland. He was thus the first anthroposophical curative teacher. Later he assisted in the establishment of curative establishments in Germany and other countries.

SCHWARZ, LINA (d.1947)
Met Anthroposophy in 1912 and was one of the pioneers of anthroposophical work in Italy. Worked in the Milan branch, which she represented at the Christmas Foundation Conference. She took over the leadership after the death of the founder, Charlotte Ferreri. She made excellent translations of Rudolf Steiner's works.

SCHWEBSCH, DR ERICH (Frankfurt/Oder 1889 – 1953 Freiburg i.Br.)
Writer about music, teacher. Member from about 1919. At the request of Friedrich Rittelmeyer, he contributed the essay 'Goethe und Rudolf Steiner' to his anthology *Vom Lebenswerk Rudolf Steiners* (On the Life's Work of Rudolf Steiner). This drew him to the attention of Rudolf Steiner who requested him to join the Waldorf School in Stuttgart. He taught there from 1921. Its re-institution after the Second World War was largely due to his initiative. In 1946 he brought the Waldorf schools in Germany together in the Association of Waldorf Schools, of which he was the chairman.

SCHWEIGLER, KARL RICHARD
Brother of the painter Emil Schweigler. Member from 1918 (St Gallen). Founded a working group in Rorschach in 1921. Lived in Dornach from 1922.

STEFFEN, ALBERT (Murgenthal/Aargau 1884 – 1963 Dornach)
Swiss poet. Met Rudolf Steiner in 1907 in Munich. Lived in Dornach from the autumn of 1920 onwards. Became editor of the weekly *Das Goetheanum* when it was established in 1921. From Christmas 1923 till 1925 Vice-president of the General Anthroposophical Society and Leader of the Section for Belles-Lettres. From Christmas 1925 President of the Society. Writer of poetry and plays, eg *In Memoriam Rudolf Steiner*, 1925, and *Begegnungen mit Rudolf Steiner* (Meetings with Rudolf Steiner), 1955.

STEIN, DR WALTER JOHANNES (Vienna 1891 – 1957 London)
Member from 1913. From 1919 to 1932 teacher of history at the

Waldorf School in Stuttgart. From 1923 to 1928 a member of the council of the German Anthroposophical Society. Later he worked in England.

STEINER, MARIE, NÉE VON SIVERS (Wloclawek/Russia 1867 – 1948 Beatenberg/ Switzerland).
From 1902 Rudolf Steiner's closest colleague in building up the Movement and the Society. At Christmas 1914 they married. With him she developed the Goetheanistic stage arts of speech formation and eurythmy. At Christmas 1923 she became the Leader of the Section for the Spoken Arts and Music. With the Philosophisch-Anthroposophischer Verlag, which she founded in 1908, she ran the editing and publishing of Rudolf Steiner's written works and his lectures. In 1943 she founded the *Rudolf Steiner Nachlassverwaltung* to continue with this work. See Rudolf Steiner *The Course of my Life*; Marie Steiner von Sivers *Correspondence and Documents 1901-1905*; Hella Wiesberger *Aus dem Leben von Marie Steiner-von Sivers* (From the Life of Marie Steiner), Dornach 1956; *Marie Steiner, ihr Weg zur Erneuerung der Bühnenkunst durch Anthroposophie. Eine Dokumentation* (Marie Steiner. Her Path to a Renewal of Stagecraft through Anthroposophy. A Documentation), Dornach 1973.

STIBBE, MAX (b. Padang 1898 – d. 1983)
Teacher. Member from 1920. In 1923 he became co-founder and teacher at the first Dutch Waldorf school 'De Vrije School' at The Hague.

STOKAR, WILLY (Schaffhausen 1893 – 1953 Zurich)
Member from about 1916. Writer. 1921-23 colleague of Willy Storrer in the smaller working committee at the Goetheanum, among other things for tours of the building and as a lecturer. From time to time he was also a member of the management committee of Futurum AG, Dornach.

STORRER, WILLY (Töss bei Winterthur 1896 – 1930 Dornach)
From 1919 onwards worked with Roman Boos in the threefold movement and in his secretarial and organizational work at the Goetheanum. In the early summer of 1921 he took on the responsibility for Dr Boos's work in this area. After the founding of the weekly journal *Das Goetheanum*, Rudolf Steiner entrusted him with the administrative side. He thus became manager of the *Verlag am Goetheanum*. In 1920 he was a founder-member and the secretary of the branch at the Goetheanum. In 1923 he co-founded the *Neue Generation* branch.

Belonged to the smaller working committee at the Goetheanum till the Christmas Foundation Conference in 1923. From time to time he was also a member of the management committee of Futurum AG. On 3 May 1930 he met with a fatal accident in his private aeroplane on the Gempen in Dornach.

STUTEN, JAN (Nijmegen 1890 – 1948 Arlesheim)
Musician. Member from about 1910. From 1914 he was a permanent musician at the Goetheanum (composing and conducting). He portrayed a number of roles on the stage under the direction of Rudolf Steiner, among others that of Faust. Later he also created scenery (in 1928 for the first and second Mystery Dramas). Composer of various works, above all stage music for *Faust, Parts One and Two* and for Rudolf Steiner's funeral. Member of the *Rudolf Steiner Nachlassverwaltung*.

THUT, PAUL (b.1872 – 1955 Bern)
Engineer. Director of the power station at Bern. Member in Bern for many years.

TRIMLER, DR

TRINLER, KARL (d.1964)
Arlesheim and Basel.

TYMSTRA, FRANS (b.1891 – 1979 Arlesheim)
From Holland.

UNGER, DR CARL (Bad Cannstatt 1878 – 1929 Nuremberg)
Member from 1902/03. Till his death he was the leader of the main branch in Stuttgart, which he had founded in 1905 together with Adolf Arenson. From 1913 to 1923 he was a member of the central Vorstand of the Anthroposophical Society. From 1923 he was a member of the council of the German national Society. At the Christmas Foundation Conference he represented that council and also the Porto Alegre group in Brazil. From January 1914 to September 1915 he was the technical building manager of the first Goetheanum and from 1913 to 1925 in the council of the *Bauverein*. Before beginning a public lecture on Anthroposophy in Nuremberg on 4 January 1929 he was shot dead by a mentally ill man. His collected works have been published in three volumes.

USTERI, DR ALFRED (Säntis area of Switzerland 1869 – 1948 Reinach)
Papers on botany. Plant drawings; lectures at the Goetheanum.

VREEDE, DR ELISABETH (The Hague 1879 – 1943 Ascona)
Member of the Theosophical Society as early as about 1902. From April 1914 she worked at the Goetheanum where from 1919 onwards she set up the archive of Rudolf Steiner's lectures. In 1920 she became a founder-member and later the secretary of the branch at the Goetheanum. In 1922/23 she was a member of the smaller working committee at the Goetheanum and from Christmas 1923 till 1935 she was a member of the founding Vorstand of the General Anthroposophical Society and the Leader of the Section for Mathematics and Astronomy.

WACHSMUTH, DR GUENTHER (Dresden 1893 – 1963 Dornach)
Permanently in Dornach from 1921. In 1922/23 in the smaller working committee at the Goetheanum. From Christmas 1923 till 1963 he was a member of the Vorstand of the General Anthroposophical Society in the capacity of Secretary and Treasurer, and Leader of the Natural Science Section. He wrote, among other things: *Rudolf Steiners Erdenleben und Wirken. Eine Biographie* (Rudolf Steiner's Life and Work), Dornach 1941 and 1951; *Die ätherischen Bildekräfte in Kosmos, Erde und Mensch* (The Etheric Formative Forces in Cosmos, Earth and Man), Stuttgart 1924.

WACHSMUTH, DR WOLFGANG (Dresden 1891 – 1953 Arlesheim)
Worked for various publishing companies. He met Anthroposophy towards the end of the First World War. In Stuttgart from 1920 he took over the management of the publishing company *Der Kommende Tag AG* until it was dissolved in 1924/25. From time to time he was a member of the council of the Anthroposophical Society in Germany.

WEGMAN, DR MED ITA (Java 1876 – 1943 Arlesheim)
Member from approximately 1903. Studied medicine in Zurich. In 1921 she founded the *Klinisch-Therapeutisches Institut* in Arlesheim which resulted in close collaboration with Rudolf Steiner in the field of medicine. From 1922 to 1924 she was on the council of management of the International Laboratories in Arlesheim. From 1922-23 in the smaller working committee at the Goetheanum. From Christmas 1923 to 1935 she was the Recorder of the Vorstand of the General Anthroposophical Society and Leader of the Medical Section. From 1924-25

she was Rudolf Steiner's physician. Together they wrote *Fundamentals of Therapy*.

WEISS, FRAU

WERBECK, LOUIS MICHAEL JULIUS (Hamburg 1879 – 1928 Hamburg)
Member from 1910. From 1917 leader of the Pythagoras branch in Hamburg. From 1923 he was a member of the council of the German Anthroposophical Society. He wrote *Die wissenschaftlichen Gegner Rudolf Steiners und der Anthroposophie durch sie selbst widerlegt* (The Scientific Opponents of Rudolf Steiner and Anthroposophy Disproved by Themselves) and *Die christlichen Gegner Rudolf Steiners und der Anthroposophie* (The Christian Opponents of Rudolf Steiner and Anthroposophy), Stuttgart 1924.

WINDELBAND, WILHELM
See Note 41.

WULLSCHLEGER, FRITZ (Zofingen 1896 – 1969 Zofingen)
Teacher. Member from 1920. Member of the School Association for Independent Education in Switzerland. (See Note 56).

ZAGWIJN, HENRI (d.1954)
Composer and writer from Rotterdam. Set to music Rudolf Steiner's verses 'Im Seelenaug' . . .' and 'Die Sonne schaue . . .' Wrote *Die Musik im Lichte der Anthroposophie* (Music in the Light of Anthroposophy). Teacher at the Waldorf school in The Hague.

ZEYLMANS VAN EMMICHOVEN, DR MED F W WILLEM (Helmond 1893 – 1961 Johannesburg)
Member from 1920. Founder of the Rudolf Steiner Clinic in The Hague, co-founder of the Anthroposophical Society in Holland and from November 1923 its General Secretary. Wrote, among other works, *Rudolf Steiner, Eine Biographie* (Rudolf Steiner, A Biography), Stuttgart 1961.

RUDOLF STEINER

MANUSCRIPTS

&

BLACKBOARD SKETCHES

Statuten der anthroposophischen Gesellschaft.

1. Die anthroposophische Gesellschaft soll eine Vereinigung von Menschen sein, die das seelische Leben im einzelnen Menschen und in der menschlichen Gemeinschaft auf der Grundlage einer wahren Erkenntnis der geistigen Welt pflegen wollen. ~~Der~~

2. Den Grundstock dieser Gesellschaft bilden die in der Weihnachtzeit 1923 am Goetheanum in Dornach versammelten Persönlichkeiten, sowie diejenigen Einzelnen oder zu Gruppen gehörigen, in deren Auftrag sie erschienen sind. Sie sind von der Anschauung durchdrungen, dass es gegenwärtig eine wirkliche Wissenschaft von der geistigen Welt schon giebt und dass der heutigen Civilisation die Pflege einer solchen Wissenschaft fehlt. Die anthroposophische Gesellschaft soll diese Pflege zu ihrer Aufgabe haben. Sie wird diese Aufgabe so zu lösen versuchen, dass sie die im Goetheanum zu Dornach gepflegte anthroposophische Geisteswissenschaft ~~zum Mittelpunkt~~ mit ihren Ergebnissen für die Brüderlichkeit im menschlichen Zusammenleben, für das moralische und religiöse, sowie für das künstlerische und Allgemein-Geistige im Menschenwesen zum Mittelpunkte ihrer Bestrebungen macht.

3. Die als Grundstock der Gesellschaft in Dornach versammelten Persönlichkeiten erkennen zustimmend die Anschauung der Goetheanum-Leitung in Bezug auf das Folgende an: Die im Goetheanum gepflegte Anthroposophie führt zu Ergebnissen, die jedem Menschen ohne Unterschied der Nation, des Standes, der Religion als Anregung für das geistige Leben dienen können. Sie kann zu einem wirklich auf brüderliche Liebe aufgebauten sozialen Leben führen. Ihre Aneignung als Lebensgrundlage ist nicht an einen wissenschaftlichen Bildungsgrad gebunden, sondern nur an das unbefangene Menschenwesen. Ihre Forschung und die sachgemäße Beurteilung ihrer Forschungsergebnisse unterliegt aber der geisteswissenschaftlichen Schulung, die stufenweise zu erlangen ist. Diese Ergebnisse sind auf ihre Art so exact wie die Ergebnisse

der wahren Naturwissenschaft. Wenn sie in derselben Art wie diese zur allgemeinen Anerkennung gelangen, werden sie auf allen Lebensgebieten einen gleichen Fortschritt wie diese bringen, nicht nur auf geistigem, sondern auch auf ~~geistigem~~ praktischem Gebiete."

4. Die anthroposophische Gesellschaft ist keine Geheimgesellschaft, sondern eine durchaus öffentliche. Ihr Mitglied kann jedermann ohne Unterschied der Nation, des Standes, der Religion, der wissenschaftlichen oder künstlerischen Überzeugung werden, der in dem Bestand einer solchen Institution, wie sie das Goetheanum in Dornach als freie Hochschule für Geisteswissenschaft ist, etwas Berechtigtes sieht. Die Gesellschaft lehnt jedes sektiererische Bestreben ab. Die Politik betrachtet sie nicht als in ihren Aufgaben liegend.

5. Die anthroposophische Gesellschaft sieht ein Zentrum ihres Wirkens in der freien Hochschule für Geisteswissenschaft in Dornach. Diese wird in drei Klassen bestehen. In dieselbe werden auf ihre Bewerbung hin aufgenommen die Mitglieder der Gesellschaft, nachdem sie eine durch die Leitung des Goetheanums zu bestimmende Zeit die Mitgliedschaft inne hatten. Sie gelangen dadurch in die erste Klasse der freien Hochschule für Geisteswissenschaft. Die Aufnahme in die zweite, beziehungsweise in die dritte Klasse erfolgt, wenn die um dieselbe Ansuchenden von der Leitung des Goetheanums als geeignet befunden werden.

6. Jedes Mitglied der anthroposophischen Gesellschaft hat das Recht, an allen von ihr veranstalteten Vorträgen, sonstigen Darbietungen und Versammlungen unter den von dem Vorstande bekannt zu gebenden Bedingungen teilzunehmen.

7. Die Einrichtung der freien Hochschule für Geisteswissenschaft obliegt zunächst Rudolf Steiner, der seine Mitarbeiter und

seinen eventuellen Nachfolger zu ernennen hat.

8. Alle Publikationen der Gesellschaft werden öffentlich in der Art wie diejenigen anderer öffentlicher Gesellschaften sein. Von dieser Öffentlichkeit werden auch die Publikationen der freien Hochschule für Geisteswissenschaft keine Ausnahme machen; doch nimmt die Leitung der Schule für sich in Anspruch, dass sie von vorneherein jedem Urteile über diese Schriften die Berechtigung bestreitet, das nicht auf die Schulung gestützt ist, aus der sie hervorgegangen sind. Sie wird in diesem Sinne keinem Urteil Berechtigung zuerkennen, das nicht auf entsprechende Vorstudien ebenso gestützt ist, wie das in der anerkannten wissenschaftlichen Welt üblich ist. Deshalb werden die Schriften der freien Hochschule für Geisteswissenschaft den folgenden Vermerk tragen: „Als Manuscript für die Angehörigen der freien Hochschule für Geisteswissenschaft, Klasse ….. Goetheanum gedruckt. Es wird niemand für diese Schriften ein competentes Urteil zugestanden, der nicht die von dieser Schule geltend gemachte Vor-Erkenntnis durch sie oder auf eine von ihr selbst als gleichbedeutend erkannte Weise erworben hat. Andere Beurteilungen werden insofern abgelehnt, als die Verfasser der entsprechenden Schriften sich in keine Discussion über dieselben einlassen."

9. Das Ziel der anthroposophischen Gesellschaft wird die Förderung der Forschung auf geistigem Gebiete, das der freien Hochschule für Geisteswissenschaft diese Forschung selbst sein. Eine Dogmatik auf irgend einem Gebiete soll von der anthroposophischen Gesellschaft ausgeschlossen sein.

10. Die anthroposophische Gesellschaft hält jedes Jahr um die Zeit des Jahresbeginns im Goetheanum eine ordentliche Jahresversammlung

ab, in der von dem Vorstande ein vollständiger Rechenschaftsbericht gegeben wird. Die Tagesordnung zu dieser Versammlung wird mit der Einladung an alle Mitglieder drei Wochen vor der Tagung von dem Vorstande bekannt gegeben. Ausserordentliche Versammlungen kann der Vorstand berufen und für sie die Tagesordnung festsetzen. Er soll drei Wochen vorher die Einladungen an die Mitglieder versenden. Anträge von einzelnen Mitgliedern oder Gruppen von solchen sind eine Woche vor der Tagung einzusenden.

11. Die Mitglieder können sich auf jedem örtlichen oder sachlichen Felde zu kleineren oder grösseren Gruppen zusammenschliessen. Die anthroposophische Gesellschaft hat ihren Sitz am Goetheanum. Der Vorstand hat von da aus das an die Mitglieder oder Mitglieder-Gruppen zu bringen, was er als die Aufgabe der Gesellschaft ansieht. Er tritt in Verkehr mit den Funktionären, die von den einzelnen Gruppen gewählt oder ernannt werden. Die einzelnen Gruppen besorgen die Aufnahme der Mitglieder; doch sollen die Aufnahmebestätigungen dem Vorstande in Dornach vorgelegt und von diesem auf das Vertrauen zu den Gruppenfunctionären unterzeichnet werden. Im Allgemeinen soll sich jedes Mitglied einer Gruppe anschließen; nur wem es ganz unmöglich ist, die Aufnahme bei einer Gruppe zu finden, sollte sich in Dornach selbst als Mitglied aufnehmen lassen.

12. Der Mitgliedsbeitrag wird durch die einzelnen Gruppen bestimmt; doch hat jede Gruppe für jedes ihrer Mitglieder ...... an die centrale Leitung am Goetheanum zu entrichten.

13. Jede Arbeitsgruppe bildet ihre eigenen Statuten; nur sollen diese den Statuten der anthroposophischen Gesellschaft nicht widersprechen.

14. Gesellschaftsorgan ist das „Goetheanum", das zu diesem Ziele mit einer Beilage versehen wird, die die offiziellen Mitteilungen der Gesellschaft enthalten soll. Diese vergrösserte Ausgabe des „Goetheanum" wird nur an die Mitglieder der anthroposophischen Gesellschaft abgegeben.

STATUTEN
der anthroposophischen Gesellschaft

1. Die anthroposophische Gesellschaft soll eine Vereinigung von Menschen sein, die das seelische Leben im einzelnen Menschen und in der menschlichen Gesellschaft auf der Grundlage einer wahren Erkenntnis der geistigen Welt pflegen wollen.

2. Den Grundstock dieser Gesellschaft bilden die in der Weihnachtszeit 1923 am Goetheanum in Dornach versammelten Persönlichkeiten, sowie die Einzelnen, wie auch die Gruppen, die sich vertreten liessen. Sie sind von der Anschauung durchdrungen, dass es gegenwärtig eine wirkliche Wissenschaft von der geistigen Welt schon gibt und dass der heutigen Zivilisation die Pflege einer solchen Wissenschaft fehlt. Die anthroposophische Gesellschaft soll diese Pflege zu ihrer Aufgabe haben. Sie wird diese Aufgabe so zu lösen versuchen, dass sie die im Goetheanum zu Dornach gepflegte anthroposophische Geisteswissenschaft mit ihren Ergebnissen für die Brüderlichkeit im menschlichen Zusammenleben, für das moralische und religiöse, sowie für das künstlerische und allgemein geistige Leben im Menschenwesen zum Mittelpunkte ihrer Bestrebungen macht.

3. Die als Grundstock der Gesellschaft in Dornach versammelten Persönlichkeiten erkennen zustimmend die Anschauung der Goetheanum-Leitung in Bezug auf das Folgende an: Die im Goetheanum gepflegte Anthroposophie führt zu Ergebnissen, die jedem Menschen ohne Unterschied der Nation, des Standes, der Religion als Anregung für das geistige Leben dienen können. Sie können zu einem wirklich auf brüderliche Liebe aufgebauten sozialen Leben führen. Ihre Aneignung als Lebensgrundlage ist nicht an einen wissenschaftlichen Bildungsgrad gebunden, sondern nur an das unbefangene Menschenwesen. Ihre Forschung und die sachgemässe Beurteilung ihrer Forschungsergebnisse unterliegt aber der geisteswissenschaftlichen Schulung, die stufenweise zu erlangen ist. Diese Ergebnisse sind auf ihre Art so exakt wie die Ergebnisse der wahren Naturwissenschaft. Wenn

sie in derselben Art wie diese zur allgemeinen Anerkennung gelangen, werden sie auf allen Lebensgebieten einen gleichen Fortschritt wie diese bringen, nicht nur auf geistigem sondern auch auf praktischem Gebiete.

4. Die anthroposophische Gesellschaft ist keine Geheimgesellschaft, sondern eine durchaus öffentliche. Ihr Mitglied kann jedermann ohne Unterschied der Nation, des Standes, der Religion, der wissenschaftlichen oder künstlerischen Überzeugung werden, der in dem Bestand einer solchen Institution, wie sie das Goetheanum in Dornach als freie Hochschule für Geisteswissenschaft ist, etwas berechtigtes sieht. Die Gesellschaft lehnt jedes sektiererische Bestreben ab. Die Politik betrachtet sie nicht als in ihren Aufgaben liegend.

5. Die anthroposophische Gesellschaft sieht ein Zentrum ihres Wirkens in der freien Hochschule für Geisteswissenschaft in Dornach. Diese wird in drei Klassen bestehen. In dieselbe werden auf ihre Bewerbung hin aufgenommen die Mitglieder der Gesellschaft, nachdem sie eine durch die Leitung des Goetheanums zu bestimmende Zeit die Mitgliedschaft inne hatten. Sie gelangen dadurch in die erste Klasse der freien Hochschule für Geisteswissenschaft. Die Aufnahme in die zweite, beziehungsweise in die dritte Klasse erfolgt, wenn die um dieselbe Ansuchenden von der Leitung des Goetheanums als geeignet befunden werden.

6. Jedes Mitglied der anthroposophischen Gesellschaft hat das Recht, an allen von ihr veranstalteten Vorträgen, sonstigen Darbietungen und Versammlungen unter den von dem Vorstande bekannt zu gebenden Bedingungen teilzunehmen.

7. Die Einrichtung der freien Hochschule für Geisteswissenschaft obliegt zunächst Rudolf Steiner, der seine Mitarbeiter und seinen eventuellen Nachfolger zu ernennen hat.

8. Alle Publikationen der Gesellschaft werden öffentlich in der Art wie diejenigen anderer öffentlicher Gesellschaften sein. Von dieser Öffentlichkeit werden auch die Publikationen der freien Hochschule für Geisteswissenschaft keine Ausnahme machen; doch nimmt die Leitung der Schule für sich in Anspruch, dass sie von vorneherein jedem Urteile über *diese* Schriften die Berechtigung bestreitet, das nicht auf die Schulung gestützt ist, aus der sie hervorgegangen sind. Sie wird in diesem Sinne

wahren

Geiste der Gegenwart entsprechenden Ausgang

schaffen.

keinem Urteil Berechtigung zuerkennen, das nicht auf entsprechende Vorstudien gestützt ist, wie das in der anerkannten wissenschaftlichen Welt üblich ist. Deshalb werden die Schriften der freien Hochschule für Geisteswissenschaft den folgenden Vermerk tragen: »Als Manuskript für die Angehörigen der freien Hochschule für Geisteswissenschaft, Goetheanum Klasse... gedruckt. Es wird niemand für diese Schriften ein kompetentes Urteil zugestanden, der nicht die von dieser Schule geltend gemachte Vor-Erkenntnis durch sie oder auf eine von ihr selbst als gleichbedeutend erkannte Weise erworben hat. Andere Beurteilungen werden insofern abgelehnt, als die Verfasser der entsprechenden Schriften sich in keine Diskussion über dieselben einlassen«.

9. Das Ziel der anthroposophischen Gesellschaft wird die Förderung der Forschung auf geistigem Gebiete, das der freien Hochschule für Geisteswissenschaft diese Forschung selbst sein. Eine Dogmatik auf irgend einem Gebiete soll von der anthroposophischen Gesellschaft ausgeschlossen sein.

10. Die anthroposophische Gesellschaft hält jedes Jahr ~~um die Zeit des Jahresbeginns~~ im Goetheanum eine ordentliche Jahresversammlung ab, in der von dem Vorstande ein vollständiger Rechenschaftsbericht gegeben wird. Die Tagesordnung zu dieser Versammlung wird mit der Einladung an alle Mitglieder drei Wochen vor der Tagung von dem Vorstande bekannt gegeben. Ausserordentliche Versammlungen kann der Vorstand berufen und für sie die Tagesordnung festsetzen. Er soll ~~drei~~ Wochen vorher die Einladungen an die Mitglieder versenden. Anträge von einzelnen Mitgliedern oder Gruppen von solchen sind eine Woche vor der Tagung einzusenden. -

11. Die Mitglieder können sich auf jedem örtlichen oder sachlichen Felde zu kleineren oder grösseren Gruppen zusammenschliessen. Die anthroposophische Gesellschaft hat ihren Sitz am Goetheanum. Der Vorstand hat von da aus das an die Mitglieder oder Mitgliedergruppen zu bringen, was er als die Aufgabe der Gesellschaft ansieht. Er tritt in Verkehr mit den Funktionären, die von den einzelnen Gruppen gewählt oder ernannt werden. Die einzelnen Gruppen besorgen die Aufnahme der Mitglieder; doch sollen die Aufnahmebestätigungen dem Vorstande in Dornach vorgelegt und von diesem im Vertrauen zu den Gruppenfunktionären unterzeichnet werden. Im

Allgemeinen soll sich jedes Mitglied einer Gruppe anschliessen; nur wem es ganz unmöglich ist, die Aufnahme bei einer Gruppe zu finden, sollte sich in Dornach selbst als Mitglied aufnehmen lassen.

12. Der Mitgliedsbeitrag wird durch die einzelnen Gruppen bestimmt; doch hat jede Gruppe für jedes ihrer Mitglieder .... an die zentrale Leitung am Goetheanum zu entrichten.

13. Jede Arbeitsgruppe bildet ihre eigenen Statuten; nur sollen diese den Statuten der anthroposophischen Gesellschaft nicht widersprechen.

14. Gesellschaftsorgan ist ~~das~~ die Wochenschrift »Goetheanum«, das zu diesem Ziele mit einer Beilage versehen wird, die die offiziellen Mitteilungen der Gesellschaft enthalten soll. Diese vergrösserte Ausgabe des »Goetheanum« wird nur an die Mitglieder der anthroposophischen Gesellschaft abgegeben.

15.

1

Menschenseele!

Du lebest in den Gliedern
Die dich durch die Raumeswelt
Im Geistesmeereswesen tragen:
Übe Geist-Erinnern
In Seelentiefen
Wo in waltendem
Weltenschöpfer-Sein
Das eigne Ich
In Gottes-Ich
Erweset
Und du wirst wahrhaft leben
Im Menschen-Welten-Wesen.

Menschenseele!

Du lebest in dem Herzens-Lungen-Schlage
Der dich durch den Zeitenrhythmus
Ins eigne Seelenwesensfühlen leitet:
Übe Geist-Besinnen
Im Seelengleichgewichte
Wo die wogenden
Welten-Werde-Taten

Das eigne Ich
Dem Welten-Ich
Vereinen
Und du wirst wahrhaft fühlen
Im Menschen-Seelen-Wirken.

Menschenseele!
Du lebest im ruhenden Haupte
Das dir aus Ewigkeitsgründen
Die Weltgedanken erschliesset:
Übe Geist-Erschauen
In Gedanken-Ruhe
Wo die ew'gen Götterziele
Welten-Wesens-Licht
Dem eignen Ich
Zu freiem Wollen
Schenken
Und du wirst wahrhaft denken
In Menschen-Geistes-Gründen.

In der Zeitenwende
Trat das Welten-Geistes-Licht
In den irdischen Wesensstrom;
Nacht-Dunkel hatte ausgewaltet
Taghelles Licht
Erstrahlte in Menschenseelen

Licht, das erwärmet
Die armen Hirten~~seelen~~herzen
Licht, das erleuchtet
Die weisen Königshäupter –

Göttliches Licht
Christus-Sonne
Erwärme unsre Herzen
Erleuchte unsre Häupter

Dass gut werde
Was wir aus Herzen
Gründen
aus Häuptern
Zielvoll führen wollen.

Den es waltet der Vater-Geist der Höhen
In den Weltentiefen Sein-erzeugend
S. Ch. Th.
Lasset aus den Höhen erklingen
Was in den Tiefen das Echo findet:
Das spricht:
E. D. N.

Das hören die Elementengeister im O. W. N. S. Menschen mögen es hören.

Denn es waltet der Christus-Wille im Umkreis
In den Weltenrhythmen Seelen-begnadend
K. D. E.
Lasset vom Osten befeuern
Was durch den Westen sich gestaltet:
Das spricht.
I. Ch. M.

5.

Denn es walten des Geistes-Weltgedanken
Im Weltenwesen licht-erflehend

A. AA. A.
Lasset aus den Tiefen erbitten
Was in den Höhen erhöret wird:

Das spricht.

P.. S. S. R.

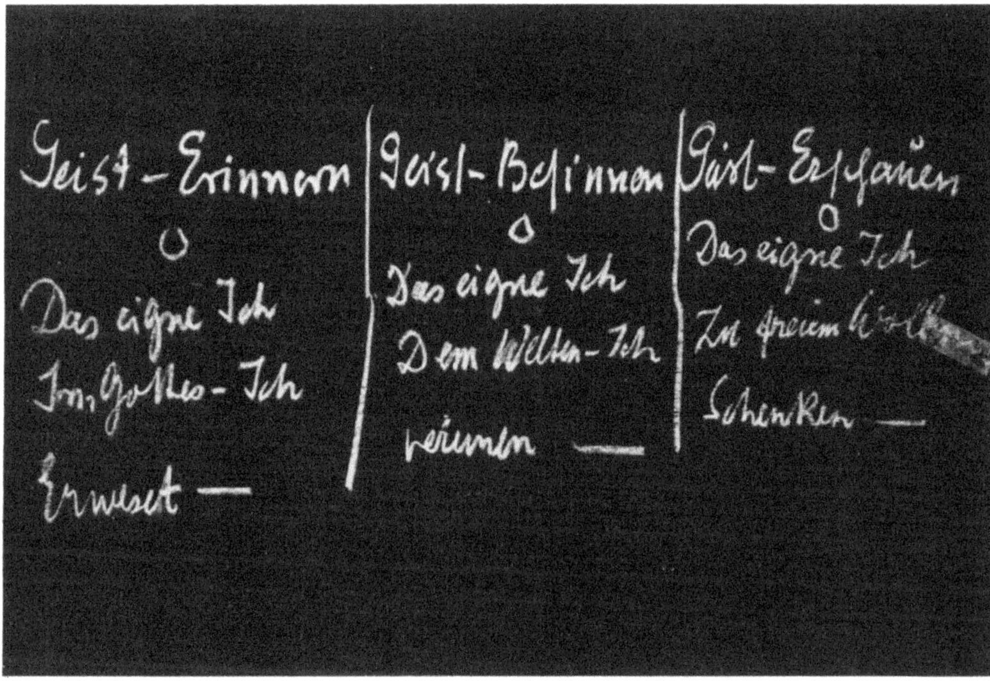
Geist-Erinnern
Das eigne Ich
Im Gottes-Ich
Erweset —
Geist-Besinnen
Das eigne Ich
Dem Welten-Ich
vereinen —
Geist-Erschauen
Das eigne Ich
Zu freiem Woll
Schenken —

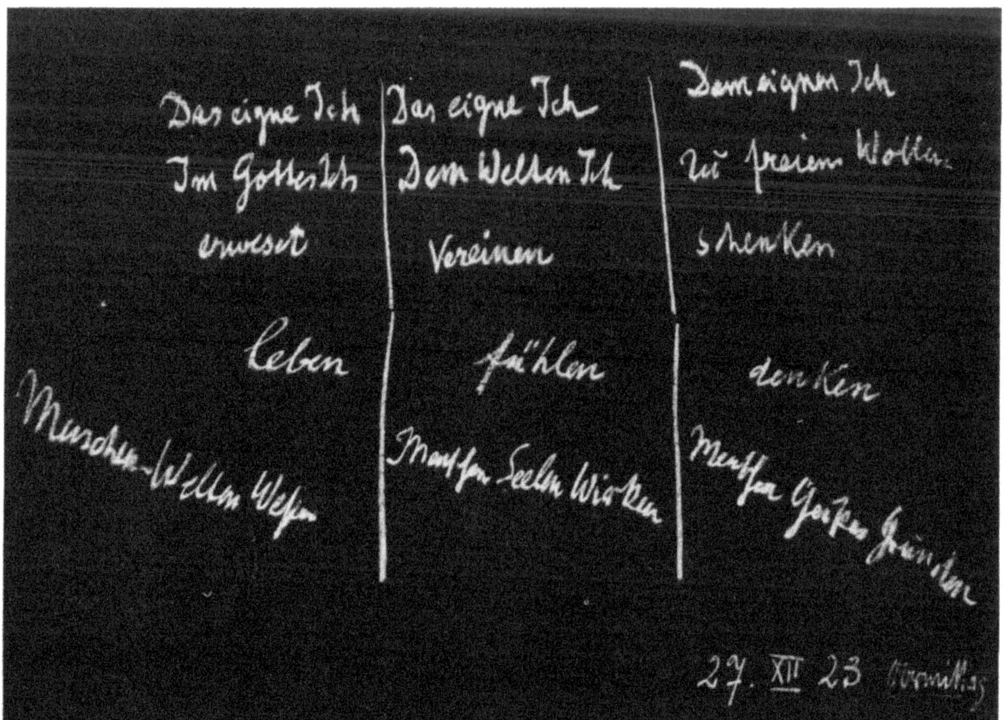
Das eigne Ich
Im Gottes-Ich
erweset
leben
Menschen-Welten-Wesen
Das eigne Ich
Dem Welten-Ich
Vereinen
fühlen
Menschen-Seelen-Wirken
Dem eignen Ich
Zu freiem Wollen
schenken
denken
Menschen-Geistes-Gründen
27. XII 23 Vormittags

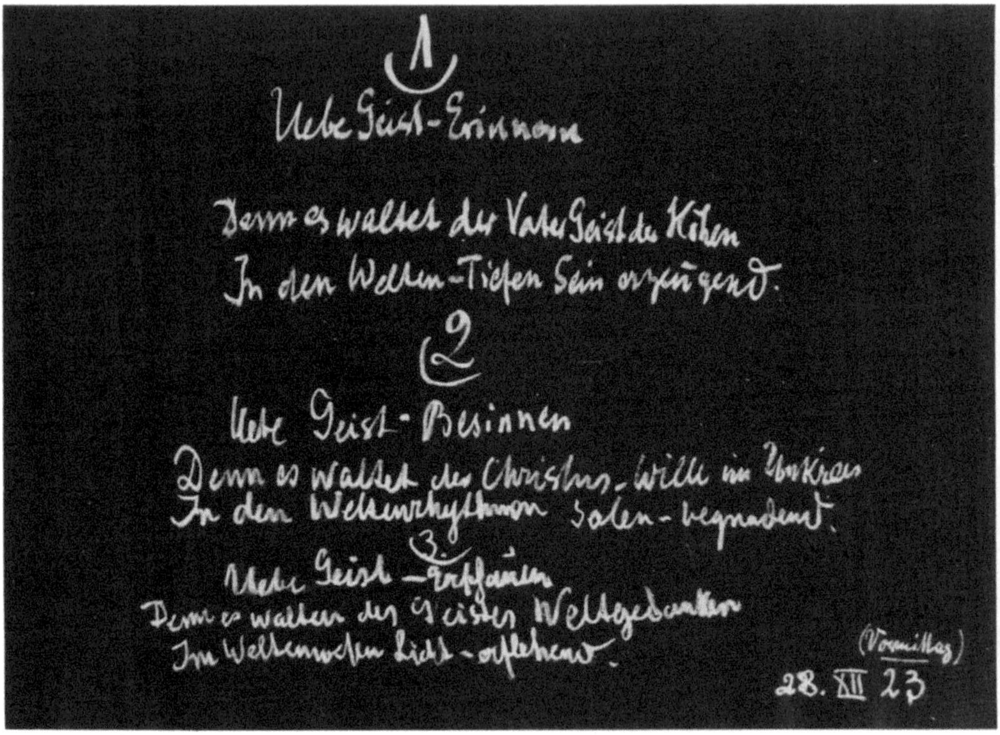
1
Übe Geist-Erinnern
Denn es waltet der Vater-Geist der Höhen
In den Welten-Tiefen Sein erzeugend.
2
Übe Geist-Besinnen
Denn es waltet der Christus-Wille im Umkreis
In den Weltenrhythmen Seelen-begnadend.
3.
Übe Geist-Erschauen
Denn es walten des Geistes Weltgedanken
Im Weltenwesen Licht-erflehend.
(Vormittag)
28. XII 23

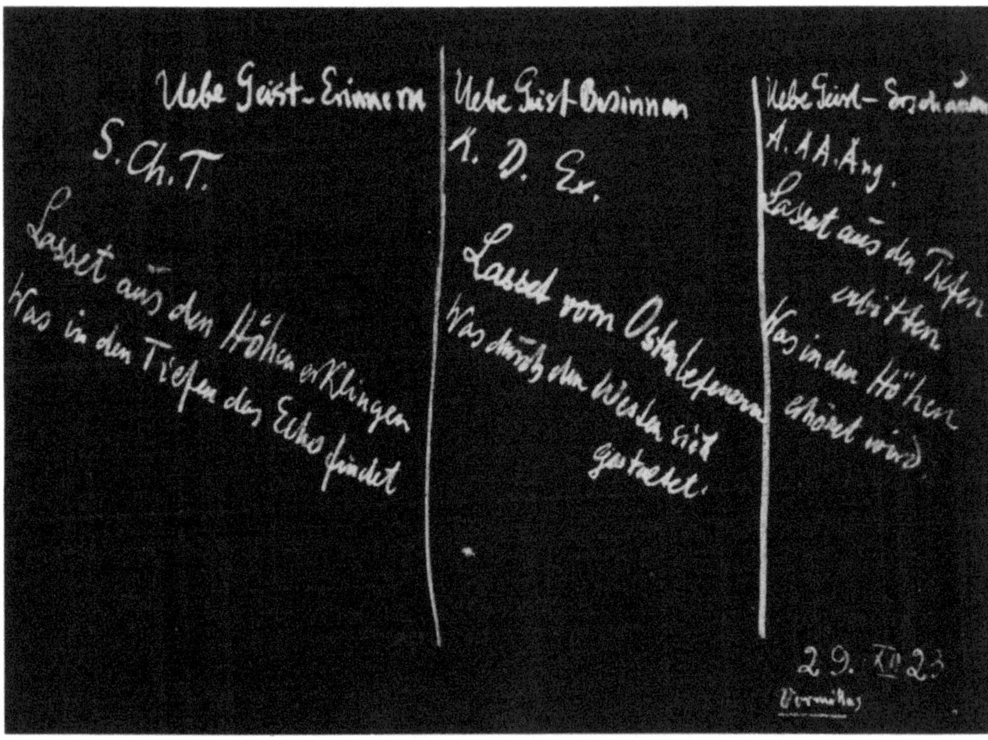
Übe Geist-Erinnern
S. Ch. T.
Lasset aus den Höhen erklingen
Was in den Tiefen das Echo findet
Übe Geist-Besinnen
K. D. Ex.
Lasset vom Osten befeuern
Was durch den Westen sich gestaltet.
Übe Geist-Erschauen
A. A. A. Ang.
Lasset aus den Tiefen erbitten
Was in den Höhen erhöret wird
29. XII 23
Vormittag

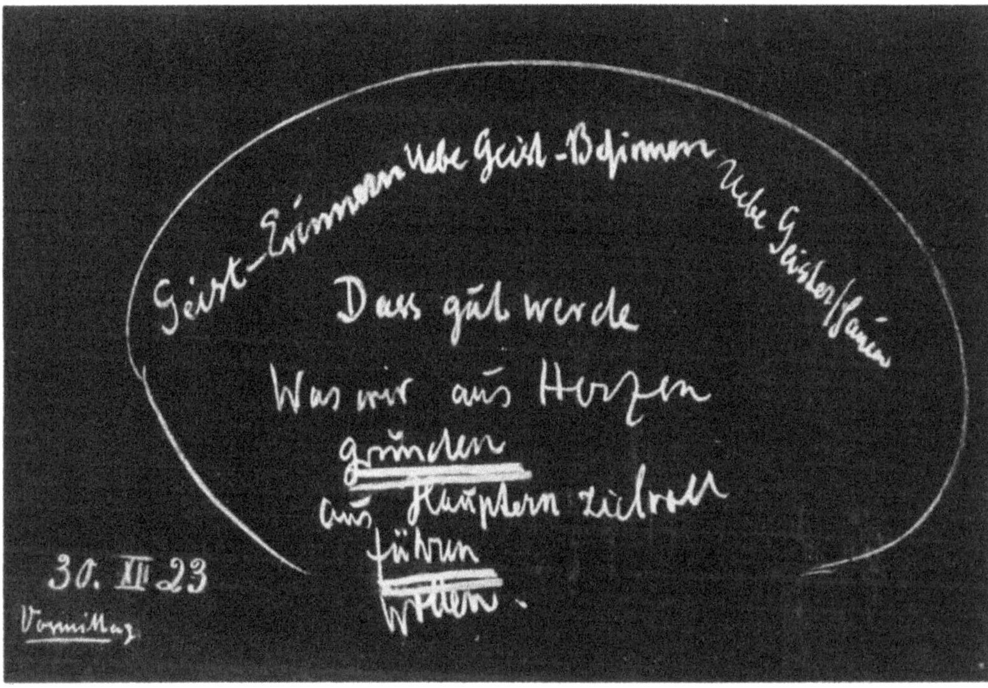
Geist-Erinnern Uebe Geist-Besinnen Uebe Geisterschauen
Dass gut werde
Was wir aus Herzen
gründen
aus Häuptern zielvoll
führen
wollen.
30. XII 23
Vormittag

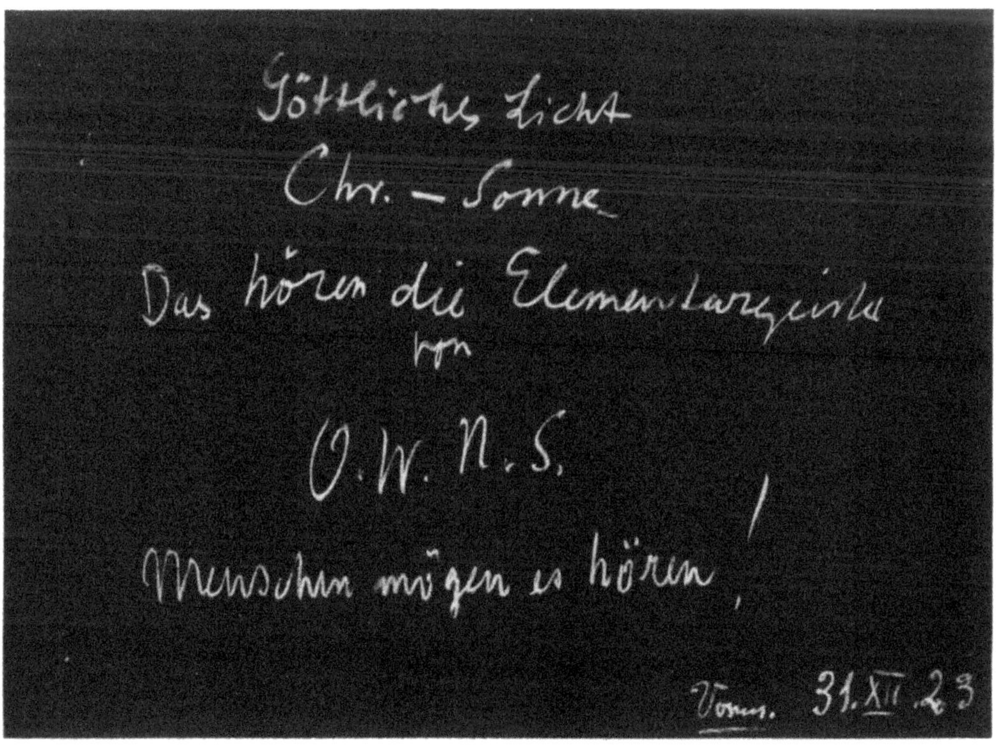
Göttliches Licht
Chr. – Sonne
Das hören die Elementargeister
von
O. W. N. S.
Menschen mögen es hören!
Vorm. 31. XII. 23

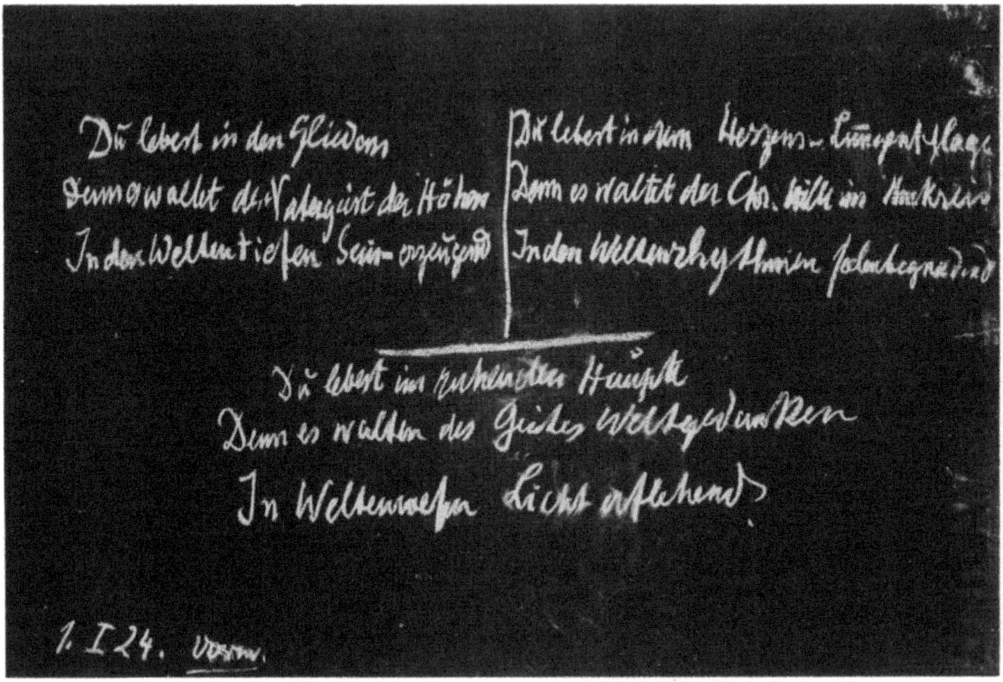
Du lebest in den Gliedern
Denn es waltet der Vatergeist der Höhen
In den Weltentiefen Sein-erzeugend
Du lebest in dem Herzens-Lungen-Schlage
Denn es waltet der Chr. Wille im Umkreis
In den Weltenrhythmen Seelenbegnadend
Du lebest im ruhenden Haupte
Denn es walten des Geistes Weltgedanken
In Weltenwesen Licht erflehend
1. I 24. vorm.

III
II
I
Allg. anth. Ges.
Dr. Steiner 27. XII 23

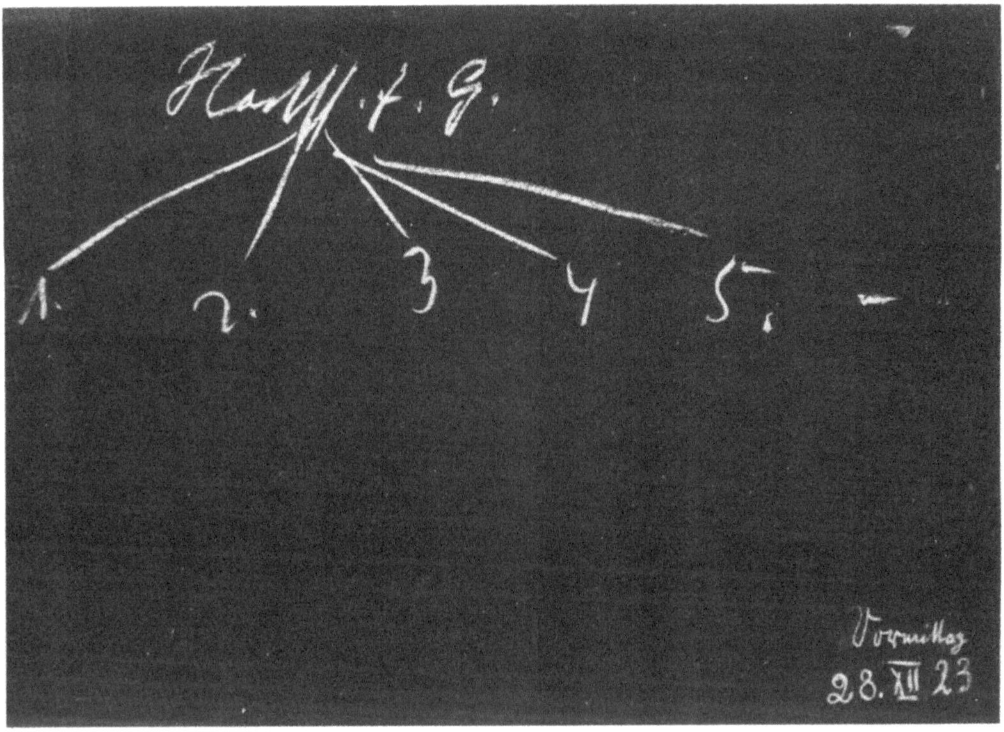
1. 2. 3 4 5.
Vormittag
28. XII 23

31. XII. 23

1. Jan. 1924. Vorm.

Menschenseele!
Du lebest in dem Herzens-Lungen-Schlage,
Der dich durch den Zeitenrhythmus
In's eigne Seelenwesensfühlen leitet:
Übe <u>Geist</u>-<u>Besinnen</u>
Im Seelengleichgewichte,
Wo die wogenden
Welten-Werde-Taten
Das eigne Ich
Dem Welten-Ich
Vereinen;
Und du wirst wahrhaft <u>fühlen</u>
Im Menschen-Seelen-Wirken.

Denn es waltet der Christus-Wille im Umkreis
In den Weltenrhythmen Seelen-begnadend
~~Die~~ Ihr Lichtes-Geister
Lasset vom Osten befeuern,
Was durch den Westen sich formet;
Dieses spricht:
In dem Christus wird Leben der Tod.
Das hören die Geister in Ost, West, Nord, Süd:
Menschen mögen es hören.

Menschenseele!
Du lebest in den Gliedern,
Die dich durch die Raumeswelt
In das Geistesmeereswesen tragen:
Übe *Geist* = *Erinnern*
In Seelentiefen,
Wo in waltendem
Weltschöpfer-Sein
Das eigne Ich
Ins Gottes-Ich
Erweset;
Und du wirst wahrhaft *leben*
Im Menschen = Welten = Wesen.

Denn es waltet der Vater-Geist der Höhen
In den Weltentiefen Sein-erzeugend:
Ihr Kräfte = Geister
Lasset aus den Höhen erklingen,
Was in den Tiefen das Echo findet;
Dieses spricht:
Aus dem Göttlichen weset die Menschheit.
Das hören die Geister in Ost, West, Nord, Süd:
Menschen mögen es hören.

Menschenseele!
Du lebest im ruhenden Haupte,
Das dir aus Ewigkeitsgründen
Die Weltgedanken erschließet:
Übe <u>Geist</u> - <u>Erschauen</u>
In Gedanken - Ruhe,
Wo die ew'gen Götterziele
Welten - Wesens - Licht
Dem eignen Ich
Zu freiem Wollen
Schenken;
Und du wirst wahrhaft <u>denken</u>
In Menschen - Geistes - Gründen.

Denn es walten des Geistes - Weltgedanken
Im Weltenwesen Licht - erflehend.
~~Die~~ Ihr Seelen = Geister
Lasset aus den Tiefen erbitten,
Was in den Höhen erhöret wird:
Dieses spricht:
In des Geistes Weltgedanken erwachet die Seele.
Das hören die Geister in Ost, West, Nord, Süd;
Menschen mögen es hören.

x x x

In der Zeiten Wende
Trat das Welten-Geistes-Licht
In den irdischen Wesensstrom;
Nacht-Dunkel [illegible]
Hatte ausgewaltet;
Taghelles Licht
Erstrahlte in Menschenseelen;
Licht,
Das erwärmet
Die armen Hirtenherzen;
Licht,
Das erleuchtet
Die weisen Königshäupter.

Göttliches Licht,
Christus-Sonne
Erwärme
Unsere Herzen;
Erleuchte
Unsere Häupter;

Dass gut werde,
Was wir
Aus Herzen gründen,
Was wir
Aus Häuptern führen,
Wollen.